GLOBAL TURBULENCE

The International Political Economy of New Regionalisms Series

The International Political Economy of New Regionalisms Series presents innovative analyses of a range of novel regional relations and institutions. Going beyond established, formal, interstate economic organizations, this essential series provides informed interdisciplinary and international research and debate about myriad heterogeneous intermediate level interactions.

Reflective of its cosmopolitan and creative orientation, this series is developed by an international editorial team of established and emerging scholars in both the South and North. It reinforces ongoing networks of analysts in both academia and think-tanks as well as international agencies concerned with micro-, meso- and macro-level regionalisms.

Other Titles in the Series

Political Aspects of the Economic and Monetary Union
Edited by Søren Dosenrode

Transforming East Asian Domestic and International Politics
Edited by Robert W. Compton, Jr.

Thailand, Indonesia and Burma in Comparative Perspective
Priyambudi Sulistiyanto

Global Turbulence:

Social activists' and state responses to globalization

Edited by
MARJORIE GRIFFIN COHEN
Simon Fraser University

STEPHEN McBRIDE
Simon Fraser University

ASHGATE

Published by
Ashgate Publishing Limited
Gower House
Croft Road
Aldershot
Hants GU11 3HR
England

Ashgate Publishing Company
Suite 420
101 Cherry Street
Burlington, VT 05401-4405
USA

Ashgate website: http://www.ashgate.com

British Library Cataloguing in Publication Data
Global turbulence : social activists' and state responses
to globalization. - (The international political economy of
new regionalisms)
1. International economic relations - Political aspects
2. International economic relations - Social aspects
3. Globalization - Political aspects 4. Globalization -
Social aspects 5. Social movements
I. Cohen, Marjorie Griffin, 1944- II. McBride, Stephen
Kenneth
338.9

Library of Congress Cataloging-in-Publication Data
Global turbulence: social activists' and state responses to globalization / edited by
Marjorie Griffin Cohen, Stephen McBride.
p.cm. -- (International political economy of new regionalisms series)
"Most of the chapters in this book were originally presented at a conference on Global turbulence: instability in national and international political economy held at Simon Fraser University (SFU) in July 2001" -- Ackn.
Includes bibliographical references and index.
ISBN 0-7546-3271-7 (alk. paper)
1. Globalization--Economic aspects. 2. Globalization--Social aspects. 3. Globalization--Political aspects. 4. Free trade--Government policy. 5. Social action. 6. International economic relations. I. Cohen, Marjorie Griffin, 1944- II. McBride, Stephen, 1947- III. Series.

HF1359 .G578 2002
337--dc21

2002027920

ISBN 0 7546 3271 7

Printed and bound in Great Britain by MPG Books Ltd, Bodmin, Cornwall

Contents

List of Figures *vii*
List of Tables *viii*
List of Contributors *ix*
Acknowledgements *xii*

1 Introduction
Marjorie Griffin Cohen and Stephen McBride 1

PART I: CHANGING NATURE OF STATE OBJECTIVES AND POWER

2 Globalization Begins (and Ends) at Home:
Bringing the State Back In
Leo Panitch 13

3 International Economic Agreements as Systems of Power
Stephen McBride 26

4 Regulatory Games States Play:
Managing Globalization Through Sectoral Policy
Anil Hira 41

5 Tax Expenditures:
The Social Policy of Globalization?
Lois Harder 59

6 National Politics and Globalization:
Varieties of Neo-Liberal Youth Labour Market Policy
Under Thatcher and Blair
Nigel Boyle and Ravi Roy 72

PART II: STRATEGIES FOR DEALING WITH GLOBAL TURBULENCE

7 Contesting Neoliberalism:
The Political Economy of Transnational Protest
Jeffrey M. Ayres 89

8 Trade Unions and Competitive Nationalism:
A House of Mirrors
Peter Graefe 105

9 Emerging Transnational Coalitions
Around Diamonds and Oil in Civil Conflicts in Africa
J. Andrew Grant, Sandra J. MacLean and Timothy M. Shaw 124

10 Foreign Migrant Workers and Civil Society in South Korea:
The Search for Power in an Era of Global Turbulence
Timothy C. Lim 140

11 Shaping 'Best Practice'? Union Responses to
Lean Production in the North American Automotive Industry
Chris Roberts 156

12 'Decent Work': The Shifting Role of the ILO and
the Struggle For Global Social Justice
Leah F. Vosko 174

Index *191*

List of Figures

Figure 4.1:	Structural Constraints on State Autonomy	45
Figure 9.1:	UNITA's Income from Diamond Sales, 1992-2000	129
Figure 9.2:	Recent Trends in World Oil Prices, 1999-2001	130
Figure 11.1:	Technical, Social and Organizational Dimensions of Lean Production	160
Figure 11.2:	Work Ownership Provisions	165

List of Tables

Table 4.1: Factors Determining State Autonomy from Globalization 46
Table 4.2: Examples of Sectoral Policy Interventions 50

List of Contributors

Jeffrey M. Ayres is an associate professor of Political Science at Saint Michael's College in Colchester, Vermont, and an adjunct professor of Canadian Studies at the University of Vermont. He is the author of *Defying Conventional Wisdom: Political Movements And Popular Contention Against North American Free Trade* (1998), and several articles on Canadian politics, political economy and social movements.

Nigel Boyle is associate professor of Political Studies at Pitzer College, Claremont. He is also Deputy Director of the European Union Center of California. His Ph.D. is from Duke University. He taught at University College, Oxford prior to teaching at Pitzer. His research has focused on the welfare state, with particular reference to British labour market policy.

Marjorie Griffin Cohen is an economist who is a professor of Political Science and Women's Studies at Simon Fraser University. She is an activist who has served on the executive board of the National Action Committee on the Status of Women, the Coalition Against Free Trade and the Canadian Centre for Policy Alternatives. She is the author of *Women's Work, Markets And Economic Development In Nineteenth Century Ontario* (1988), *Free Trade And The Future Of Women's Work* (1987), *From Public Good To Private Exploitation* (2001), and is co-author of a two volume series, *Canadian Women's Issues* (1993, 1995).

Peter Graefe is a doctoral candidate in Political Science at the Université de Montréal. He has published articles on Québec's economic development strategy, *Studies In Political Economy* (2000), and on the social economy, *Policy And Politics*, forthcoming, *Critical Social Policy* (2001), *Lien Social Et Politiques* (1999).

J. Andrew Grant is a SSHRC Doctoral Fellow and Ph.D. candidate in Political Science at Dalhousie University, Halifax. Grant has presented papers at several major international conferences, such as the meetings of the International Studies Association and the International Political Science Association. Grant is also a Doctoral Fellow in the Centre for Foreign Policy Studies at Dalhousie University, and his current research is on development, democratization, civil conflict, and the political economy of violence in Africa.

Lois Harder is an assistant professor of Political Science at the University of Alberta where she teaches Canadian political economy and gender and politics. Her current research concerns the social policy uses of tax expenditures and the democratic consequences of this mode of policy delivery. Her recent publications include 'Social Policy for the Postmodern Condition: Early Intuitions', published in French in the *Canadian Review Of Social Policy* (2000), and 'Whither the Social Citizen?' in *Canada In A Globalizing Era: Politics In The 21st Century*, J. Brodie and L. Trimble (eds.), forthcoming.

Anil Hira is assistant professor of Political Science and Latin American Studies at Simon Fraser University. He holds a Ph.D. in Political Science from Claremont Graduate University and has held numerous policy positions. His principal focus is Latin American economic and energy policy. His book, *Ideas And Economic Policy In Latin America*, was published in 1998.

Timothy C. Lim is an assistant professor of Political Science at California State University, Los Angeles. He specializes in East Asian political economy, about which he has published numerous articles. Professor Lim is currently working on two books: *Understanding The New Global Political Economy* and *Thinking Comparatively: An Introduction To Comparative Method And Theory.*

Sandra J. MacLean is an assistant professor of Political Science and a Fellow at the Centre for Foreign Policy Studies, Dalhousie University, Halifax. She is co-editor of *Crises Of Governance In Asia And Africa* (2001), and has contributed recently to *Canadian Foreign Policy*, *Third World Quarterly*, *Canadian Journal Of Development Studies*, *New Political Economy*, and *Journal Of Contemporary African Studies*, as well as to several edited collections.

Stephen McBride is a professor of Political Science, Simon Fraser University. He has published widely on political economy and public policy. His current research is focused on the domestic political and constitutional impact of international economic agreements and on the sustainability of neo-liberal globalization. His most recent books are *Paradigm Shift: Globalization and the Canadian State* (2001), and *Globalization and its Discontents*, co-edited with John Wiseman (2000).

Leo Panitch is a Distinguished Research Professor of Political Science at York University and Fellow of the Royal Society of Canada. He is the editor of the *Socialist Register*, and author of many books, including *The End Of Parliamentary Socialism*, *Social Democracy and Industrial Militancy* (1997), and *The Canadian State: Political Economy and Political Power* (1977).

Chris Roberts is a doctoral candidate in Political Science at York University in Toronto, completing a study of the postwar auto industry in Canada. His research interests lie in the area of trade unions, globalization and competitiveness.

Ravi Roy is a Postdoctoral Fellow at Claremont Graduate University. He earned his Ph.D. at Claremont Graduate University in 2000. He has taught at the University of California, Riverside and California State University, Fullerton. His research has focused on fiscal policy in the US and Britain, with particular reference to the role of normative belief systems.

Timothy M. Shaw is Director of the Institute of Commonwealth Studies at the University of London. He has been a faculty member at Dalhousie University for three decades and has been a visiting professor in Nigeria, South Africa, Uganda, Zambia and Zimbabwe. He has held research grants from CIDA, DFAIT, IDRC, Ford Foundation, SSHRC, UN, UNU, etc. His recent essays have appeared in *Canadian Foreign Policy*, *International Insights*, *New Political Economy*, and *Third World Quarterly*.

Leah F. Vosko is Canada Research Chair in Feminist Political Economy, School of Social Sciences, Joseph E. Atkinson School of Liberal and Professional Studies, York University, Toronto, Canada. She is author of *Temporary Work: The Gendered Rise Of A Precarious Employment Relationship* (2000), University of Toronto Press, and co-editor, with Wallace Clement, of *Changing Canada: Political Economy As Transformation*, McGill Queen's University Press, forthcoming.

Acknowledgements

Most of the chapters in this book were originally presented at a conference on Global Turbulence: Instability in National and International Political Economy held at Simon Fraser University (SFU) in July 2001. The conference was organised by the Department of Political Science at SFU and funded by the Boag Foundation, the Social Sciences and Humanities Research Council of Canada, and Simon Fraser University. This collection publishes a selection of the best papers from the conference, which have since been extensively reviewed and revised, together with other chapters that were commissioned for the volume. We would like to thank all those who made the conference possible, as well as those who assisted in the preparation of the book manuscript.

Special thanks go to Margaret Manery and Randi Drevland for their diligent editorial work and assistance in preparing camera ready copy. Finally, we would like to thank Kirstin Howgate and Pamela Bertram at Ashgate, as well as Tim Shaw, the Series Editor at Ashgate, for their support and assistance in the completion of this project.

Vancouver, BC, Canada	Marjorie Griffin Cohen
North Vancouver, BC, Canada	Stephen McBride

Chapter 1

Introduction

Marjorie Griffin Cohen and Stephen McBride

Introduction

Within living memory turbulence has been a constant feature of world developments. Historically, global turbulence has reflected the clash of different civilizations, different systems of thought, different political objectives. The most obvious examples in the 20th century were the turbulences occasioned by the rise of fascism and Nazism. And, of course, there was the turbulence generated by the rivalry between the Soviet and the American plans for the world. Most recently, the political turbulence associated with September 11th and the divergent view of Islam and the West highlight the chasm between different systems of thought and belief.

The turbulence of this book, however, is not brought about by the clashes between cultures or civilizations. The turbulence of this book is about the dislocations that arise within a system that is characterized by its sameness throughout most of the world. Globalization represents a uniform system of thought and practice, based on a 'consensus' originating in Washington, that all nations and all people within nations throughout the world should root their decisions and actions in one type of economic system. It is a system based on the American model and has unfolded as a world system that is codified, albeit fairly primitively at present, in international economic law, but is also backed up by military might of the U.S. superpower.

That sameness should occasion turbulence is counterintuitive, because the point of sameness is to avoid conflict. And this probably is the objective of those who want uniform economic policies to blanket most of the globe. But the results of these policies have created serious dislocations that have undercut the efforts made by countless people in many countries to construct democratic institutions that would provide a modicum of economic and social security. The world has not become a better place because of the policies and institutions of globalization. Over the last 20 years of the project of globalization most countries in the world are worse off, and within the countries that can be technically be deemed successes, the divergence in the experiences of people has increased dramatically.[1]

The divergence between poor and wealthy countries has widened considerably. Most telling is the dramatic slowdown in economic growth for most poor countries, and an absolute decline in growth for the poorest countries in the world. But even in areas where progress is expected, such as life expectancy (probably the most significant indication of well-being), it has slowed significantly in all but the wealthiest countries. Similarly, progress in reducing infant mortality and improving education and literacy in middle-level and poor countries declined significantly.

People are conscious of the changes that globalization brings, and they are conscious of an acceleration of these changes to reflect an intensification of market principles in all decision-making. This is occurring despite outright failures on many levels of performance, even in wealthy countries. But most contentious is the shift in the perception that something can be done. The 'consensus' has been presented as though there is something inevitable .and unwavering about the development of a uniform economic system, regardless of the objectives, needs and resources of different people throughout the world.

During the 1990s, the term 'globalization' became the flavour of the decade among many journalists and academics. From the beginning, the term had both empirical and ideological characteristics. Empirically, globalization referred to economic, political and cultural developments that were said to constitute a new era. Economically, the key referents were heightened levels of international trade and investment, deregulation of financial and capital flows, and the emergence of global production networks connected to transnational corporations. Politically, the collapse of the Soviet Union seemed to mark the end of an alternative to capitalism and liberal democracy. With the removal of this alternative, liberal capitalist ideas were triumphant, the 'end of history' was proclaimed, and the newly ascendant neoliberals moved quickly to construct a world of freer markets, with a transformed and restricted role for political institutions like the state. Culturally, a rather chaotic mix of homogenization and fragmentation was said to result (Waters, 2001; McBride, 2001, Ch.2).

However, the use of the term 'globalization' stretched far beyond these descriptive or empirical claims. It was an idea that aimed to shape the world more than describe it (Steger, 2002, Ch. 3.)[2] As an ideology, globalization makes several heroic claims. The over-arching claim rests on the superior performance of markets for decision-making in all circumstances, in both the national and the international setting. The implication for the state, at least rhetorically, is that its role ought to be limited to facilitating marketization. Another claim is that globalization is both inevitable and irresistible. The implication for states, individuals and groups is that resistance is futile, since adaptation to the discipline of the global market is the only rational available choice. This claim is related to the notion that markets and technology generate the process of change and that human agency is absent as the driving force of 'globalization'. The central claim of globalist ideology is that everyone throughout the world benefits both in economic terms (as a positive sum game) and in human terms (democracy). This relates to the underlying assumption that markets are inherently efficient, competitive and democratic. The promise of democracy throughout the world as a result of the adoption of unregulated markets highlights the futility of any attempt to characterize globalization as either 'good' or 'bad'. The ideology declares it inherently good and leaves little space for debate. This ideology of the globalists is a powerful force in shaping the nature of international institutions – institutions whose dictates make the globalist ideology self-fulfilling within nations.

The editors of this book challenge the claims of the globalist ideology. While we recognize that globalization is a real process that is attended by upheaval and turbulence in the international political economy, we will show, throughout this book, that none of the claims of the globalist ideology can be accepted as true. Compared to the 'certainties' of the globalist ideology, this book charts a dramatically different perspective of the process by which globalization has developed, of the state's implication in that process, and of the possibilities of resistance and posing of alternatives to neoliberal globalization. This book focuses on these issues in two main ways: first by dealing with the state's role under globalization; and second by showing how various major groups assess the changing climate of globalization and strategize to deal with turbulence in markets and regulatory regimes.

The first section of this book moves beyond the usual claim that the state is a victim of the power of globalization to show that the state is heavily involved as a catalyst and facilitator of globalization. States certainly have changed their roles but, as Leo Panitch in chapter two shows, the transformation is 'from welfare states to states that would facilitate and police the free flow of capital around the globe'. This represents change, but not a reduced significance in the power or role of the state. And, it certainly contradicts the notion that globalization is just happening and 'no one is in charge': Panitch's main point is that states, rather than being victims of globalization, are themselves the authors of global transformation and are a part of a system that facilitates and polices the institutional changes that support it. This analysis sees the state as retaining considerable power, but does not feel that the future is immutable, if states themselves can be made responsive to democratic power.

This new role of the state is one that fits the classic liberal conception of state. Liberals envisage a strong, but limited state. In particular, the state should defend rather than interfere with the operation of markets. While the need for some degree of economic regulation is conceded, great care should be taken to ensure that this is enabling, rather than restrictive, as far as markets are concerned. This conception of the state's role is being locked into place through the requirements of new international economic agreements. The urgency with which this project is pursued itself suggests that states remain quite capable of playing other roles, were political forces aligned differently. The effect of the 'quasi-constitutional' provisions of economic agreements is to make it more difficult for this to happen.

In the process of structurally reinforcing the liberal concept of the state through international economic law, the possibility of democratic governance is reduced. Regardless of formal voting procedures and the like, the effect of the politically constructed 'conditioning framework' embodied in international economic agreements, is to constrain the scope of democracy (Grinspun and Kreklewich, 1994). As Stephen McBride shows in chapter three, these agreements define many matters as being beyond the reach of democratic decision-making and, as a result, the decisions of people within nations become confined to a narrower range of activity. Even the possibility of moderating the outcomes of market actions is critically reduced. What remains is a liberalism that is stripped of some of the democratic elements that had been grafted onto it over the past century and a half. McBride sees that state capacity for policy-making has been diminished, but like Panitch, he sees this as a situation that involved not just the willful cooperation of the states themselves, but their leadership in bringing about this situation.

Politics is still about who gets what, when, and how, and these issues should be settled within the democratic political system, not by outside forces. A focus on the interests that have promoted the state's advocacy of globalization is overdue. Those who promote it have something to gain from a realignment of economic and political forces in the world. Any hard look at the benefits of globalization makes it clear that they are at best, asymmetrical. But clearly there are losers and even among the winners the distribution is uneven. The convenience of globalization, for the elites, is that political decisions that benefit one group of countries or one class of people can appear to be impartially derived from the forces of international competition. These elites do not have to take responsibility, then, for the outcomes that clearly favour their interests.

This book claims that political choices still exist and the policies of individual states can make a difference in outcomes for people. Despite the constraints of the institutions of globalization, empirical studies suggest considerable policy divergence exists between states (Hoberg, 2000; McBride and Williams, 2001; Reiger and Leibfried, 1998). As Anil Hira shows in chapter four, this clearly indicates the continued capacity for the state to take an active role in policy making. But, as Hira points out, how a state will respond depends on both its own understanding of its domestic economy and a clearly articulated national strategy. Hira is interested in regulatory policy as a middle-ground in which capable states can use regulatory policy to pursue sectoral and national competitiveness policies, as well as a host of domestic policy concerns.

Where convergence does appear to exist, as with neoliberal continuities between 'right' and 'left' governments within states, it can often be explained by recourse to domestic politics, rather than the inexorable pressures of globalization. This is the argument advanced by Nigel Boyle and Ravi Roy in chapter six where they analyze youth labour market policy in Britain. This chapter explores the neoliberal policy paradigm that underlies the consistencies in youth labour market policies over time and from governments with different policy claims – i.e. from Thatcher to Blair. These youth labour policies were clearly motivated by domestic choices, rather than by the pressures of globalization. This chapter reinforces the general theme of the book that political decisions are at the heart of the neoliberal directions that states take.

States increasingly engage in opaque and complex maneuvers to adapt their citizens to the discipline of globalism. Lois Harder, in chapter five explains one aspect of this in her analysis of the increased use of tax expenditures to achieve social policy aims. This choice of the state also can be attributed to domestic neoliberalism as easily as to the impact of globalization. Making a distinction between the two is important, however, because it does not allow states and politicians to escape from taking responsibility for the many undesirable outcomes of policies they claim are necessary to deal with globalization. Harder's point (using U.S. and Canadian data) is that the tax system is playing an increasingly significant role as a delivery vehicle for social policy. This elevation of the role of the tax system has been undertaken in an attempt to reduce state involvement in direct funding and provision of social programs. Proponents of this shift away from directly funded programs toward tax expenditures argue that citizens, as consumers, are better able to address their specific needs when they have access to services through the market. Among the casualties of this increased use of the tax system are public debates about social responsibility and the desired outcomes of collective social programs.

The clear message of this book is that states continue to 'matter'. The assertion, in globalist ideology, that their day is over both hides the truth and, to the extent it enters into popular consciousness, serves to disable opposition to neoliberal globalization. A focus on the progressive role that nation-states could play may not be a sufficient platform for anti-globalism activism, but it remains a necessary part of the puzzle of what to do about globalization.

The second part of this book focuses on how different groups of people, both within countries and in trans-national alliances, assess the changing climate of globalization and strategize to deal with the turbulence it creates. These groups implicitly understand that there is nothing inherently inevitable about globalization, despite its almost universal reach. They see globalization and the neoliberal policies associated with it as a creation of power – much as is any specific political institution.

The shift in the structure and location of power means that for those who want to contest the unfolding of the world in the shadow of a super-market, the target for action is often not firmly in focus. The state and corporations, the normal targets for action in a power structure where the rule of law is situated within the state, become more nebulous entities as radical changes occur in global political cultures and institutions. The kinds of strategies that had been effective for groups on the margins in capitalist societies (labour, women, racial minorities) have less effect, as states are able to sidestep social responsibilities in the name of competitiveness. Similarly, the hyper-mobility of capital makes the normal constraints on corporations that had been built up over a century, more easily evaded as they shift, or threaten to shift their activities to nations that ensure minimal constraints on corporate activity.

The very intention of 'liberalization' of markets is to undo the work of millions of women and men within the boundaries of nations whose specific project over the last couple of centuries has been to get the law to intervene on their behalf to bring about results that were not possible with a self-regulating market. The result is that the state-oriented arena for debate and action is shifting substantially with the growth of international institutions that condition the action of nations.

This does not mean that strategies for dealing with globalization within states is dormant or is confined to protests to hold on to the gains made in the past. As this section of the book will show, 'despite the dismal ratcheting-down of states', and taste for new programs to protect people from the vagaries of the market, some space is being created by people for innovative change within states themselves. The strategies used range from those that begin within the conditions established by globalization and try to maneuver within this framework, to those that challenge the very parameters that are being established and that insist on democratic representation in deciding what the parameters for social and economic life will be.

Peter Graefe, in chapter eight, pursues the argument that the hollowing out of the nation-state has opened spaces for minority nations to assert themselves, particularly by deploying regional development strategies. For labour movements in minority nations, this shift promises a more inclusive development model based on social partnerships and high wages. This promise is nevertheless threatened as capital mobility and competition tilt the cross-class compacts of regional strategies and of the nationalist movement towards business interests. Using 'competitive nationalism' to obtain representation for the labour movement, therefore, may fail by leading labour to accept a one-sided partnership. His chapter illustrates this dynamic using the experience of the labour movement in Quebec, Canada.

Timothy Lim's examination of foreign migrant workers in chapter eleven provides an understanding of the process by which seemingly powerless social groups – in conjunction with a network of globally-oriented and socially-conscious NGOs – can take advantage of ongoing changes in the global system to challenge and perhaps overturn historically reproduced practices of exploitation and subordination. Specifically, this chapter focuses on the relationship between foreign migrant workers – historically, one of the weakest and most marginalized of social groups – and Korean NGOs. He shows how and why this relationship has led to significant and progressive changes for foreign migrant workers in context of South Korea's national policies.

Is globalization forcing national industries to converge willy-nilly towards a single model of work and employment relations? Chris Roberts discusses this issue through an analysis of the diffusion of lean manufacturing. Lean manufacturing is thought to be driving a world-wide convergence on 'global best practice', narrowing the competitive gap, restoring balanced trade, and restabilizing employment in the North American auto industry. However, neither uniformity nor stability is likely to result from the diffusion of lean techniques, since lean production itself continues to diffuse through experimentation and incremental change. Roberts argues that trade unions play a key role in shaping this process of uneven development, as the example of the Canadian Auto Workers suggests.

Political action to contest globalization is most obvious on the international scene, particularly as international financial and trade institutions seem to be on the run and hiding from visible protests from people who demonstrate their strong distaste for the unfair manipulation of the world's economic and social organizations. Jeffrey Ayres, in chapter seven, analyses how, over time, popular contention has undergone a noticeable transnational innovation, in forms of association, tactics adopted and targets identified. For Ayres the strength of transnational protest highlights the problems of legitimacy that the international regulatory regimes face. But with the state responses to September

11th, particularly with a renewed push for neoliberal policies as part of state responses to terrorism, it is far from clear whether this re-scripting of protest strategies will succeed in redirecting efforts towards containing and regulating corporations and capital on a global scale.

The transnational protest analyzed by Ayres has parallels, albeit in less dramatic forms, to the instability that globalization has created in Africa and the problems of creating transnational alliances. As Grant, MacLean and Shaw show in chapter nine, the extraordinary value of diamonds and oil represent huge challenges for transnational coalition building, an action that will be essential to change the dynamic of extreme instability through civil war in Africa. Their main point is that the civil strife can be understood only within the context of ever-changing national, international, and global political economies. This 'political economy of violence' approach explores the multi-level, transnational nature of Africa's civil conflicts as well as the networks of multiple formal and informal actors who are helping to fuel them. The strategies for change these authors find promising relate to the innovative initiatives undertaken by 'mixed-actor' transnational coalitions of state and non-state actors that have emerged as a response to these conflicts.

The proliferation of supranational trade agreements brings with them the simultaneous de-regulation of national labour markets. This has resulted in increased calls for some type of international body to protect labour. One outcome of these developments is that international organizations, like the International Labour Organization (ILO), are engaged in a process of rethinking their roles under globalization. Leah Vosko in chapter twelve examines the ILO's new platform of action known as *Decent Work*. Vosko argues that *Decent Work* is emblematic of the evolving political struggles within the ILO that mirrors many of the challenges to the prevailing order ushered in by globalization. *Decent Work* represents an effort at mediating tensions inside the ILO between global capital and various industrialized states and an increasingly vocal group of member states, trade unions, women's organizations and other NGOs concerned with improving the lives of marginalized workers. Two sets of initiatives underpinning *Decent Work* highlight its mediating role: the new Social Declaration – the ILO's attempt to compel member states to abide by 'core labour standards' – and the commitment by the ILO to craft standard-setting instruments to improve the situation of marginalized workers. The chapter examines these initiatives in depth and tries to discern if there really is space at the ILO to advance progressive labour standards and controls on capital.

Social activists' and state responses to globalization are on radically different trajectories. For the most part the unfolding of the world under globalization is structured to meet the needs of states that want to pursue neoliberal practices without the inconvenience that domestic debate and messy democratic struggles would entail. With the codification of neoliberal practice in international trade and investment law, the superstructure for state behaviour is established. The role of the state then shifts from being a champion of its people in the international arena to ensuring that its citizens conform to the dictates of international economic law.

While the mechanisms of globalization are complex and its politics often opaque, the effects of the changes it brings about are not obscure to many people and often these changes provoke the kind of outrage that can foster extreme political dissent. This danger is clear to political and corporate elites: increasingly they hide their meetings from the scrutiny of the public but also they now try, occasionally, to mediate the anger directed toward them by agreeing to more inclusive practices in their decision-making. While activists are skeptical about the sincerity of the responses to democratic pressure in institutions at the international level, and suspect that conciliatory actions are mainly lip-service to advert bad publicity, it is clear that conditions that currently exist will not remain the status quo. The nature of states are changing, but so too is the nature of international society. While people have been short-changed in the marketization of the globe, the indications are that the demands on states will not diminish, nor will the demands of activists at the international level.

Notes

1 The figures that follow come from Mark Weisbrot, Dean Baker, Egor Kraev and Judy Chen, 2001.

2 The following borrows from Steger's typology.

References

Grinspun, Ricardo and Kreklewich, Robert (1994), 'Consolidating Neoliberal Reforms "Free Trade" as a Conditioning Framework', *Studies in Political Economy*, Vol. 43.

Hoberg, George (2000), 'Canada and North American Integration', *Canadian Public Policy*, Vol. XXVI, Supplement 2.

McBride, Stephen (2001), Paradigm Shift: Globalization and the Canadian State, Fernwood, Halifax.

McBride, Stephen and Williams, Russell A. (2001). 'Globalization, the Restructuring of Labour Markets and Policy Convergence: The OECD "Jobs Strategy"', *Global Social Policy*, Vol. 1, No. 3, December, pp. 283-311.

Rieger, Elmar and Leibfried, Stephan (1998), 'Welfare State Limits to Globalization', *Politics and Society*. Vol. 26, No. 3, September.

Steger, Manfred B. (2002), *Globalism: The New Market Ideology*, Rowman and Littlefield, Oxford.

Waters, Malcolm (2001), *Globalization*, 2nd Ed, Routledge, New York.

Weisbrot, Mark, Baker, Dean, Kraev, Egor and Chen, Judy (2001), *The Scorecard on Globalization 1980-2000: Twenty Years of Diminished Progress*, Washington Center for Economic and Policy Research, Washington, D.C.

Part I

Changing Nature of State Objectives and Power

Chapter 2

Globalization Begins (and Ends) at Home: Bringing the State Back In[1]

Leo Panitch

Every time the winter or summer Olympics roll around, I am struck by how much the evident tension they reflect between nationalism and internationalism is relevant for the understanding of globalization. On the one hand, a showcase for international cooperation and solidarity; on the other, an opportunity for the expressions of national pride and boosterism. On the one hand, global interdependence in a world economy; on the other, each state scrambling to advance its economic competitiveness, to beat its rivals at maximizing exports. On the one hand, the fall of tariff walls, and the Berlin Wall; on the other, new nationalisms 'exploding like fire-crackers across much of the world'.[2] On the one hand, American governments leading the drive to break down barriers to trade and investment; on the other hand, the same governments raising higher and higher the barriers to the movement of people across their borders. (This was true long before September 11th, as seen in the Clinton administration's commitment to massively increasing the size and resources of the patrol policing the border with Mexico at the same time as legislation was advanced in Congress to establish extensive entry controls at the Canadian border.)

In order to understand what globalization actually amounts to in the real world, in light of such apparent contradictions, we had better begin with some careful reflections on the proper meaning of the term. It is important to recall that the clearest description of the process now called globalization rolled off the press of a London publisher over a hundred and fifty years ago.

> ...the world-market [has] given a cosmopolitan character to production and consumption in every country... it has drawn from under the feet of industry the national ground on which it stood. All old-established industries have been destroyed or are daily being destroyed. They are dislodged by new industries, whose introduction becomes a life and death question for all civilised nations, by industries that no longer work up indigenous raw material, but raw material drawn from the remotest zones; industries whose products are consumed, not only at home, but in every quarter of the globe. In place of the old wants, satisfied by the productions of the country, we find new wants, requiring for their satisfaction the products of distant lands and climes. In place of the old local and national seclusion and self-sufficiency, we have intercourse in every direction, universal inter-dependence of nations. And as

> in material, so also in intellectual production. The intellectual creations of individual nations become common property. National one-sidedness and narrow-mindedness become more and more impossible, and from the numerous national and local literatures, there arises a world literature (Marx, 1988, pp.58-9).

This is, of course, Karl Marx, whose Communist Manifesto was printed in London between February 14th and 18th, 1848. In good part because of that kind of description of capitalism, it became the 19th century text that exercised more influence on the twentieth century than any other.

So is there really anything new about globalization today? Or is it just 'globaloney', as some wags have suggested, designed to convince people at the end of the 20th century what they couldn't be convinced of for most of it – that is, that there is nothing that can be done to stop ruthless economic competitiveness and commodity fetishism taking over every aspect of our lives and encompassing the whole world. And for those of us who discern that behind (or should we really say at the forefront?) of globalization lies the imperial American state, does the word globalization only provide a cover for what President Truman meant when he said, in his famous speech at Baylor University on March 6th, 1947, that 'the American system could survive in America only if it became a world system' (Jagan, 1994, p.1).

There is something distinctive, I think, in what is being called globalization today, different from what it meant in 1848 at the birth of modern free trade, liberal nationalism and internationalist communism, or a century later just after World War Two when most of the world was just escaping from the old European imperialisms and when a different kind of American imperialism (whose power penetrates but does not directly colonize) was just emerging. There are five senses in which the processes we call globalization today really means something distinctive – if not exactly new, then at least, an important new stage in modern world history:

i) The first sense is geo-political and has to do with the collapse of Communism in the former USSR and Eastern Europe, as well as the turn to capitalism in China and Vietnam by Communist elites that continue to rule those countries. What this means is the spatial extension of capitalism into areas of the globe largely closed to it for much of the 20th century.

ii) The second sense is cultural, and pertains to the broad global sweep of the capitalist ideas and values that define our neo-liberal era. The bourgeoisie is making 'the world in its own image' with impunity almost unparalleled since Marx used this phrase to describe that class's growing dominance 150 years ago.

iii) The third sense has to do with the actual formation of a transnational capitalist class, one that putatively stands above the various national identities and affiliations of the capitalist classes in the past (although it is generally admitted that this transnational capitalist class formation process is by no means yet very far advanced).

iv) The fourth and much the strongest sense that globalization connotes might be termed the new capital accumulation on a world scale, a system of world-wide production and finance, made technologically possible by computerization and the information-communications revolution in the means of production in our time, and characterized by a vast increase in the size, flow and speed of foreign direct investment and trade, and accompanied by an even more vast creation of international credit, currency flows, speculation, futures markets, and private and public debt.

v) Finally, the fifth sense pertains to the internationalization of the state, which, properly speaking, must be understood not in terms of transnational capital escaping the nation-state, but rather in terms of states becoming more and more attuned to fostering and/or accommodating to capital accumulation on a world scale.

Each of these meanings of globalization deserves very close analysis. And the first thing that must be said is that as regards each of them, one particular state stands at the centre of the process. In the geo-political sphere, the USA stands as the police force of world order, the only surviving superpower after the Cold War. In the cultural arena, American media conglomerates are predominant in terms of global penetration. The world gets its news from CNN, and the US Motion Picture Association is ever vigilant to make sure that when it goes to the movies the world watches Hollywood. The man who owns Fox, Rupert Murdoch, was an Australian who changed his citizenship to American so he could own a network in the USA – which only goes to show that even while America batters down the walls of cultural protection around the world, if you want to do big media business in America, nationality remains important. In terms of the formation of a transnational capitalist class, Americans also stand front and centre. While only about a third of Fortune Magazine's Global 500 corporations are owned by Americans (still far more than any other country), let us not forget that the rest of the world sends its ambitious would-be capitalists to study there. A Wharton School of Business spokesman has been quoted as saying: 'We want to be a school of management of the world that just happens to be in Philadelphia' (Sklar, 1997, p.522).

But it doesn't *just* happen – and the reason why it happens is that at the centre of the processes of capital accumulation and speculation on a world scale stands American capital. American manufacturing industry is not the basket case that so many people thought it was back when Japan, before the demise of its economy in the1990s, was being extolled as the new workshop of the world. American productivity increases in the 1990s were no mirage; they reflected the incorporation of its 'new economy' into its 'old economy'. The USA is at the same time both the largest source, and the largest recipient, of world investment. The predominance of New York's financial institutions over all others, and the senior position of the dollar among world currencies, both reflect and sustain this. The size of the American trade deficit is less a sign of the weakness of American capital than evidence that every other country's exports are deeply dependent on the American domestic consumer market. Capital continues to flow into New York despite the size of the American trade deficit, and while this capital account coverage of the trade deficit hardly means that American economic crises are a thing of the past, it is clear that when a recession occurs in the

USA, it becomes a world recession, and that when the American speculative bubble threatens to burst, so does every other.

As for the political structures that oversee globalization, it is also no accident that Washington is the home of the World Bank and IMF, where the US Treasury's influence is overwhelming. The global predominance of the American state's military apparatus hardly needs stressing in the wake of the war on Afghanistan after September 11th, but this had already been evident in the Gulf War that opened the decade of the 1990s, and in the war on Yugoslavia that closed it. If there is a global ruling class, it is one very closely related to the American state.

This already signals the need for an important qualification to the claim that globalization is a process that transcends the nation-state, as so many people have mistakenly claimed. And this is only the first of many such qualifications that need to be made. Alongside global economic integration, we also see the emergence of new nationalisms, and we see strong and atavistic reactions, not least in the form of Islamic fundamentalism (the clash between *Jihad vs. McWorld*, as Ben Barber (1995) put it in his marvellously prescient book title). But it must also be noted that even the multinational corporations retain a national identity. If over 150 of the world's leading MNCs in the 1990s were American, in terms of the nationality of their owners and boards of directors, by the same measure we could identify the others: 114 Japanese, 42 French, 40 German, 32 British, 16 Swiss, 12 Italian, 11 Dutch, and six Canadian. Of course, the fact that even multinational corporations are still in a very important sense national does not itself gainsay the real significance of the increasingly large proportion of global GDP that takes the form of international trade in goods and services, nor the vast increase in recent decades in foreign direct investment (multiplying by 10 times over the 1970s and 1980s and then doubling again in the 1990s). All of this has been aided and abetted by the emergence of a global market in currencies, credit, futures, stocks, bonds and derivatives of enormous size as well as range. But it does suggest that we need to be careful in associating any of this with the end of the state, or the even declining significance of national identities and affiliations.

This is all the more the case if we recognize that despite its remarkable dynamism, the uneven and unstable nature of global capitalism is – or ought to be – no less unmistakable. Just how uneven it is can be seen from the fact that two-thirds of foreign direct investment is accounted for by only five countries (the USA, Japan, Germany, France and the UK). The proportion of foreign direct investment going to the lesser developed countries actually fell from 30 per cent to 20 per cent over the two decades up to1990, and while there was a major increase in the flow of investment to the developing world in the 1990s (after the recession that began this decade in the advanced capitalist countries), some four-fifths of the enormous amounts of capital flowing to the third world in that decade was confined to only ten countries – eight in East Asia (above all China) and two in Latin America. Even those countries, many of which were seen as the great 'success stories' of our era, were soon famously caught in the throes of the major economic crisis that engulfed Mexico in 1994, East Asia in 1997, and Argentina in 2001.

Most countries, of course, were never success stories amidst globalization. If anything, it is notable how many countries global capitalism merely cast aside rather than integrated. The share of trade in GDP *fell* in 44 of 93 developing countries between the mid-1980s and mid-1990s, while the level of foreign investment in Africa actually *dropped* by 50 per cent (sub-Saharan Africa's share of world trade declined from four per cent to one per cent, even while its foreign debt increased to $160 billion).[3]

In this context, the long term implications of globalization are hard to read in any straightforward way – and they become all the more so once we introduce the highly contradictory direct relationship between global capitalism and the nation-state. It sometimes appears that nation-states are losing control in the context of globalization; yet as I have argued before, far from escaping the state or not needing states, global capitalism has had to effect globalization through their agency and very much must rely on them to manage global capitalism's contradictions.[4]

The British historian Eric Hobsbawm's much celebrated history of the twentieth century claimed that 'the most convenient world for multinational giants is one populated by dwarf states or no states at all' (Hobsbawm, 1996, p.281).

This has become a conventional view fostered by the fact that globalization has developed under the ideological umbrella of neo-liberalism. We constantly have heard the despairing refrain, especially from those who dislike neo-liberalism's free market rhetoric, that the global economic system lies beyond the control of any state, and that the state has lost power to the multinational corporations and financial markets. In so far as democracy exists at the level of nation-states, the ability of an internationally mobile capital to browbeat elected governments into compliance with its interests is no small cause of concern. But the view that capital has gone international and by-passed the state is misguided. We can understand this better if we use the concept of class rather than market when we think about the relationship between capitalism and the state

Far from not needing states any longer, all capitalists and especially multinational corporations, always need states. They need them to guarantee contracts and private property, to provide legal tender, to build infrastructure, to educate workers, to maintain order and to fight wars. We cannot understand the development of capitalism without the transformation of pre-capitalist states to serve all the above purposes. Historically, when capital moved around the globe in the era of imperialism, it came to rely on colonies of imperial states to do the very things – and more – that the state did to make capitalism viable at home. Today when foreign capital moves from one independent nation-state to another, it almost always becomes a powerful actor on the terrain of the state to which it has moved. And if it finds itself discriminated against, it is still likely to call to aid the more powerful states from which this capital emanated to protect it and advance its interests. What all this tells us is that while states remain important in the era of globalization, some states remain more important than others.

Far from being the victims of globalization, states are often better seen as the authors of it. The end of the post-war boom era in the early 1970s was a crucial turning point. Increased inter-capitalist competition, inflation and speculation against the dollar were accompanied by 'third world' revolts against a new American imperialism as well as by worker, youth and black militancy in the core capitalist countries. But this was also a conjuncture marked by the growing power of international finance that was straining against the limits of the old post-war regime. Under these conditions, the 1944 Bretton Woods agreement governing international finance crumbled and the Keynesian welfare state came under severe strain. Radical anti-capitalist political alternatives for democratizing the economy were on the agenda of social democratic parties, involving proposals for controls on multinational corporations and foreign investment, planning agreements with leading firms and unions, nationalization of banks and extension of exchange and capital controls. Even the left of the Democratic Party was able to bring some of these kinds of proposals onto the agenda of the US Congress in 1974. And the United Nations enacted in that year a Charter of Economic Rights and Duties of States which proclaimed that member nations had the right to 'regulate and exercise authority over foreign investment' and to 'regulate and supervise the activities of multinational corporations', the Charter went so far as to explicitly allow states to 'nationalize, expropriate or transfer ownership of foreign property' (Clarke and Barlow, 1997, p.13).

Against such radical proposals was arrayed a group of forces in the early 1970s which looked to states to resolve the crisis by more strongly supporting, rather than further controlling, international finance and multinational corporations. Especially important in this respect were a group of officials who had come into the Nixon White House in the late 1960s with close ties to Wall Street and armed with Milton Friedman's free market theories. They believed that what was needed, as the famous Trilateral Commission put it at the time, was to put a stop to governments being 'overloaded' by popular demands. But this did not mean that states were to be cashiered. Rather they had to be transformed from welfare states to states that would facilitate and police the free flow of capital around the globe.

This was to be done via coordinated state policies, a coordination led by the American state, which facilitated and policed the free flow of capital. What Robert Cox (1987) called the internationalization of the state does not mean the creation of a transnational 'superstate', but rather each state's acceptance of its responsibilities to global capitalism. Over the past two decades this has involved the removal of capital controls, the 'big bang' that attenuated financial market supervision, and the privatization of various industries (most important being telecommunications). While a common term for this is deregulation, it is a misleading term. The 1997 World Bank Report tried to make this clear when it insisted that 'liberalization is not the same as deregulation'. Free markets actually require more, not less, rules (Vogel, 1996). To ensure the effective operation of markets, states must legalize and juridify relations among market actors both in the domestic arena and in the international arena (through treaties like NAFTA).

States have certainly restructured themselves to make all this possible, both in terms of a shift in ideology and function within departments and agencies, and also in terms of a shift of power in favour of those, like Treasuries and Central Banks, which are most closely linked and directly responsible for managing the global economy. (A probably unconscious reference to such a shift was made when the economist Rudi Dornbusch noted, while being interviewed on CNBC on 8 January 1998 that the 'positive side' of the financial crisis in East Asia was that Korea was now 'owned and operated by our Treasury'. It used to be the State Department and the Pentagon, rather than Treasury that held such a franchise.)

The role that states are increasingly playing today in 'bail-outs'– whether of domestic banks or investment funds or of whole economies – reflects not only the financial instability globalization fosters, but also just how much states are needed in the era of globalization. This is not just a matter of this particular moment of crisis – this role for the state in the era of globalization was present all along. The American journalist Kevin Phillips has aptly sketched the considerable history of what he called 'financial socialism' over the past twenty years:

> Multinational corporations and Texas and Illinois banks got bailed out in the 1970s and early 1980s. By the late 1980s, federal bailouts had spread – at an eventual cost of hundreds of billions of dollars – to run-amok savings and loan and commercial banks... One expert pointed out that the share of US bank deposits held by financial institutions rescued by post-1986 federal insurance pay-outs exceeded the percentage held by banks that actually failed between 1928 and 1933, the Depression nadir...The new financial socialism – considerably more popular in Palm Beach than San Pedro – now collectivizes the perils of insolvency, not the means of production (Phillips, 1997).

Indeed, ever since the 1987 stock market crash, there has been a remarkable degree of planning on the part of the 'free market' states, singly and together, to try to prevent similar crashes – and they have been quite successful in keeping the chaos of the financial markets in bounds. None of this should be understood as functionally automatic; far from it, all this takes place through trial and error, negotiation and compromise, including a marked increase in corruption and the buying of political favours, as individual capitalists, faced with the insecurities and rigours of global competition, are tempted to secure from particular politicians what industrial subsidies, banking monopolies and tariff protections used to provide to whole sectors of capital (Tsoukalas, 1999).

The contradictions of globalization are such today that the political and ideological leadership of the neo-liberal right is increasingly vulnerable to challenge. Given the contradictions of globalization, a change in the nature of state sponsorship of it, both ideological and material, is in fact on the agenda. Neo-liberalism has reached its limits, even if globalization has not. This was presciently observed by the World Bank's *The State in a Changing World* report, released in June 1997 at the Bank's 'Global Knowledge' conference in Toronto. This was a momentous intervention, a bid to do no less than displace the Trilateral Commission's famous 1976 report with a new strategic perspective designed to carry globalization into the

21st century. In explicit contrast with the 'overloaded government' thesis of the former report, and in place of its advocacy of a 'minimalist state' (which the new Report suggests led many countries to 'overshoot the mark'), the World Bank now advocated a large role for the state *in protecting and correcting markets.*

The World Bank's central message was that 'globalization begins at home'. Not only does it see the state as a necessary 'partner, catalyst, facilitator', it goes further in recognising that 'markets cannot develop without effective property rights'. The World Bank's goal was to shift 'attention from the sterile debate of state and market to the more fundamental crisis of state effectiveness'. Effectiveness is defined primarily in terms of developing the kind of public rules and institutions that 'allow markets to flourish'. Thus while very much still in favour of the removal of restrictions on trade and capital flows, this was not sufficient if most countries were going to be successfully integrated into the global economy rather than marginalized. Even as regards the advanced capitalist states of Western Europe, the report cited opinion polls that showed a clear majority believed that governments should maintain current social benefits and protection levels (as opposed to only 12 per cent who thought they should be cut to enhance competitiveness in world markets). It cited similar orientations in Latin America and Asia, and in contrasting these with anti-egalitarian and anti-welfare state opinion in the United States, it makes the latter look like the exceptional case.

This World Bank's new perspective has generated considerable enthusiasm over the past few years on the part of many social democrats who have been troubled by the nostrums of neo-liberalism. But such enthusiasm is misplaced. It is not only that the IMF and the US Treasury have never been quite happy with this new 'post-Washington Consensus' perspective (with obvious implications for how far the World Bank has since been willing or able to act on it). It is also that there were plenty of passages in the 1997 Report that, despite the insistence that states must bring themselves closer to the people, make themselves more accountable to civil society, and reflect 'the full panoply of a society's interests', showed that the World Bank was not making too sharp a turn. It constantly warned states against biting off more than they could chew. States were advised to constrain themselves, to match their role to their capacities, so that when it actually came to advancing specific reforms, the World Bank carefully tied these to what, in keeping with the old 'Washington Consensus, it still called the "fundamentals"' insisting that 'maintaining *liberal trade, capital markets and investment regimes* is essential for economic growth'.

What this has meant is that even the World Bank has largely restricted itself to 'safe' reforms, that is, to the development of those state capacities that facilitate rather than hinder integration into capitalist globalization. Its 1997 Report had already rationalized the regressive shift in taxation from corporate and personal income taxes, and trade taxes, towards consumption-based taxes like VAT as an inevitable consequence of global integration. It also endorsed the discipline in the area of fiscal deficits that financial markets impose on 'open economies exposed to external risk', while wanting to reinforce this with 'the need to comply with the rules and conventions of international treaties [as] another spur to good behaviour'. Even in the areas of urban hospitals, clinics, universities, and transport, where governments concentrate their spending on infrastructure and social services, the World Bank has taken the view that markets and private spending can meet most needs, except for those of the very poorest minority of the population. 'Most curative health care is a (nearly) pure private good – if government does not foot the bill, all but the poorest will find ways to take care of themselves'. The Bank's concern with the social dimension of globalization is further tempered by its resignation to the fact that developing countries cannot afford western social programs as well as by its claims that greater social security can be achieved at lower costs by relying on communities and households to take up the slack.

What then really distinguished this new globalization cookbook from the old neo-liberal one? The goal of market liberalization now became explicitly linked to the development of effective regulatory state capacity to sustain private markets. In the crucial case of the financial sector, this was presented by the World Bank in terms of moving from 'control to prudential regulation...The case for the regulation of banking is as compelling as ever. Only the purpose has changed, from channelling credit in preferred directions to safeguarding the heath of the financial system'. But the World Bank's major concern was the endemic corruption that attends the state-capital interface in so much of the world. The Bank undertook a survey of 3,685 firms in 69 countries in an attempt to measure the extent of such corruption and their perception of the harm that it does to investment; and it found that 'high and unpredictable corruption' especially had this effect. Strengthening mechanisms for juridical monitoring and punishment, making rules more transparent, reducing the scope for official discretion, introducing competitive bidding processes into government – all these were advanced as administrative reforms that would help to contain the problem, albeit always in conjunction with 'policies that lower controls on foreign trade, remove entry barriers for private industry, and privatize state firms in a way that ensures competition'. One of the factors identified as most highly correlated with corruption is the erosion of civil servants wages relative to average manufacturing wages. The remedy advanced, notably, was the decompression of public sector salary structures, paying senior officials more while still constraining the overall total public sector wage bill through layoffs and wage restraint at the lower levels. Those at the top are to be given the material compensation to stop them lining their pockets. When it comes the lower levels, we see an appeal to 'worker dedication and commitment', stressing 'the importance of non-monetary rewards – recognition, appreciation, prestige, and awards – in motivating staff, over and above the adequacy of pay and meritocratic recruitment and promotion'.

Clearly, the international institutions that sponsor globalization do not now see themselves, if they ever did, as by-passing or displacing the state, but rather as operating to guarantee a certain type of state restructuring. Among these are international commercial or currency treaties through which the state commits themselves, as the World Bank put it, to 'self-restricting rules, which precisely specify the content of policy and lock it into mechanisms that are costly to reverse'. What are we to conclude, then, about the future of the nation-state? It is clear that there is a future for the nation-state, not only despite globalization but rather because of it. But as to what kind of a future, we hardly have to accept the limited vision of the World Bank. Rather, the more radical options advanced in the early 1970s, when the compromises made with the capitalist classes in the post-war era became so badly unstuck, deserve to be brought back on the agenda and extended. Given the limits of those compromises and the great costs to social justice of what came to succeed them in recent decades, it makes eminent sense to opt once again for radical strategies of democratizing the nation-state to the end of democratizing the economy. This can only happen in the wake of a radical shift in the balance of class forces within each state, one that actually leads to taking power away from the capitalist classes rather than just trying to compensate the people for leaving capital in control. It is only such a strategy, it seems, that offers the prospect of an alternative to the state being turned completely over to facilitating and codifying global capitalism while socializing only the financial investors and speculators 'perils of insolvency'.

It is very important to make this point now when the IMF and the 'Washington Consensus' have come under such sharp criticism from many diverse quarters in recent years, and when the bloom has come off neo-liberal globalization everywhere, including in the USA, let alone Argentina. For solutions are not going to found in trying to turn the IMF into some sort of beneficent super-state, nor even in attaching side agreements on labour or environmental rights to international treaties, a strategy which will at best reinforce the type of second-order state reforms advanced by the World Bank. The overarching priority of the state, despite such reforms, will remain that of fostering the penetration of capitalist values into every dimension of state-society relations as well as every corner of the globe and every facet of human life.

Nor will a solution be found in social democratic strategies that accommodate themselves to globalization by undercutting social benefits in order to advance labour-market flexibility. Social democratic economic strategies that increasingly rely on export competitiveness for 'success' ignores the ethical dilemmas this inevitably entails in terms of the more successful countries exporting their unemployment to the countries that are less successful. And even what they have to say by way of encouraging their own citizens to be more competitive is ethically suspect. It is as though, seeing a man on the street, hungry and homeless, you approach his problem only through the optic of his not being motivated enough, entrepreneurial enough, skilled enough to get a job, rather than through the optic of there being something fundamentally wrong with the capitalist system. There is nothing much to do with social justice in a value system that begins with the competitiveness optic. But there is also a pragmatic problem with such a competitiveness strategy. For it aggravates the crisis-ridden nature of globalization, both in terms of the overproduction that must attend a system where everyone is trying to increase their exports and limit their imports, and in terms of the financial instability that attends capital movements attuned to free exchange rates in such a system.

The types of reforms that are needed are indeed radical ones. They begin with capital controls coordinated among as many countries as possible so as to increase their viability. But these must be accompanied by a shift towards more inward-oriented economic strategies, planning trade to allow for different orientations to production, environmental standards, and the distribution of work and working time in the various communities and regions that make up each nation-state (Albo, 1997). And none of this can happen unless it reflects what Tony Benn in the early 1970s called 'a fundamental shift in wealth and power towards working people and their families', recognising that this too would require a strategy to develop the democratic and planning capacities of people at their places of work and in public institutions so they could actually effectively exercise greater popular power.

All this would entail, of course, a far more extensive restructuring of the state than has taken place amidst globalization, including a very different kind of shift in the hierarchy of state departments and agencies and a very different transformation in the ideology and purpose of state personnel in every branch. The former American Secretary of Labour, Robert Reich's book about life inside the Clinton Administration, *Locked in the Cabinet,* contains a humorous passage that is very relevant to the point I am making here. After describing a lunch with Alan Greenspan at the Federal Reserve, Reich reveals to his readers what he really had wanted (but did not have the courage) to ask Greenspan, and how he believes Greenspan himself would have replied had he been completely honest:

> *Q: What's your purpose in life?*
> *A: To stamp out inflation.*
> *Q: Even if that means high unemployment.*
> *A: You bet.*
> *Q: Even if it requires slow growth and stagnant wages?*
> *A: Right you are.*
> *Q: Even if it means drastic cuts in federal programs that help working people and the poor?*
> *A: Absolutely, if that's what it takes to balance the budget and remove all temptation to inflate away the government debt.*
> *Q: But why? A little inflation never hurt anybody.*
> *A: You're wrong. It hurts bond traders and lenders.*
> *Q: But why place their interests over everybody else's interest in good jobs?*
> *A. Because I'm a capitalist and capitalism is driven by the filthy rich. They make their money off bonds. Your constituents are just plain filthy. They have to work for a living.*
> *Q: You're the nation's central banker. You should be accountable to all Americans.*
> *A: But I'm not and neither is the Fed...*
> *Q. Well you can take your crummy lunch and cram it, you robber-baron pimp.*
> *A: Go suck on a pickle, you Bolshevik dwarf* (Reich, 1997, pp.82-3).

But what if Clinton had made Reich head of the Federal Reserve rather than Greenspan? Would that have solved the problem? Don't start by imagining the reaction on Wall Street. Think first of all of the reaction inside the Federal Reserve itself. Reich knows this – that is why he has Greenspan say that not only is he primarily accountable to capitalists, but *so is the Fed.* It is not only that particular individuals would need to go, it is the very purpose and structure of the agencies themselves that would need to be transformed.

Such a transformation of the state can only be brought about by powerful movements outside the state, but such movements also arise in a dialectical relationship with states and may be consciously fostered rather than repressed by new left-wing governments. Nicos Poulantzas (1973) used to define the function of the capitalist state as that of organizing the ruling classes and disorganizing the subordinate classes. We need to elect the kinds of governments and develop the kind of state personnel who will try to reverse that – who will try to disorganize the capitalists, while helping the people get organized. The struggle for this will necessarily take place within each state, although it will also be encouraged and even inspired by linkages with movements engaged in similar struggles across the globe. Radical alternatives to global capitalism, in other words, will also reflect their own dialectic between the national and the global.

Notes

1 This essay draws on a lecture delivered at Bucknell University, February 18, 1998, parts of which, although considerably revised here, were previously published in *Monthly Review* (1998) and in *Working Papers in Local Governance and Democracy* (1999).

2 The phrase is Anderson's, p.367.

3 All these figures are from The World Bank's World Development Report for 1997, Chapter 8. See also, Bond, 2001.

4 See, for instance, Panitch, 1996.

References

Albo, Gregory (1997), 'A World Market of Opportunities? Capitalist Obstacles and Left Economic Policy', in L. Panitch (ed), *Ruthless Criticism of All that Exists,* The Socialist Register, Merlin, London.

Anderson, Perry (1992), *Zones of Engagement*, Verso, London.

Barber, Benjamin R. (1995), *Jihad vs. McWorld*, Random House, New York.

Bond, Patrick (2001), *Against Global Apartheid,* University of Cape Town Press, Cape Town, South Africa.

Clarke, Tony and Barlow, Maude (1997), *MAI*, Stoddart, Toronto.

Cox, Robert (1987), *Production, Power and World Order*, Columbia University Press, New York.

Hobsbawm, Eric (1996), *The Age of Extremes*, Penguin, London.

Jagan, Cheddi (1994), *Forbidden Freedom*, 3rd edn, Hansib, London.

Marx, K. (1988), *The Communist Manifesto*, F.L. Bender (ed), Norton, New York.

Panitch, Leo (1996), 'Rethinking the State in an Era of Globalization', in J. Mittelman (ed), *Globalization: Critical Reflections*, Lynne Rienner, Boulder.

Panitch, Leo (1998), *Monthly Review*, Vol. 50, No.5.
Panitch, Leo (1999), *Working Papers in Local Governance and Democracy,* Vol. 1.
Phillips, Kevin (1997), 'The Bailout Bubble', *The Los Angeles Times*, 28 December.
Poulantzas, Nicos (1973), *Political Power and Social Classes*, New Left Books, London.
Reich, Robert B. (1997), *Locked in the Cabinet*, Vintage, New York.
Sklar, Leslie (1997), *Review of International Political Economy*, Vol. 4, No. 3, Autumn.
Tsoukalas, Konstantinos (1999), 'Globalization and the Executive Committee: Reflections on the Contemporary Capitalist State', in Leo Panitch and Colin Leys (eds), *Global Capitalism versus Democracy*, The Socialist Register, Merlin, London.
Vogel, Stephen (1996), *Freer Markets, More Rules*, Cornell University Press, Ithaca, New York.
World Bank (1997), *The State in a Changing World*, World Development Report for 1997, presented at the World Bank's 'Global Knowledge' conference, Toronto, June, Ch. 8.

Chapter 3

International Economic Agreements as Systems of Power

Stephen McBride

International economic agreements are often presumed to be positive sum games in which all participants make gains, even if not necessarily to the same extent. In particular weak states may gain through participation since they then operate under a set of rules, binding on both strong and weak, rather than in a Hobbesian context of the war of each against all. International agreements thus substitute the 'rule of rules' for the rule of power. In contrast to this view, this chapter demonstrates how the rules established by international economic agreements establish a system of power in which economic liberalism is entrenched to the disadvantage of states that have traditionally, or might in future want to use the state to moderate the effects of markets. In achieving this result international economic agreements also disadvantage many of those social forces that have relied on state power to moderate market outcomes. In this way international economic agreements replicate the power relations of domestic liberal democratic regimes, except that the balance between liberalism and democracy is redrawn to advantage the former.

The International Political Economy as a System of Power

C. B. Macpherson (1965, 1977) once noted that many theorists of liberal democracy were reticent about that regime's status as a *double* system of power. The first aspect of a system of power, that it was a system by which people were governed, was widely acknowledged. But the second aspect – that in a liberal democracy the democratic government 'exists to uphold and enforce a certain kind of society, a certain set of relations between individuals, a certain set of rights and claims that people have on each other both directly, and indirectly through their rights to property' (1965, p.4) – was less widely noticed. Liberal democracy existed to maintain property-based relations between people; these were power relations that needed 'a superior power to keep them in order' (Ibid., p.40) because in a market economy a transfer of powers from property-less individuals to the propertied occurred (Ibid., pp.46-55). In short, liberal democracy and capitalism tended to go together and, for Macpherson, the political system of liberal democracy was there to uphold the power relations embedded in the capitalist society that historically preceded it.

Macpherson, whose focus was on the domestic political system, argued that the two elements of a liberal democratic system, liberalism and democracy, were separable logically and historically. Liberalism was linked, perhaps inextricably, to capitalist market economies, and came first historically. Democratic elements were subsequently grafted onto the existing liberal society to form the system of government known as liberal democracy. In the process though, democracy became liberalized by losing its original focus on class rule, rule by the common people, and becoming instead a market-like mechanism of choice between competing suppliers of political goods, with citizens largely cast in the role of consumers. Macpherson's point was that there has been a reluctance to recognise that the outcomes of political processes within liberal democratic institutions are less than open and in practice serve to enforce 'a certain type of relations' between people.

In later works Macpherson argued that the future of liberal democracy depended 'on a downgrading of the market assumptions and an upgrading of the equal right to self-development' within liberal thought (1977, p.2). However, anticipating the argument to be made about international economic agreements, we may note that the content of those agreements moves in precisely the opposite direction. The connection between liberalism and market capitalism has tightened rather than loosened, and the scope for democratic decision-making has correspondingly narrowed.

In the international sphere, scholars who talk of a 'new constitutionalism' and 'disciplinary neoliberalism' that results from international economic agreements (Gill, 1995, p.412; Grinspun and Kreklewich, 1994, p.33; Schneiderman, 2000; Clarkson, 1991; Schneiderman, 1996; see also O'Brien, 1995) provide an equivalent to Macpherson, and other domestically oriented theorists of the state whose work runs contrary to the conventional (liberal) wisdom. Such IPE accounts deal in differing degrees with how international agreements reflect differential power relations between *states* and between *social classes*.

The dominant school of thought in international political economy (IPE), liberalism, seems unable to acknowledge the second aspect of the 'systems of power' image – that the global market society is one of structured inequality which international institutions exist to maintain. That is, the global market society may be a negative – rather than a positive sum system; or, alternatively, that the distribution of relative gains may be so unequal as to threaten the long-term interests of some participants (Grieco, 1990). Liberal international political economy for the most part proceeds on positive sum assumptions. In this view, the reason for the popularity of the new generation of economic agreements is that all parties gain or, at a minimum are no worse off than they would have been had they not entered the agreement. Thus international economic agreements are driven by mutual gain and there are no losers, except possibly particular sectors of national economies which may require temporary assistance to adjust to new circumstances.

States' willingness to participate, given this efficiency rationale, is thus unproblematic. Indeed, Gilpin has argued that neoliberal institutionalism generally assumes that 'the state is a liberal, market-oriented state in the American sense, more interested in co-operation and absolute gains than in conflicts over relative gains' (Gilpin, 2001, p.379). In the liberal view, then, international institutions merely serve states' purposes and there is thus no conflict between the creation of supranational governance structures and state sovereignty. More critical observers might argue that liberal international institutions seek to create that which they assume already exists – liberal, market-oriented states in the American sense. For countries that have traditionally relied, or might wish at a future date to rely upon a different state-model, the result is sovereignty diminishing (McBride, 2002).

Realist theorists put greater emphasis on inter-state disagreements and do integrate the concept of 'power' into their accounts (Carr, 1964).[1] The propensity of dominant powers to define their own interests as being beneficial to all is certainly part of this story (Ibid., pp.44-5). During the period of British hegemony in the nineteenth century, for example, the British state favoured free trade and sought to convince others of its generally beneficial character. Critics considered that such a policy was self-interested on the part of a hegemon: '*Laissez-faire*, in international relations as in those between capital and labour, is the paradise of the economically strong' (Ibid., p.60). Indeed, Britain's rivals seem to have taken the same view and concluded that protectionism was the route to catching up with the hegemonic power.

More recently, however, international regimes dominated by a single hegemon, which might be assumed to promote its own interests, are often depicted by benign versions of hegemonic stability theory as promoting the common interests of all or virtually states in the international system. Thus, even realists within that school of thought, assume, with liberals, 'that the cooperative equilibria that emerge once … distributional conflicts are resolved leave all participants, strong and weak alike, at least as well off as they would have been had the original, pre-cooperation status quo remained in effect' (Gruber, 2000, p.3, 28, n.46). Under such conditions there would seem only a limited need for a superior power to enforce the relationships entered into voluntarily; the logic of mutual advantage, reinforced by transparency measures to detect cheating, and with a limited enforcement apparatus, should ensure widespread compliance. A corollary of this argument is that complaints about democratic deficits or vacuums in international economic organizations like the European Union (EU), North American Free Trade Association (NAFTA), or World Trade Organization (WTO) are misplaced.

This benign view of the increasing incidence and reach of international economic collaboration seems to be the dominant one within IPE. However, there are strong grounds for questioning the assumptions which lie behind the approach.

First, working backwards, if we examine the texts of recent international economic agreements it is clear that they reach far beyond the transparency, surveillance, monitoring package of measures that might be sufficient to police compliance with generally perceived positive-sum agreements. One account describes international organizations as acting 'as agenda setters', serving to 'tie the hands' of domestic policy-makers and undercut the power of pro-protection interests; organizations such as the WTO facilitate the bundling or linking of issues within and across issue areas, increasing the probability of creating a majority in favour of free trade; and international institutions can cause a shift in domestic normative discourse' (Goldstein, 1998, p.134). Moreover, the terms of international economic agreements go beyond these intrusions into the balance of domestic political forces by significantly diminishing the legal potential for states to take (sovereign) decisions on matters of concern to their citizens. As well as influencing outcomes they serve to preclude certain outcomes.

The WTO and NAFTA seek to embed economic liberalism as the key reference point for state decision-makers. The WTO Agreement on Technical Barriers to Trade,[2] permits government regulation of matters such as national security, prevention of deceptive practices, and protection of human health and safety, animal or plant life or health provided the regulations are not more trade-restrictive than necessary, are non-discriminatory, and respect the national treatment principle. This establishes a hierarchy of principles which privileges trade above other legitimate policy goals. For example, the least trade restrictive health or environmental regulations may not be the best regulations, if viewed from health or environmental value systems.

In signing the WTO agreement, countries committed to a 'built-in' agenda from the Uruguay Round that promotes further liberalisation of trade in services (Das, 1998, p.110). Under the General Agreement on Trade in Services (GATS) the process is tilted towards progressive 'opting-in' of services for liberalisation. The WTO Secretariat is explicit about the GATS's capacity to intrude into national decision-making: 'the reach of the GATS rules extends to all forms of international trade in services. This means that the GATS agreement represents a major new factor for a large sector of world economic activity. It also means, because such a large share of trade in services takes place inside national economies, that its requirements will from the beginning necessarily influence national domestic laws and regulations in a way that has been true of the GATT only in recent years' (WTO, 1999a). The ideological roots of this are also explicit – in a related document the secretariat cited as advantages the ability of bindings, once undertaken, to 'lock in a currently liberal regime or map out a future liberalization path' (WTO Secretariat, 1999, p.1) while overcoming domestic resistance to change. NAFTA applies the same principles to services as well as goods, investment as well as trade, and strengthen intellectual property rights.

The argument that liberal democratic policies are being liberalized at the expense of their democratic elements has been illustrated by efforts to bind the state permanently to a particular (liberal) conception of the state's role. One dimension of this process is entrenching the values of economic liberalism in international agreements that have constitutional effect. This results in diminished state capacity and increased reliance on international rules and norms, liberal in nature, and difficult to alter, once ratified. Barry Appleton (1994) argues that: 'The NAFTA represents the supremacy of a classical liberal conception of the state with its imposition of significant restraints upon the role of government. All international trade agreements entail some self-imposed limitation on government authority, for example governments regularly agree not to increase their tariff rates. However, the NAFTA appears to approach an extreme. It does this by the extensiveness of its obligations which attempt to lock-in one perspective of governmental role for all successive North American governments' (Ibid., p.207).

Similarly, the extension of GATT into the WTO produced an intensification of the liberalization of world trade. Shallow or negative integration based on reciprocal reduction of border measures (GATT) has been transformed into ' "deeper", positive or "behind the border" integration which can require analysis of almost any national policy likely to have spill over or external effects across borders' (Wolfe, 1996, pp.692-3).[3]

Enhanced protection for property rights is a significant part of the liberalisation process. In NAFTA, for example, a form of property rights, even of limited citizenship, has been conferred on foreign investors through NAFTA. NAFTA Article 1116 permits investors to directly launch a claim without 'their' government acting as an intermediary. Such provisions confer rights on multinational corporations, in particular, that strengthen their hand vis-à-vis states and also privilege 'corporate citizens' in relation to 'natural' or human citizens. This provision was a breakthrough for U.S. policy and established a precedent in international economic agreements by giving corporations, for certain purposes, equal status with states.

Chapter 11 provides that an investor may initiate a suit against a member government alleging that it has breached its obligations under Article 11. Chapter 11 obligations are broadly defined and: 'virtually all types of ownership interests, either direct or indirect, actual or contingent' (Appleton). Obligations include national treatment and most-favoured nation status, together with a prohibition on nationalization or expropriation of an investment except on a number of identified grounds. Cases are heard by a tribunal, which applies the rules of international rather than national law governing commercial disputes. Notably, it provides investors with enforcement rights under a treaty to which they are neither party nor under which they have obligations (Shrybman, 1999, pp.135-6).

A second line of attack on the benign interpretation of international economic agreements is that the positive sum assumptions of liberal and newer realist political economy may be unjustified. The idea that neoliberal globalization fails to meet positive-sum expectations, is widespread among its critics. For example, growing inequality between states and classes is often attributed to globalization. Even the assumption that liberalization of trade and capital movements improves economic growth rates has come under challenge. A cross-national comparison of performance in the 1960-80 and 1980-2000 periods (the latter seen as one of intensifying globalization) found that rates of economic growth declined compared to those of the earlier twenty-year period (Weisbrot, Baker, Kraev and Chen, 2001). The same study revealed that on a number of other socio-economic indicators – life expectancy, infant and child mortality and education and literacy – progress was much slower in the later than the earlier period. The authors were careful to note they had not proven that the policy changes associated with neoliberal globalization had produced slower progress. Rather, they argued that their findings 'present a very strong *prima facie* case that some structural and policy changes implemented during the last two decades are at least partly responsible for these declines. And there is certainly no evidence in these data that the policies associated with globalization has improved outcomes for most low to middle-income countries'(Ibid., p.3). Other studies have highlighted the growth in social inequality with which globalization has been associated (Petras and Veltmeyer, 2001, pp.20-22; 50-53). From this perspective, the closer economic integration that globalization produces is zero-sum in its effects, both between nations but, even more so, within nations.

Such research lends little credibility to the notion that sovereignty is being sacrificed for broadly based economic gains or that international institutions are efficient, Pareto-improving responses to collective action problems. Indeed, rather than demonstrating Pareto-improvement outcomes empirically, these are often assumed by virtue of the fact of increased co-operation. But, if outcomes are negative rather than positive sum: 'Why would a "sovereign" state – or, more precisely, the collection of individuals who exercise governmental authority within it – ever be willing to relinquish that prerogative?'(Gruber, p.62). Gruber's explanation is that the hegemonic state or coalition possesses 'go it alone' power that removes the status quo as an option for other states. This induces them to get on board to cut their losses. Thus, the actors who initiate and drive today's international economic agreements, that is the powerful actors, are 'free to impose their own institutional choices on other actors in the system. Because the "enacting coalition" can shift the institutional status quo unilaterally, its members do not need to take account of their current partners' institutional preferences. When it comes to matters concerning institutional design, the enacting coalition is in the driver's seat, and everyone else better look out' (Ibid., p.81). Essentially, powerful states leave weaker states no palatable option but to get 'on board'.

The effect of the institutional design choices made by the enacting coalition is to erode sovereignty, and thus the scope for democratic decision-making, in countries outside the enacting coalition. Even more importantly, to preclude future defections should the domestic political leadership change; this applies to some countries inside the enacting coalition. Thus, institutional design of international economic agreements produces constitution-altering effects for most participants. Through these changes the international power relations between states are defined; but more importantly, domestic power relations, both institutional and more broadly political, are redefined. It would be wrong to depict the constraints thus created as primarily external in origin. The extent to which the re-ordering of domestic power relations through international economic agreements is driven by domestic factors, such as the desire of governing elites to lock-in place policy changes, has received insufficient attention in the literature (Krasner, 1999, p.22; Gruber, pp.82-4).[4]

Others regard globalization simply as a synonym for contemporary imperialism (Petras and Veltmeyer; Guyat, 2000). In this picture the United States is the imperial power, and internationally oriented capital, much of it U.S. based, the social force behind it. Gramscian accounts present an alternative explanation. In this version of events international economic integration is driven by a transnational historic bloc comprised of large corporations, sectors of national state apparatuses, international institutions, and private think tanks and other forums, but incorporating, too, privileged workers, elements of small business, and professionals. It is this bloc that 'generates the ideas, institutions and material capabilities that are associated with the global shift towards more neoliberal forms of state. The broad political aim is to restructure and consolidate state forms so that they become internally and externally more hospitable to the dominant forces in modern capitalism (notably large transnational corporations, financial services firms and institutional investors)' (Gill, 1998, p.11). The hegemony established by the bloc is a system of power that empowers and advantages some, but not others.

These accounts of international economic agreements hold that they are systems of power designed to sustain the power of some actors and limit that of others. Their effect is to enhance liberalism and the liberal market society and to diminish democracy – insofar as that concept includes the potential to go against or even modify significantly the results of market processes.

International economic agreements accomplish this result through their impact on the sovereignty of states and through a *de facto* re-writing of national constitutions. In the process, economic liberalism is privileged at the expense of potential and future democratic choice. Notwithstanding the key role that the state has played in promoting neoliberal globalization, limiting certain of its capacities is a central goal of international economic agreements. This is because of the 'tremendous potentialities of the state as a centre for alternative forms of economic organization' (Petras and Veltmeyer, p.55). Clearly, considered at the level of *states*, international economic agreements have increased the external constraint on policy-making. In particular, resort to state activism is far more problematic than formerly. Considered at the level of *class interests* within countries this situation may be unproblematic and even welcome for some interests (capital); and deeply disempowering for others (labour).

Ensuring Rule Observance

A series of processes and institutions have been established to 'police' the liberal rules now embedded in international economic agreements. Three examples are provided here: the moral suasion exercised by organizations like the OECD; the growth of external scrutiny and accountability mechanisms; and the transfer of authority to adjudicate disputes to international tribunals and panels.

Moral Suasion: The Example of the OECD Jobs Study/Strategy[5]

The OECD describes itself as a 'forum to discuss, develop and perfect economic and social policies' which 'helps member governments identify good practice in managing their own economies' and where 'peer pressure can act as a powerful incentive to improve policy' (OECD, 2002). Its reports and initiatives range over a wide variety of policy issues. Here I summarize the OECD's efforts to promote deregulation in the area of labour market policy.

Responding to high unemployment levels that emerged in the 1980s, the OECD directed its Economic Secretariat to conduct a study and make substantive proposals for policy reform. Recommendations produced by the 'Jobs Study' subsequently formed the basis of the OECD 'Jobs Strategy' (1994a) – a detailed set of policy prescriptions for each member state. The theoretical basis of the Jobs Study was neoliberal and rested on the non-accelerating inflation rate of unemployment, or NAIRU. This led (OECD, 1998a, pp.7-9) to an identification of the bulk of contemporary unemployment as structural rather than cyclical. By NAIRU-based estimates, in 1996, structural unemployment accounted for an average of 91 per cent of actual unemployment in OECD member countries. The residual amount might be considered cyclical. The policy implication of this, for the OECD, was that the vast majority of unemployment, being structural, was impervious to macroeconomic management (OECD, 1994b, pp.66-9). The core hypothesis, and central policy implication then was that labour market rigidities such as employment protection legislation, or financial inducements which cushioned workers from changing market conditions (unemployment benefits, early retirement schemes, and social programmes generally) served ultimately to reduce employment and harm the workers they were intended to help (Kuhn, 1997). Thus grounded in neo-classical economic theory, the Jobs Study represented a sustained plea for policies to promote greater labour market flexibility by removing politically constructed obstacles to the unfettered operation of market forces (OECD, 1994b, p.7).

The OECD identified social policies as a key area for change if adequate flexibility was to be achieved. Members should examine, 'the full range of policies that have been put in place over the last 30 years to see where, and to what extent, each may have contributed to ossifying the capacity of economies and the will of societies to adapt; and then to consider how to remove those disincentives without harming the degree of social protection that it is each society's wish to provide' (OECD, 1994b, p.30). OECD officials believed that the performance of the US labour market in the 1990s vindicated the superiority of 'liberal' market-based approaches to labour market policy. While the early 1990s were bad times for European countries, which experienced increased structural unemployment, the US was going through a period of improved performance. Thus, liberal policies emerged as a 'flavour of the decade' – a somewhat ironic outcome given the events of the 1980s (Kuhn). Then, the United States was a poor performer; all eyes were focused on the more successful Japanese approach which embraced precisely the kind of 'rigidities' which are now so passé.

Based on these assumptions, the OECD outlined a broad, ten-point programme of action, or 'Jobs Strategy' to be implemented in a 'coordinated manner' by member states. The strategy covered, macroeconomic policy, technology diffusion, competition policy and, most centrally labour market and social policy.

General principles were subsequently operationalized into some forty-five specific policy recommendations that might be applied to each member government. The focus was on deregulation, reflecting the OECD's belief that rigidities like union strength, social benefits, and legislation and regulations on employment conditions, were responsible for increased unemployment in the OECD area.[6] The OECD deemed that, '. . . governments . . . can introduce comprehensive reforms along the lines of the recommendations in the OECD Jobs Strategy which will expand employment opportunities and reduce structural unemployment' (OECD, 1997a, p.7).

Armed with this strategy, the OECD launched a surveillance project aimed at encouraging member states to adopt the study's specific recommendations. There is a growing literature on compliance with international treaty obligations (Weiss and Jacobson, 1998; Chayes and Chayes, 1995). Still, the length to which the OECD has gone in proselytizing the Jobs Study's recommendations, an exercise in pure moral suasion rather than treaty adherence, is striking. Follow-up studies extended the analysis and were presented to ministers. The OECD ministers mandated the organization's Economic and Development Review Committee (EDRC) to examine the extent of implementation in each member countries with a view to exerting 'peer pressure on the policies pursued by individual OECD Member countries' (OECD, 1998b). The results were published in the OECD's regular country surveys. As well, special publications dealing with implementation have been issued (OECD, 1999; OECD, 1998c; OECD, 1997b; OECD, 1997a). This represents a major effort to keep the deregulatory labour market strategy on the political agenda in member countries. Indeed, eight years after the project was launched, the EDRC's work on the Jobs Strategy is unfinished as the OECD, dissatisfied with the rate of implementation, continues to criticize recalcitrant member states and reiterate its belief that the strategy works and should be adopted universally (Globe and Mail, 1999; OECD, 1999).

So, in this case, moral suasion must be judged only partly successful. This is, however, but one part of a number of such exercises, covering many areas of public policy, conducted by the OECD and other international organizations.

Accountability: Monitoring /Review

New forms of scrutiny and accountability are emerging. Domestic policy is continuously monitored by the international organizations to which the country belongs. Conducted in the name of 'transparency' this exercises strong pressure for compliance with the letter, but also with neoliberal spirit of the agreements.

The Uruguay Round of GATT established a Trade Policy Review Mechanism (TPRM) under which the trade policies of member nations are regularly reviewed to improve their adherence to WTO rules and commitments, to achieve greater transparency surrounding trade policy and practices, and to facilitate collective evaluation of the impact of individual trade policies on the multilateral trading system of the WTO (Qureshi, 1999, p.314). The agreement contains provisions that state that the mechanism is not there to enforce specific obligations, and trade officials deny that TPRM is an enforcement mechanism (Ibid., pp.318-22). Interestingly, these measures are depicted simply at improving public policy through transparency and information about each other's practices. However, it can be argued that the TPRM has 'enforcement characteristics' because it is compulsory, and occurs within a normative framework against which national trade policies are judged, implicitly or explicitly. The effect is to condition state behaviour: 'It inculcates at the earliest possible moment a 'WTO' approved pattern of behaviour – both through the impregnation of the national policy framework by substantive WTO trade prescriptions, as well as through the provision of conditions, including institutional, necessary for the evolution of WTO approved trade policies. The 'conditioning' stems particularly from the probing of policy, policy formulation and the objectives of policies' (Ibid., p.320).

Whether viewed as enforcement or transparency mechanisms, the TPRMs seem to have been effective. Increased use of anti-dumping measures, detecting use of subsidies, state aids and tax concessions in support of industrial and regional development policies, and drawing attention to the importance of domestic deregulation to ensure that the effects of trade reforms were not offset by domestic firms' strategies, have been credited to the TPRM process. Through its monitoring role trade policy review process has 'not only contributed to the fulfilment of commitments in the multilateral trading system but has also contributed to the development of national policies' (Laird, 1999, p.760). If so, there is a case for arguing that these extra-territorial monitoring mechanisms are more effective in influencing policy than elected domestic institutions in some countries.

Members of the Quad, the inner circle of the WTO, undergo a Trade Policy Review every two years (WTO, 2001b, 1999c, 1997). Having reviewed the TPRM's for Canada, a Quad member, it is apparent that the procedure involves a mixture of praise for Canada's policies, since it is acknowledged to be committed to liberalization, combined with expressions of concerns about remaining deviations from liberal principles. Concerns fall into a number of categories. First, WTO members who consider themselves harmed by particular Canadian practices like supply management systems for food products, or remaining tariffs in textiles, footwear and shipbuilding raise these issues and call for adjustments on Canada's part. Secondly, concerns are expressed about Canada's constitutional arrangements and the ability of the federal government to overcome internal trade barriers, provincial government procurement policies, and the like. Those outside NAFTA draw attention to the need for trade diversification and worry those regional agreements may create infringements on trade, for example through rules of origin provisions. Similarly there are calls for greater respect for intellectual property rights and for Canada's concern about protecting its culture to express in the least trade restrictive manner possible. In responding to questions and concerns Canadian delegates sometimes acknowledge that the TPRM has an impact on the domestic policy process. In 1998, for example, a Canadian representative stated that the TPR contributed to public support for Canada's trade policy and that initiatives like the tariff simplification exercise were a concrete expression of the influence of the TPR (WTO, 1999c, p.ix).

Adjudication

Under NAFTA a by-national review panel displaced judicial review of most issues concerned with dumping and anti-dumping, at least for disputes between NAFTA members. And, in the investment chapter, foreign investors are given the option of pursuing disputes through domestic courts or arbitration panels. Whereas under the anti-dumping and countervailing subsidies provisions the panels are applying domestic law, under the investment chapter they apply international law and are able to award damages and impose other sanctions (Lemieux and Stuhec, 1999, p.146).

Chapter 11 provides that an investor may initiate a suit against a member government alleging that it has breached its obligations, which are broadly defined and cover: 'virtually all types of ownership interests, either direct or indirect, actual or contingent' (Appleton). Obligations include national treatment and most-favoured nation status, together with a prohibition on nationalization or expropriation of an investment except on a number of identified grounds. Cases are heard by a tribunal that applies the rules of international rather than national law governing commercial disputes. A tribunal has ruled recently that Canada must ignore its freedom-to-information law and withhold documents requested by a member of the public concerning a U.S. forest company's claim for compensation under NAFTA Chapter 11 (Chase, 2002, p.A 10). Regardless of whether Canada ultimately complies with the tribunal's ruling, the decision illustrated the potentially wide scope of the trade agreement. Notably, Chapter 11 provides investors with enforcement rights under a treaty to which they are neither party nor have obligations (Shrybman, p.135-6).

Over these very broad issues, states have essentially ceded decision-making to an international tribunal. As important issues have been transferred to the jurisdiction of international trade panels, national courts have been diminished. Moreover, the enforcement of property rights has been partially transferred to investors themselves.

Disputes arising under the WTO are referred to dispute panels once attempts at consultation and mediation have failed to produce a mutually acceptable resolution. The Uruguay Round strengthened dispute resolution mechanisms to eliminate delays and the right of the 'guilty' party to eventually veto decisions. Enforcement mechanisms include elimination of the regulation or legislation found to be in breach of WTO provisions, payment of compensation or, should the offending party fail to implement panel findings, sanctioned retaliation by the injured party. For example, the WTO has already deemed Canadian magazine legislation, promoted as defence of Canadian culture, and the Auto Pact, to be contrary to WTO provisions. These examples alone indicate the scope of the WTO and its extra-territorial adjudication mechanisms.

Countries do not have to comply with rulings on such matters, of course and can opt to pay compensation or endure sanctioned retaliatory measures instead. This serves as a disincentive for all states but may be more intrusive for small and medium states that are less able to bear the costs of retaliation, and less enforceable by them if they are unable to mount effective retaliatory measures. Not all states are created equal. And certainly they are more intrusive for states that are less committed to the neoliberal view of the proper relationship between states and markets.

In disputes over the scope of the rules, few cases so far have sustained the ability of nation-states to regulate on health, environmental, labour or other issues that might stand in the way of economic liberalization.[7] For example, analysis of WTO cases related to labour standards and health issues showed that the private interest prevailed over the public interest in the great majority of cases. That is, free traders generally prevailed over those who wished to erect social regulations, where these were judged to have infringed on free trade (Drache et al, 2000, pp. 39-45, 71-2). Mostly, therefore, although countries may enter disputes about specific cases according to their perceived interests, and 'win' or 'lose' their case, the pattern of the outcomes reinforces the liberal rules that constrain state action. If these are democratic states, the scope for future exercise of democratic decision-making is also constrained.

Conclusion

In these ways the contents of international agreements, ostensibly dealing with trade, have become part of the constitutional system. The agreements function to constrain, limit, direct and 'condition' decision-making in areas far removed from trade as traditionally understood. States are no longer available for as wide a range of purposes as formerly.[8]

The argument has been that in re-balancing the liberal democratic order by accentuating the liberal and diminishing its democratic elements, the new generation of international economic agreements operate as a system of power, which serves to discipline states. But by so doing they limit, structure and discipline the citizens of those states. Citizens are confined to a limited range of choices and thus bound to existing property and power relations embodied in the agreements. Continued participation may be rational if the alternatives are demonstrably worse. However, little serious academic attention is given to whether this would, in fact be the case, or for whom.

In any case the disempowerment of states is likely to have a more severe impact in those countries where use of the state for national development and social security purposes was more significant than in the American hegemon.

Notes

1 For a classic account see Carr.

2 Texts of all WTO agreements can be found in World Trade Organization, 1999b.

3 Wolfe (p.693) notes the familiar line-up of social forces around this issue. Business groups are supporters of deep integration, social and environmental groups oppose it.

4 Krasner cites this as a reason why rulers sometimes 'invite' diminution of their country's sovereignty, and Gruber considers that the institutional design of international economic agreements is configured with a view to offset future defection of members of the enacting coalition.

5 This discussion is based on McBride and Williams.

6 One weakness of the theory is that the economy was highly regulated (and thus 'inflexible') in previous periods of full-employment, see Britton.

7 The main exception to date is the failed Canadian action against French regulations prohibiting the use of asbestos, see World Trade Organization, 2001a.

8 It is important not to exaggerate the purposes for which it has been used in the past. Nevertheless, its constitutional room for action was wider in the past than it has recently become.

References

Appleton, B. (1994), *Navigating NAFTA: A Concise User's Guide to the North American Free Trade Agreement*, Carswell, Scarborough, Ontario.

Britton, A. (1997), 'Full Employment in a Market Economy', in J. Philpott (ed), *Working for Full-Employment*, Routledge, London.

Carr, E.H. (1964), *The Twenty Years' Crisis 1919-1939: An Introduction to the Study of International Relations*, Harper and Row, New York.

Chase, S. (2002), 'NAFTA forces Canada to break own law, critics say', *Globe and Mail*, 21 March, p. A 10.

Chayes, A. and Chayes, A.H., (1995), *The New Sovereignty: Compliance with International Regulatory Agreements*, Harvard University Press, Cambridge, Massachusetts.

Clarkson, S. (1991), 'Disjunctions: Free Trade and the Paradox of Canadian Development', in D. Drache and M.S. Gertler (eds), *The New Era of Global Competition: State Policy and Market Power*, McGill-Queens University Press, Montreal.

Das, B.L. (1998), *An Introduction to the WTO Agreements: Trade and Development Issues and the World Trade Organisation*, Zed Books, London.

Drache, D. Guan, Y. Arnott A. and Grayson, K. (2000), *An Analysis of WTO Rulings With Respect to Labour Standards and Health*, Robarts Centre for Canadian Studies, York University, Toronto.

Gill, S. (1995), 'Globalisation, Market Civilisation and Disciplinary Neoliberalism', *Millennium*, Vol. 24.

Gill, S. (1998), 'European Governance and New Constitutionalism: Economic and Monetary Union and Alternatives to Disciplinary Neoliberalism in Europe', *New Political Economy*, Vol. 3, No. 1, March.

Gilpin, R. (2001), *Global Political Economy: Understanding the International Economic Order*, Princeton University Press, Princeton.

Globe and Mail (1999), Report on Business, 17 September.

Goldstein J. (1998), 'International Institutions and Domestic Politics: GATT, WTO, and the Liberalization of International Trade', in A.O. Krueger (ed), *The WTO as an International Organization*, University of Chicago Press, Chicago.

Grieco, J.M. (1990), *Cooperation among Nations: Europe, America, and Non-Tariff Barriers to Trade*, Cornell University Press, Ithaca, New York.

Grinspun, R. and Kreklewich, R. (1994), 'Consolidating Neoliberal Reforms: "Free Trade" as a Conditioning Framework', *Studies in Political Economy*, Vol. 43.

Gruber, L. (2000), *Ruling the World: Power Politics and the Rise of Supranational Institutions*, Princeton University Press, Princeton, New Jersey.

Guyat, N. (2000), *Another American Century? The United States and the World after 2000*, Zed Books, London.

Krasner, S. (1999), *Sovereignty: Organized Hypocrisy*, Princeton University Press, Princeton, New Jersey.

Kuhn, P. (1997), 'Canada and the "OECD Hypothesis": Does Labour Market Inflexibility Explain Canada's High Level Of Unemployment?', Working Paper 10, Canadian International Labour Network, Department of Economics, McMaster University, Hamilton, Ontario, April.

Laird, S. (1999), 'The WTO's Trade Policy Review Mechanism – From Through the Looking Glass', *The World Economy*, Vol. 22, No. 6, August.

Lemieux, Denis and Stuhec, Ana (1999), *Review of Administrative Action under NAFTA*, Carswell, Scarborough, Ontario.

Macpherson, C.B. (1965), *The Real World of Democracy*, CBC Publications, Toronto.

Macpherson, C.B. (1977), *The Life and Times of Liberal Democracy*, Oxford University Press, Oxford.

McBride, S. (2002), 'Quiet Constitutionalism in Canada: The International Political Economy of Domestic Institutional Change', *Canadian Journal of Political Science*, forthcoming.

McBride, S. and Williams, R.A. (2001), 'Globalization, the Restructuring of Labour Markets and Policy Convergence: The OECD "Jobs Strategy"', *Global Social Policy*, Vol. 1, No. 3, pp. 283-311.

O'Brien, R. (1995), 'North American Integration and International Relations Theory', *Canadian Journal of Political Science*, Vol. 28.

OECD (Organization for Economic Cooperation and Development) (1994a), *The Jobs Study: Facts, Analysis, Strategy*, OECD, Paris.

OECD (1994b), *The OECD Jobs Study: Evidence and Explanations: Part 1: Labour Market Trends and Underlying Forces of Change*, OECD, Paris.

OECD (1997a), *Implementing the OECD Jobs Strategy: Lessons from Member Countries' Experience*, OECD, Paris.

OECD (1997b), *Implementing the OECD Jobs Strategy: Member Countries' Experience*, OECD, Paris.

OECD (1998a), *The OECD Jobs Strategy: The Policy Implications of Estimates of Structural Unemployment*, Report on a Consultation between Trade Union Experts and the Chairman and the Bureau of the Economic and Development Review Committee held under the OECD Labour/Management Programme, Paris, OECD, 23 October.

OECD (1998b), 'The OECD Jobs Strategy: Progress Report on Implementation of Country-Specific Recommendations', Working Paper No. 196, OECD, Paris, Foreword.

OECD (1998c), 'The OECD Jobs Strategy: Progress Report on Implementation of Country-Specific Recommendations', Working Paper No. 196, OECD, Paris.

OECD (1999), *Implementing the OECD Jobs Strategy – Assessing Performance and Policy*, Paris: OECD.

OECD, (2002), *About OECD*, OECD web page.

Petras, J. and Veltmeyer, H. (2001), *Globalization Unmasked: Imperialism in the 21st Century*, Fernwood, Halifax.

Qureshi, Asif H. (1999), *International Economic Law*, Sweet and Maxwell, London.

Schneiderman, D. (1996), 'NAFTA's Takings Rule: American Constitutionalism Comes to Canada', *University of Toronto Law Journal*, Vol. 46.

Schneiderman, D. (2000), 'Investment Rules and the New Constitutionalism', *Law and Social Inquiry*, Vol. 25.

Shrybman, Steven (1999), *Citizens Guide to the World Trade Organization*, J. Lorimer, Toronto.

Weisbrot, M., Baker, D., Kraev, E. and Chen, J. (2001), *The Scorecard on Globalization 1980-2000: Twenty Years of Diminished Progress*, Center for Economic and Policy Research, Washington D.C.

Weiss, E. Brown and Jacobson, H.K. (eds) (1998), *Engaging Countries: Strengthening Compliance with International Environmental Accords,* Harvard University Press, Cambridge, Massachusetts.

Wolfe, R. (1996), 'Global Trade as a Single Undertaking: The Role of Ministers in the WTO', *International Journal*, Autumn..

World Trade Organization (1997), *Trade Policy Review: Canada 1996*, WTO, Geneva.

World Trade Organization (1999a), *About the WTO*, WTO, Geneva.

World Trade Organization (1999b), *The Legal Texts: The Results of the Uruguay Round of Multilateral Trade Negotiations*, Cambridge University Press, Cambridge.

World Trade Organization (1999c), *Trade Policy Review: Canada 1998*, WTO, Geneva.

World Trade Organization (2001a), *European Communities – Measures Affecting Asbestos and Asbestos-Containing Products AB-2000-11: Report of the Appellate Body*, WTO, Geneva, 12 March.

World Trade Organization (2001b), *Trade Policy Review: Canada 2000*, WTO, Geneva.

World Trade Organization Secretariat (1999), *The GATS: Objectives, Coverage and Disciplines*, WTO, Geneva.

Chapter 4

Regulatory Games States Play: Managing Globalization Through Sectoral Policy[1]

Anil Hira

Defining Globalization

'Globalization' is a term used for a growing set of international-level movements, exchanges, and pressures. Each of these phenomena is changing and pressuring national economies towards both specialization and convergence, sometimes simultaneously in different trajectories. For example, the increased investment of international corporations in certain developing countries is pushing those countries towards specialization in production. Thus, factories in northern Mexico are part of a global 'commodity chain'[2] of production of automobiles, since some auto parts are made there. At the same time, illegal international labour migration from developing countries puts downward pressure on wage levels in First World countries. The development of the internet and satellite television, meanwhile, is creating a global information community. Yet though U.S. companies dominate traditional media, smaller groups with minimal resources have the ability to create their own web pages that ensure virtually universal access to their messages. In political economy terms, much of the focus of the analysis of globalization has been on the growing constraints on state economic policies. Using the example of regulatory policy, this paper will demonstrate that while those pressures are growing, there are still specialized spaces within the domestic political economy where a state can shape its domestic economy.

Globalization: New Pressures on State Economic Policy

During the last 20 years there have been growing pressures on states' ability to pursue economic policies. The result has been an increasing pressure towards convergence of economic policies, thus limiting states' scopes for action on the domestic level.[3] For developing countries, the pressure towards convergence is multiplied.[4]

These pressures can be understood through understanding changes in international financial markets and international trade. Changes in international financial markets are well-documented in the international political economy literature.[5] The breakdown of the Bretton Woods system in the early 1970s in combination with the creation of petrodollar capital and Eurobanks signaled the beginning of a burgeoning international capital market. In the last decade, the need for investment led to the creation of equity markets in many developing countries.

Essentially, the rise of a global capital market has led to pressures on states to accommodate the interests of international investors as much as possible. Investment is key to business activity and increasing production. International investment comes in two forms: portfolio and direct investment. Portfolio capital is mobile, short-term investments. Portfolio capital creates pressures for effective international interest rate convergence,[6] and high volatility should business conditions change. Portfolio capital tends to have a well-noted herd-like quality, in the sense that a noted outflow of capital by a prime investor can lead to a rush by many others. Investment in equity markets can be considered akin to portfolio capital in terms of the high levels of volatility and long-term unpredictability of such markets. The point is that states are not only constrained by the demands of portfolio capital, but also by the fear of setting off waves of harmful speculation. The explosive growth of the portfolio capital market thus has important effects on monetary policy.

Direct investment is investment in property or equipment and implies the purchase of a local company or the creation of an agricultural, industrial, or service enterprise. Direct investment thus can have very important effects on employment, domestic price levels, and market structures. It may also bring transfers of technology, as well as managerial expertise and training of human resources. The competition among states for direct investment leads them to offer enticements such as direct subsidies; tax breaks; and the relaxation of business restrictions, such as environmental standards. The result of the competition for direct investment is increasing restrictions on states' tax bases and regulatory policies.

In the last two decades, there has been a wave of international trade agreements. These include the consummation of the European Union (EU), the North American Free Trade Agreement (NAFTA), and the Mercado del Sur (MERCOSUR) agreements. This process has been driven by the desire to reduce transaction costs, the desire for greater competitiveness in global markets, and the desire to lock in access to large, in some cases, growing, domestic markets. The seeds of the international integration movement lie in the rise of East Asian competition in the 1980s, which threatened U.S. and European industries. In turn, worries about the diversionary effects of first the EU, then NAFTA, spurred the MERCOSUR project forward. Similar concerns lay behind the Asia-Pacific Economic Cooperation (APEC) agreements on the regional level, and further efforts at progress in the General Agreement on Trade in Services (GATS) and the World Trade Organization (WTO) on the multilateral level.

From the U.S. point of view, the desire for integrated markets ensures easy access to natural resources, such as Mexico's or Canada's petroleum and gas.

The NAFTA agreement also gives the U.S. access to cheap pools of labour in Mexico, which enhances the U.S. ability to compete with East Asian and European producers. NAFTA also ensures liberalization and privileged access for U.S. corporations to a growing Mexican consumer market. Finally, NAFTA can be seen as part of a U.S. geo-strategy to bind other economies to its own.

As well as constraining states' economic policies, international competition for investment and trade have placed increasing pressures on the social welfare programs. Welfare programs are a huge fiscal expense, and can be construed as reducing the state's ability to offer enticements to international investment. Moreover, welfare payments, and other social protections, such as labour regulations, are linked to higher wage rates. Unless productivity is high and increasing fast enough to maintain wage disparities against international competition, there will be (and has been) strong downward pressure on wages and on social welfare policies.

If we consider developing countries in general, the pressures noted above are multiplied. Besides the fact that developing countries by definition, have a greater need for capital, they are also saddled with 'shallow' financial markets, meaning their ability to raise capital domestically is limited. The problem of capital flight because of domestic lack of confidence underscores this problem, and increases the pressures even more. Perhaps the largest constraint on aspiring developing countries is the continuing mountain of debt with which most continue to struggle. A superficial understanding of capital markets would lead us to believe that because developing countries have much more untapped potential as an investment site than developed markets they should be more attractive to investment. However, the factor of risk is much greater in the minds of international investors than potential gains over the long run. Factoring in risk, developing countries and their companies always pay higher interest rates on debt. Moreover, developing countries suffer from a much higher level of volatility of capital flows. The recent Mexican crisis (1982), Asian crisis (late 1990s), and Brazilian financial crisis (1999) of herd flight of international capital underscore this situation.

In terms of trade treaties, developing countries are in competition with each other for access to the largest markets in the First World. Therefore, countries like Mexico are all too willing to enter into a bargain in which they must make compromises in their domestic economic policy, in order to gain access to the U.S. market. The result is that developing countries find themselves forced to liberalize their own domestic markets in order to have the possibility to gain access to the largest markets in Western Europe and the U.S.

Our review of the pressures of globalization paints a grim picture for the independence of national economic policy.[7] Monetary, fiscal, and trade policy are all facing a situation of increasing convergence due to the competition for global capital. The pressures for tight monetary and fiscal policy are considerable, and probably irresistible given that expansionary policies might result in inflation, capital flight, or an inability to export to the large First World markets. In the next section, we will see why regulatory policy provides a more complex arena in which states still have some degree of autonomy in terms of how they respond to international pressures. Like all economic policies in a global economy, regulatory policy is a two-level game, but provides considerably more room for national policy manoeuvre than monetary, fiscal, trade or general investment policies.

Regulatory Policy as a Two Level Game Response to Globalization

Two Level Game Responses to Globalization

Robert Putnam's seminal work identified the games that state leaders must play in terms of reaching international agreements while maintaining winning domestic political coalitions.[8] A large body of literature also looks at how domestic coalitions re-align based on changes in international conditions (Gourevtich, 1986; Rogowski, 1989; Milner, 1988). Thus, the two-level game in economic policy can be seen as an interactive one, in which nations both create and respond to changes the international economy. The capacity of states to act independently of domestic interest groups is defined in the literature as *state autonomy* (Evans, Rueschmeyer, and Skocpol, 1985). Unlike the common definition, however, here we define state autonomy as state independence on *both* the international and domestic levels.

The existence of international trade agreements in which previously winning coalitions lose, such as the end of protected markets in Mexico with NAFTA, shows that states have autonomy from domestic coalitions. The ability of states such as the U.S. or Brazil, more recently, to ignore international dictates, such as arbitration decisions by the World Trade Organization, also demonstrates that states continue to enjoy some degree of autonomy from the international economy. The 'exceptions' built into agreements such as the GATS reflect states' continuing, if constrained, ability to limit international pressures.

Defining State Autonomy and Capacity

Merilee S. Grindle's (1996) classic study of state capacity, *Challenging the State*, encapsulates much of the conceptual logic behind state capacity and autonomy (Grindle, 1996; Arbetman and Kugler, 1997; Evans, 1995, and Haggard and Kaufman, 1992). State capacity and autonomy generally work along three lines: political, managerial, and administrative. Political capacity refers to the state's ability to carry out its decisions without resistance from society. Thus, political capacity is closely linked to the legitimacy and support of the government. We can consider autonomy as slightly different in that autonomy connotes the benefits of some degree of 'insulation' from social pressures. Therefore, a highly autonomous state is one that can operate in the good of the national interest, rather than in response to particular (lobbying) ones, whether they originate domestically or from abroad. Autonomy thus connotes the ability of the state to carry out (economic) decisions that have heavy costs of adjustment. Autonomy can also have negative connotations in the sense that a highly autonomous state has limited responsiveness to social needs and thus can become corrupt and abusive for its own purposes. Like capacity, autonomy works not only in the political sense, but also in the managerial and technical sense. Thus, a state with a large corps of well-trained economists has greater technical capacity and thus greater autonomy from external funding agencies like the International Monetary Fund (IMF). So we expect that the greater a state's autonomy and capacity, the greater will be its leverage vis-à-vis other powerful actors and the greater its ability to carry through difficult programs. While it is clear that state capacity and autonomy depend in large part on the managerial and technical capabilities of an organization, the literature does not explain the sources of state political capacity and autonomy. We do so now, focusing on the economic arena.

Factors Determining the Degree of State Autonomy from Globalization Pressures

The degree to which states have autonomy to engage in international markets thus can be thought of as depending on several factors, as demonstrated in Figure 4.1 and Table 4.1.

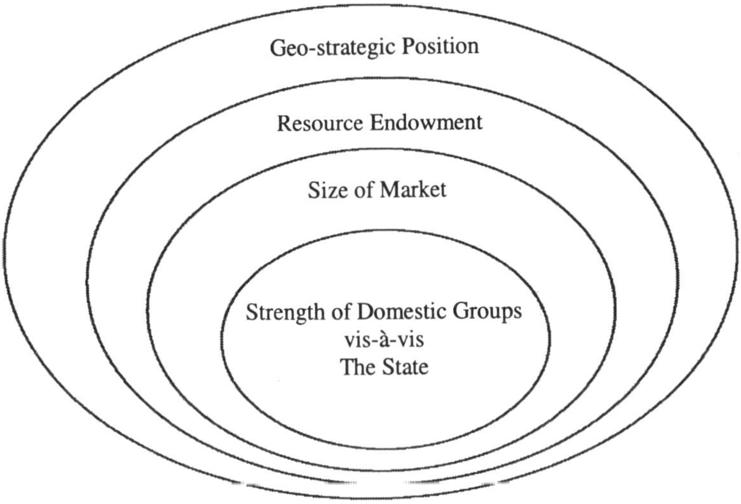

Figure 4.1: Structural Constraints on State Autonomy

Dynamic two-level factors: (examples)
Global: changes in technology, politics of other states; regional trade and investment agreements; MNC policies; levels of competition; crisis;
National: product mix; regulatory policy; quality of infrastructure; human resources; degree of national consensus; strength of domestic private sector; crisis;
Local state capacity: leadership; capacity of technical decision-makers in public and private sectors; crisis.

Table 4.1: Factors Determining State Autonomy from Globalization

Factor of Autonomy	High	Low
Geostrategic Position	Israel	Sierra Leone
Access to Resources	Saudi Arabia	Japan
Size of Domestic Market	China	Nepal
Separate International Trade Agreements	Brazil- MERCOSUR	Venezuela
Openness: Types of Exports and Imports	South Korea	Ghana
International Financial Dependency	Malaysia	Argentina
Sectoral Policy Capacity	Japan	Panama

Note: These factors could work with or against each other.

The factors creating state autonomy are independent of each other, so that we find some states that are high in some factors, and low in others, such as Japan in regard to state capacity and Saudi Arabia in regard to access to resources. Nonetheless, in general, we find that the more developed countries have several factors working in their favour.

The first factor is, of course, the geo-strategic position, including the relative international power of the state. Beyond the obvious example of the power of the U.S. to dictate international market rules, there is a whole hierarchy of degrees of international economic power. We should keep in mind that international power has regional dimensions as well, so the relative power that Brazil has vis à vis the U.S. has little to do with its power to dictate terms with smaller partners in economic negotiations, such as Paraguay.

Another classic source of international economic power and so state autonomy is access to scarce natural resources. Therefore, we see that Saudi Arabia has a very strong negotiating position in line with its petroleum wealth and ranks higher than its other attributes would suggest. Negotiating power would therefore depend in part on the relative abundance of those same resources in the partner, thus, Saudi Arabia has little leverage in negotiations with Iraq, which has its own oil resources, but can impose relatively greater pressure on Egypt, which does not.

The size and, more importantly, the potential size of a market is another important source for state autonomy from international dictates. The potential size of Brazil, China, and India's economies puts those countries in a separate category from other developing countries in terms of their bargaining power in investment and trade agreements.

Regional and bilateral trade agreements can also have the paradoxical effect of increasing the size of regional bargaining strength. Therefore, we would expect that as (if) the MERCOSUR integration process moves forward, Argentina's position is strengthened vis à vis outside investors and traders, at the same time that its position is bound with its MERCOSUR partners. The evolving MERCOSUR decision-making process thus becomes key to understanding the degree of state autonomy in the Southern Cone.

The degree of openness of an economy, in terms of degrees of contribution of exports and imports to international production is important, but the types of exports and imports traded are even more important. Both the classic writings of Raúl Prebisch in regard to Latin America and the literature on East Asian growth point to the importance of elasticities in terms of determining vulnerability to international markets. Elasticities work on both the supply and the demand side. Thus, on the supply side, the ability of suppliers to easily increase production in response to increases in price generally puts commodity producers, where there are many suppliers in a weaker position, than high technology or manufactured goods producers, where there is generally less competition. On the demand side, the willingness of consumers to pay high levels of prices for high tech and innovative goods, such as new computer equipment means that profit margins, and so international market power, is greater for nations that produce such goods. Moreover, as technology changes, demand for the latest product of high tech goods continues, while demand for basic commodity items, such as bananas, is easily satiated. Finally, basic commodity items such as strawberries may be more easily substituted for by other products, or denied, if the price somehow goes up substantially. An item like the latest semi-conductor chip is likely to be much less substitutable. The upshot is that the product mix of a country is vital to determining its degree of state autonomy.

In short, we should not underestimate the importance of the type of product a country produces. If we consider the aspects of value-added, spillover, and multiplier effects, the product mix of a country has very important implications for its standard of living. By value added, we mean the steps of the productive process that a country is able to capture. Thus, if a country only exports the raw iron ore, it is missing on the chance to gain good (high wage) employment and the profits that go along with every other step in the steel-making process. Moreover, the country is missing the spillover effects whereby a competitive steel industry may lead to the development of other product industries, such as equipment manufacturers that use steel. Last but not least, the country would lose all the income and spending multiplier effects that every worker along the rest of the production process would have on the rest of the economy in spending their wages.

What products a country produce, and how it produces them do not depend simply on comparative advantage. Instead, we see a variety of production techniques and structures among countries (and regions within them) for producing the same product. Therefore, the way that a country organizes its production is also vital to understand the degree of autonomy that it has from globalization pressures. State policies towards certain products are grouped under the label 'sectoral' policies. We now examine sectoral policies, and the implications for the sources of domestic political autonomy and capacity to choose them.

Explaining Sectoral Policy: Domestic Factors of State Autonomy

A sector is simply the amalgamation of economic activities involved in creating a certain type of economic product. Thus, we can consider the steel sector as comprising everything from mining the iron ore to producing it in factories to transporting it to buyers of the product.[9] Sectoral policy is mutually defined by state autonomy.

More autonomous states will be able to guide production in their sectors towards international competitiveness. In some cases, as with the development of Korean production in automobiles, state intervention may actually create a sector. State autonomy in sectoral policy depends not only on its level of vulnerability to international pressures noted in the previous section, but also upon the way its own domestic political economy is set up. We identify the main domestic factors as the level of development of the domestic private sector; the level of organization of domestic producers and labour; the relative and absolute levels of state capacity; and the more intangible roles of leadership and national culture.

A factor that is often overlooked or underestimated in developing countries is that the domestic private sector is also in the process of development. In most developing countries, not only is the private capital sector weak, but also labour markets and domestic human capital are also weak. Most developing countries, partly as a legacy of colonial structures, partly because of state dominance in production in the early independence years, and partly simply as a function of a lack of time, have very weak private capitalist and organized labour classes. This weakness, like all measures, occurs on a continuum. More developed countries, like Argentina, have stronger unions and stronger domestic capital owner networks, than countries like neighbouring Bolivia. However, in some less developed countries with concentrated exports, including Bolivia, the unions in the few leading sectors, such as mining, have disproportionate degrees of power compared to other private domestic actors. Thus state autonomy on a domestic level depends on the overall level of development of the private sector as well as the relative level of development of different groups within the private sector.

The level of organization of its domestic producers and skilled labour will also determine state autonomy from domestic pressures, and so its ability to move in new directions. States that face strong pressures from domestic interest groups, particularly if they are highly dependent for tax revenues from production by those groups will find it difficult to engage in building in competition within the sector or in favouring other sectors. Favouring other sectors means a commitment of scarce resources to them, so unless the sectors are somehow linked to the currently dominant sectors, or members of the dominant sectors can be factionalized and/or co-opted, introducing whole new sectors will be exceedingly difficult.

Barriers to entry are the steps and conditions needed to enter competitive production of a product. They include technological, managerial, and financial costs to enter into markets. There are other barriers beyond those related directly to production, including the need for skills among the work force, the need to learn how to market the products, the need for reputation of quality, and, not least, the need to adequate access to external markets to be able to reach economies of scale. In every case, the international market is dynamic, thus ongoing re-tooling and productivity increases in each of these competitive areas is a must. In sum, countries wishing to compete in manufacturing, high tech, or complex service sectors, such as financial services, will face heavy initial and ongoing costs.

As D. Michael Shafer (1994) points out, sectors can be divided into two general types: those with high barriers to entry and high levels of asset and factor specificity and those with low entry costs and flexible asset and factor transferability. If we added the factors of technological, managerial, and ongoing research and innovation costs, we see that some industries will have a natural tendency to move towards oligopolistic structures. If we furthermore think about the major industries that provide numerous high wage jobs and revenues in the First World countries, such as automobiles, pharmaceuticals, and airplanes, we see that the size and critical value of these industries ensures that they will have a very strong position vis à vis the state. The industries will moreover lend themselves to strong labour organization as well, since a large number of skilled workers, with barriers to entry to obtain those skills, will be needed. This explains the U.S. government's bail out of Chrysler in the 1970s, and the intensity of Canada's recent dispute with Brazil over airplane industry market shares. In these types of enterprises, timing is critical – because the later a country or company enters the market, generally the higher will be the costs for entry. Ongoing innovation and the development of vertical economies of scale, the need for access to huge pools of cheap capital, and the competition for market share leads to the mergers and acquisitions we see internationally in these industries, such as the recent Daimler – Chrysler merger.

Emerging high value-added services industries, such as financial and information technology industries are a little different in that while they have high barriers to entry and extremely high ongoing costs for innovation, they have not yet tended to result in strong lobbies or unions as large manufacturing industries. In these areas, the state could potentially have more leeway, since its provision of research and development money (even if through defence contracts) and the need for skilled workers puts it, at least for now, in a critical supporting position for the industry. The U.S. government may be the only country with a large enough pool of skilled labour and, because of timing, an already entrenched information technology industry to be less autonomous in this regard.

Finally, state autonomy will depend in good part on state capacity, in both a relative and an absolute sense. As aforementioned, state capacity refers to the analytical and managerial capabilities of the bureaucracies. In the case of Japan, since World War II, state managers have enjoyed a privileged social status, and have been able to recruit from the most capable members of the society. Japanese bureaucracy has thus been dominant to private sector capabilities until recently. Even in situations where the private sector is a match for state capabilities, a nimble, flexible, and clever state, such as those in Western Europe, including Switzerland and Sweden can play a vital role in shaping sectoral policy.[10]

We would be remiss if we underplayed the roles of leadership and culture in shaping the values and levels of trust in states that lends them a degree of autonomy. The contrast between Indonesia and Japan is telling in terms of the degrees of corruption and repression of the former, signs that the state itself was weak and internally divided. Leadership itself with economic vision, whether in the guise of Park in Korea, Pinochet in Chile, or Salinas in Mexico, can have important effects on both state autonomy and its ability to pursue sectoral policy through regulation.

Regulatory Games States Play[11]

While the degree of state autonomy varies, there are a wide variety of tools available to *all* states to pursue sectoral policies, as summarized in Table 4.2.

Table 4.2: Examples of Sectoral Policy Interventions

<table>
<tr><th>Type of Intervention</th><th>Direct (Financial or Protective)</th><th colspan="2">Indirect (Factor of Production-oriented)</th></tr>
<tr><td>Domestic Protection</td><td>Agriculture in most countries: protection + subsidization</td><td>Subsidizing Agricultural Research & Technology</td><td>Tied Aid</td></tr>
<tr><td>Financial</td><td>Chrysler bailout; Embraer vs. Bombardier</td><td colspan="2">U.S. Defence research spill-overs</td></tr>
<tr><td>Reduction of Foreign Access</td><td>Abuse of anti-dumping temporary protection; ongoing by various countries</td><td colspan="2">Japanese retail system</td></tr>
<tr><td>Improving Competitiveness of Exports</td><td>Export-Import bank loan guarantees</td><td colspan="2">Subsidizing & protecting media outlets: French film industry</td></tr>
<tr><td>Trade Agreements</td><td>Regional reduction of barriers: NAFTA, etc</td><td>Trade diversion to buy time for local manufacturers</td><td>Brazil-MERCOSUR vs. FTAA</td></tr>
<tr><td>Sectoral Targeting</td><td>Europe – Airbus</td><td colspan="2">South Korean auto industry</td></tr>
<tr><td>Subsidizing Human Resources</td><td>Canada – grants for innovation research</td><td colspan="2">Any country's educational system</td></tr>
</table>

The tools that states use to intervene are reflective of the market and natural productive structures of the sector.

Through regulatory policy, states can reduce these obstacles to entry into new sectors of production. In the broadest terms, states can engage in three regulatory strategies to affect sectoral conditions:

i) create barriers to entry in their domestic markets, thus reducing foreign competition;
ii) promote domestic producers through direct interventions;
iii) find indirect ways to promote domestic producers through manipulations of linked demand or supply markets.

While the actual policy tools used by states in these three functions are complex and imaginative, we can identify some basic prototypes. The most obvious ones, which have begun to disappear in large part due to globalization pressures, are direct subsidy or protection measures. However, none of these tools has totally disappeared, rather they have simply taken on new forms. Subsidies could take the form of favourable tax treatment, outright price supports, or indirect transfers, such as subsidized loans. An easy example is the case of agriculture in Europe and North America. Protection could include quotas or outright prohibition, as is the case with Canada's health care system. Anti-dumping is often used as a protective tool in the U.S. Another frequent accusation is the abuse of health standards to block imported goods. Globalization pessimists can make a case that these types of policies are under heavy pressure for universal liberalization.

However, even should these more obvious forms of regulatory intervention disappear, there are myriad subtle ways in which states will continue to intervene in sectors, most of which are unassailable under the provisions of international economic agreements. One of the biggest is indirect subsidization of linked markets. Thus, U.S. spending on defence technology has important spillover effects in the development of high technology products. The East Asian model of political economy has involved heavy control and taxation of consumer products, as well as highly institutionalized savings rates, so that not only is protection afforded to domestic producers, but also a lower cost of capital is provided. In other words, although taxation has important international-level effects, many of the rules about taxation are still considered exclusively domestic in scope. Subsidization and protection in one form or the other occurs in any intervention of supply or demand markets, including state financing of higher education, such as student loans on favourable terms. All of these policies are outside the conceivable scope of globalization processes, so all are fair game for state intervention.

Another way of pursuing regulatory strategy is to simply put up informal or tacit barriers to entry in the domestic market. The Japanese retail system is (in)famous not only for producing high employment, but also for creating frustrating barriers to entry for foreign competitors. However, informal barriers will exist in any regulatory system, including more favourable rulings for national producers or tacit collusion of domestic suppliers or consumers to support national producers. States have shown themselves to be open and quiet cheerleaders of the virtue of buying and supporting national production. In the myriad forms of red tape, such as licensing, required permits, or simple registration paperwork, any state can create a barrier to entry for would-be foreign producers.

One of the most interesting games most states play is to liberalize their sectors only after they have encouraged and supported the development of a national monopoly or oligopoly in their domestic markets. The oligopoly rents during the period of heavy protection give the industry time to retool and to develop the financial, productive, and technical economies of scale to compete on an international level. The U.S. government tends to be the strongest pro-liberalization lobbyist on the international scale precisely because its markets are so big and its oligopolies have already had time to develop. The numerous examples of countries that are following this strategy, include China in a variety of industries and Canada with Air Canada's privileged control of domestic airspace. Naturally, domestic consumers pay a higher price, the price of subsidization, so that their national industries have a chance on the international level.

These innumerable 'tricks' available to the state are likely to elude any ability for present and future international treaties to enforce or, in most cases even detect them. And, if they are detected, capable states will simply find other, more creative ways to favour domestic producers. The capacity of states to manage their regulatory spheres thus is a key factor in international competition. Beyond state capacity, the domestic private sector can set up its own barriers to entry for foreign competitors – an accusation frequently levelled at Japan (for example, in terms of subcontracting arrangements). Given the complexity and subtlety of the ways in which states can continue to intervene in their markets, this argument may seem difficult to demonstrate empirically. In the next section, we will present a framework for deciphering regulatory policy intentions through breaking down the effects of regulatory markets that could serve as a road map for preparing just such sectoral studies.[12]

Mapping State Regulatory Policies: A Preliminary Framework

The data for a sectoral analysis of the effects of regulation could proceed in the following steps:

i) identifying the primary economic and social groups affected by economic liberalization;
ii) identifying criteria for beneficial, neutral, and harmful effects and gauging whether those effects can be linked to certain groups as a result of liberalization;
iii) assessing the degree of those effects on the various groups;
iv) noting any discrepancies between perceived effects and measurable effects.

I would suggest a multi-step, multi-layered process of investigation for accomplishing these goals.[13] The primary focus on this process would be to examine processes of regulatory change, which will be the only way to reveal the interest groups, institutional structures, and policy ideas behind regulations. The first step would be to identify clearly each stage of the economic liberalization process in question. Liberalization of regulated industries tends to occur through distinct phases, starting with a reduction of protective policies; then proceeding to an emphasis first on deregulation – setting up regulatory codes and institutions for the market; followed by privatization; with anticipation towards an eventual free trade agreement.

The second step would be to discern the level of the policy change. The level of change could range from the incremental, such as a ruling, to a policy or code change, to an actual change in the regulatory institutions. Again, the most wide-ranging change would be the problem of harmonizing regulations under a free trade agreement.

There are a number of well-organized groups that could be affected by the change. These will vary by country, but some of the most interesting aspects of regulatory policy will come from examining interest group conflict, such as: government vs. business; large businesses vs. small businesses; domestic vs. foreign businesses; government sub-contractors vs. those who want a more open government procurement process; and business vs. consumers. In studying these areas of interest group contestation, we would want to be cognizant of both the perceived and the real effects of the regulatory change in question – keeping in mind that present harm usually results in greater potential political resistance than potential gain. Similarly, gains or losses can be considered in terms of their absolute, relative, and proportional characteristics, as well as their dynamic properties, i.e., whether they are short-term, on-going, or long-term in nature. Of course, these axes of conflict are not bi-directional, but multi-dimensional (multiple simultaneous actors along multiple issues). Moreover, the groups themselves are subject to fragmentation. Moreover, we should not discount less organized forms of feedback, such as protests, strikes, and media coverage, including opinion polls. These may coalesce into political party platforms or campaigns that lead to regulatory change.

In the end, a study of regulatory policy will want to know not just the interest group effects, but also the actual and perceived effects on public policy. This part of the study might focus on the intra-industry and intra-sectoral effects of regulatory policy, such as the levels of competition, consumer satisfaction, profits, production, debt, and international competitiveness. A secondary, but equally important step would be to look at the effects on industries and other aspects of the economy that have important linkages to the industry in question. For example, the regulatory structure of a transportation or information technology industry could have profound effects on industries throughout a country.

In sum, studying the differential effects of regulatory change is a challenging and multi-faceted task. It requires intimate knowledge of an industry; the ability to compare regulatory structures across countries; a good practical knowledge of macro- and micro-economics; and the ability to understand both the political and policy process of a country. The challenge requires the use of a wide variety of 'inside' and 'outside' sources of information on the industry, including interviews, newspapers, surveys, economic analyses, and financial statements. Studying a regulatory system requires a dedication to move beyond the often hollow claims of the need for change from academics and the overly technical and narrow analyses of consultants and practitioners who understand an industry and the difficulty of making decisions. Unfortunately, at present, there is very little in the way of training available for those who want to make a genuine contribution in this all important and increasingly prominent area of governance.

Some Very Brief Examples of Regulatory State Autonomy

In terms of regulatory policy regarding sectors, we can illustrate the application of our model using two quick examples. The first example is embodied in much of the literature surrounding the development miracle of the East Asian state. The general idea of a developmental state is one that consciously intervenes into markets in order to overcome domestic bottlenecks to economic growth and to improve its international competitiveness. Thus, Robert Wade's (1990) seminal work, *Governing the Market*, laid out the numerous ways in which the Taiwanese government intervened in its economy. His study includes documentation of a conscious industrial policy to create new productive sectors. He also recounts interventions in financial markets to direct investment and savings towards favoured sectors. Similarly, the state encouraged the development of a corps of technical and managerial experts that could manage the new enterprises. However, the nature of the state's interventions are not to simply create long-standing state-owned behemoths, but to cultivate an internationally-competitive private sector that works hand-in-hand with the state. Thus Wade's portrait of Taiwan, like Johnson's (1982) of Japan, and Amsden's (1989) of South Korea, are of states that achieve high economic growth with highly equal levels of income distribution through consciously regulatory intervention.[14] Despite the last few years of slow growth, the East Asian developmental state delivered some 30 years of quality growth, and therefore is not to be dismissed.

The general argument that is now being made is that with the collapse of the East Asian economies and the growth of bi- and multilateral trade agreements, as well as the pressures for access to international finance, interventions along the lines of those described in East Asia previously are no longer possible. While we have given a variety of examples of the regulatory games all states play, the question remains as to whether regulation can play a developmental role in the same way that state intervention once did. We might also ask whether regulatory policy can have the same potential for social and national purposes as did developmentalism. My own forthcoming research on energy markets in South America shows that regulatory policy is decidedly more limited than previous state intervention, but that there are genuine possibilities. First, estimates of the new limits on state action are highly over-rated. In the energy sector, there are several examples of states, such as Uruguay and Paraguay, who have not, and do not, intend to privatize state-owned electricity companies. Second, even where electricity systems have been privatized, the way the markets are set up affects to a great extent the levels of foreign ownership and investment, the levels of competition, and the prices that are paid by consumers. Thus, the regulatory policy of Argentina's electricity system has led to a more competitive market than that of Chile. Third, international integration offers local companies greater economies of scale. Thus we find that domestic regulatory policy has very important effects on the ability of national companies to compete internationally. For example, the high level of market concentration in Chile's electricity market can be seen as an advantage in terms of its dominant companies, Endesa and Gener, competing in other markets like Brazil and Argentina. That is, Endesa has been able to use its oligopoly profits at home to expand overseas.

The expected response to this line of inquiry will be that a privatized system can only benefit private companies. However, we should point out that in shaping market outcomes, regulation could inject a level of national and social purpose. While there is competition for international investment in strategic sectors, states can guide domestic market outcomes in a number of directions. Thus, in the example of Endesa above, some sectors of Chilean society pay higher electricity tariffs, but we should note that both the Chilean government and large domestic labour unions own large percentages of Endesa's shares. We can end with a more straightforward and indisputable example of national interest through regulation. The Brazilian government enforces a strict code that forces a regular incremental improvement in energy efficiency among its major industries through its PROCEL program, carried about by the ANEEL regulatory agency.[15] Energy efficiency helps all parties, the public, and the environment.

What Creates New Regulatory Autonomy and Capacity?

The wider question of how states can change their levels of autonomy and capacity is beyond the scope of the present effort, but we can rely upon the existing literature to give us some clues. Arbetman and Kugler (1997) discuss the importance of a state's ability to extract resources in a non-predatory way for re-direction. Thus we find that First World states have much higher effective rates of taxation on income and property than those of developing countries. Moreover, even within developing countries there are big differences in the ability to control fiscal policy. Weaker states, like those in Latin America, have great difficulty in balancing government budgets, while those in East Asia have been able to create government surpluses and otherwise re-direct government spending towards long-term investment, including the development of education and health. Peter Evans (1995), in his book *Embedded Autonomy*, points out the importance of the training and recruitment of civil servants, and the independence of productive bureaucracies. In East Asian states, there is more emphasis on meritocratic recruitment than in Latin America or Africa. What is even more important is the development of a productive partnership between the state and domestic industry and labour and the ability to carry out adjustment and redistributive policies. These require some degree of elite consensus around a long-term development strategy. While it is clear that a state with great autonomy and capacity, such as Israel, is able to use regulatory policy to develop highly productive new export manufactures and to vastly increase agricultural productivity, we do not yet know exactly how capacity and autonomy can be changed over time.

Conclusion

Our effort thus far brings us to an important research agenda of which this author is part. That is, what are the optimal regulatory policies to pursue which goals? Of course, these will depend on the specific country and sectoral context. Also, what are the trade-offs among the goals of regulatory policy and which groups are affected in which ways by certain regulatory frameworks? Last but not least, how are regulatory decisions made, and how can we develop a strong technical corps of independent but responsive regulators with the national and public interest in mind in developing countries?

By tracing the effects of regulatory policy through our framework, we can begin to answer these questions and to trace back the implicit intentions of regulatory policy makers. In some cases, to be sure, states will be inept and simply open their markets to international competition. But there will certainly be a learning curve for all states as to how to embed national purpose within the complexity of regulations over time. Just as the spread of the internet opens up new avenues for control as well as resistance/independence, so regulation opens up new avenues for global pressures as well as state autonomy from it. In this paper, we have identified the main parameters of this dynamic process, as well as set forth a research agenda by which to study it.

Notes

---

1 I would like to thank Simon Fraser University for providing the funding that made this research possible, and particularly my colleagues in the Department of Political Science for their helpful support and feedback.

2 This is now a common term in the international political economy literature for the farming out of segments of the production process to foreign countries in order to take advantage of local resources, generally cheap labour, see Gereffi and Wyman, 1990, or Dicken, 1992, for examples.

3 A more general label is neoliberalism, which defines the policy package of economic liberalization. The package is also called 'the Washington consensus,' named so by Williamson, 1994.

4 While some anti-globalization authors believe we are on the verge of a 'coming tyranny' of corporate domination, see Teeple, 1995, others believe that states themselves are deciding to move towards globalization agreements (and so can modify it), see McBride, 2000.

5 See Gilpin, 2000, and Cohn, 2000, for overviews of both international finance and trade.

6 Of course, effective interest rates must reflect exchange rates, as well as the general business climate and policy stability (perceived risk) of a country.

7 On the growing weakness of the state, see for examples, Carnoy, 1993; Strange, 1996; Rodrik, 1997; and Falk, 1992. Interesting rejoinders are found in Weiss, 1998 and Gilpin, 2000.

8 See Putnam's work in Evans, Jacobson, and Putnam, 1993.

9 For political economy discussions of sectoral policy, see Zysman 1983; Karl 1997; and Shafer 1994. None of these authors deals with regulatory policy.

10 See, Katzenstein, 1985, for studies on European states' industrial policy.

11 For obvious reasons, there are few empirical global studies of ubiquitous and universal state interference in markets. One interesting recent, if limited, example is, OECD, 1998.

12 I am in the midst of preparing such studies on the electricity sector in South America.

13 See my conference paper for a figure illustrating these steps.

14 See also, Woo-Cumings, 1999, for a contemporary review of the literature on the developmental state.

15 PROCEL stands for Programa Nacional de Conservacão de Energia Elétrica. ANEEL stands for Agência Nacional de Energia Elétrica.

References

Amsden, A.H. (1989), *Asia's Next Giant: South Korea and Late Industrialization*, Oxford University Press, New York.

Arbetman, M. and Kugler, J. (1997), *Political Capacity and Economic Behavior*, Westview Press, Boulder.

Carnoy, Martin (1993), *The New Global Economy in the Information Age: Reflections on our Changing World,* Pennsylvania State Press, University Park, Philadelphia.

Cohn, T.H. (2000), *Global Political Economy: Theory and Practice*, Longman, New York.

Dicken, P. (1992), *The Internationalization of Economic Activity*, Chapman, London.

Evans, P.B., Rueschmeyer, D., and Skocpol T. (1985), *Bringing the State Back In*, Cambridge University Press, New York.

Evans, P.B., Jacobson, H.K., Putman, R.D. (eds) (1993), *Double-Edged Diplomacy: International Bargaining and Domestic Politics*, University of California Press, Berkeley, California.

Evans, P.B. (1995), *Embedded Autonomy: States and Industrial Transformation*, Princeton University Press, Princeton.

Falk, Richard A. (1992), *Explorations at the End of Time: The Prospects for World Order*, Temple University Press, Philadelphia.

Gereffi, G. and Wyman, D. (1990), *Manufacturing Miracles: Paths of Industrialization in Latin America and East Asia*, Princeton University Press, Princeton.

Gilpin, R. (2000), *The Challenge of Global Capitalism: The World Economy in the 21st Century*, Princeton University Press, Princeton.

Grindle, M.S. (1996), *Challenging the State: Crisis and Innovation in Latin America and Africa*, Cambridge University Press, New York.

Gourevitch, P. (1986), *Politics in Hard Times: Comparative Responses to International Economic Crises*, Cornell University Press, Ithaca, New York.

Haggard, S. and Kaufman, R.R. (1992), *The Politics of Economic Adjustment: International Constraints, Distributive Conflicts, and the State*, Princeton University Press, Princeton.

Johnson, C. (1982), *MITI and the Japanese Miracle: The Growth of Industrial Policy, 1925-75*, Stanford University Press, Stanford.

Karl, T.L. (1997), *The Paradox of Plenty: Oil Booms and Petro-States*, University of California Press, Berkeley, California.

Katzenstein, P. (1985), *Small States in World Markets*, Cornell U. Press, Ithaca, New York.
McBride, S. (2000), 'The Politics of Globalization and Labour Strategies,' in S. McBride and J. Wiseman (eds), *Globalization and its Discontents*, St. Martin's, New York.
Milner, H. (1988), *Resisting Protectionism: Global Industries and the Politics of International Trade*, Princeton University Press, Princeton.
OECD (Organization for Economic Cooperation and Development) (1998), *Spotlight on Public Support to Industry*, OECD, Paris.
Rodrik, Dani (1997), *Has Globalization Gone too Far?*, Institute for International Economics, New York.
Rogowski, R. (1989), *Commerce and Coalitions: How Trade Affects Domestic Political Alignments*, Princeton University Press, Princeton.
Shafer, D.M. (1994), *Winners and Losers: How Sectors Shape the Developmental Prospects of States*, Cornell University Press, Ithaca, New York.
Strange, Susan. (1996), *The Retreat of the State: The Diffusion of Power in the World Economy*, Cambridge University Press, New York.
Teeple, G. (1995), *Globalization and the Decline of Social Reform*, Garamond Press, Toronto.
Wade, R. (1990), *Governing the Market: Economic Theory and the Role of Government*, Princeton University Press, Princeton.
Weiss, Linda (1998), *The Myth of the Powerless State: Governing the Economy in the Global Era*, Polity Press, Cambridge.
Woo-Cumings, M. (1999), *The Developmental State*, Cornell University Press, Ithaca, New York.
Williamson, J. (ed) (1994), *The Political Economy of Policy Reform*, Institute for International Economics, Washington, D.C.
Zysman, J., and Tyson L.D. (1983), *American Industry in International Competition: Government Policies and Corporate Strategies*, Cornell University Press, Ithaca, New York.

Chapter 5

Tax Expenditures: The Social Policy of Globalization?

Lois Harder

The annual discipline of tax filing seems like an unlikely site from which to access social policy and hence to learn the meaning of citizenship that social policy conveys. Paying taxes is, of course, a necessary citizenship activity. Taxation is the means through which revenues are generated for the pursuit of public goods. But welfare state theorists have generally asserted that the expression of citizenship and the state's role in disciplining that expression happen when citizens access identifiable, directly funded programs and services (or when non-citizens are prevented from doing so), once the revenues have been collected and redistributed in social programs. While this research continues to offer insights into the character of contemporary citizenship, it is missing an obscured but significant dimension of the story; the role of indirectly funded social programs in integrating citizens into the globalizing economy.

At the level of the federal government in the United States and, especially in Canada, tax expenditures are becoming increasingly important vehicles for the delivery of social policy. Indeed, in the United States, tax expenditures with social policy purposes posted an annual, real growth rate of 4.8 per cent between 1965 and 1995 and grew faster than direct expenditures between 1975-95 (Howard, 1997).[1] In Canada, the use of the personal income tax system to deliver indirect transfers is one of the broadest among industrialized countries, surpassing the U.S., the U.K., Australia and France (Ruggeri and Yu, 1999, p.551). Moreover, the most significant recent social policy developments in Canada and the U.S. (those that have involved investment rather than retrenchment) have been tax expenditures. In a recent study of the 'hidden welfare state', an American policy analyst observed that the Earned Income Tax Credit (EITC) has been hailed as the policy equivalent of penicillin (Howard, p.64). Further north, a prominent social policy analyst described the National Child Benefit as 'one of the most important advances in the history of the modern welfare state in Canada' (Battle, 1999, p.1221).

Both the data and the enthusiasm beg the questions – what accounts for this growth and what objectives are tax expenditures designed to achieve? I argue that the Canadian and American use of tax expenditures to fulfill social policy needs represents a specific response to the prescriptions of neoliberal globalism. It is not that international competitive pressures and the imposition of financial discipline from global capital markets *necessarily* give rise to this method of meeting social needs. Indeed, recent comparative literature suggests that European states have pursued markedly different social policy trajectories (Jackson; 2001, Olsen, 2001). Rather, the contemporary use of the tax system to deliver social policy in Canada and the U.S. reflects an elegant but problematic fix for a complex of ideological, institutional, economic and social pressures. The injury to democracy that results from the opacity and disciplinary effects of tax expenditures outweighs their unique capacity to sustain a role for the state in an era of diminished sovereignty and to bridge partisan divisions. In the interests of contributing to a progressive, emancipatory politics, it is imperative to interrogate the effects of tax expenditures on our self-understanding, collective sense of well-being and capacity to participate in our own governance.

What Are Tax Expenditures Anyway?

The concept of tax expenditures was first articulated in the 1940s by Stanley Surrey, a professor of tax law at Harvard and Assistant Secretary of the Treasury for Tax Policy under Presidents Kennedy and Johnson. Tax expenditures are familiarly known as loopholes or tax breaks, and they are delivered as tax deductions, credits, deferrals or outright exclusion of income from taxation (Howard, p.3). As Christopher Howard explains, 'most public finance experts consider tax expenditures to be "conceptually equivalent" to direct spending. They portray tax expenditures as a simultaneous exchange of cash: taxpayers write a check to the government for their full tax liability, and the government issues them a check to cover those activities exempted from taxation' (Howard, pp.3-4).

The basic principles of taxation are that taxes should provide horizontal and vertical equity, be simple and be neutral in their effects (Young, 2000, p.6). Tax measures that uphold these principles constitute the benchmark tax system. Tax expenditures, however, depart from each of these principles by creating inequities, adding complexity to the tax filing process and providing incentives and rewards for particular types of behaviour. The degree of departure from the benchmark tax system is determined by the particular design of the tax expenditure. In a progressive tax system, one in which people with higher earnings are expected to pay a greater percentage of their incomes in taxes, tax *deductions* are worth more to taxpayers with higher incomes. This is because tax deductions reduce the amount of income that is taxed at the highest tax rate. For example, a deduction of $5000 for a taxpayer taxed at 50 per cent is worth $2500. For a taxpayer who earns less money and hence, is taxed at a lower rate, say 20 per cent, the $5000 deduction is only worth $500.

Tax *credits*, by contrast, are worth the same dollar amount for every claimant. However, the value of the credit is generally considered higher for lower income taxpayers, because they have less disposable income. In effect, $3000 means more to someone earning $20,000 than it does to someone earning $80,000.

If the credit is *non-refundable*, however, it will only provide a benefit to people earning sufficient income to pay income tax. Here too, then, the principle of vertical equity may be strained. *Refundable* credits offer the least violation to the vertical equity principle, since these credits provide benefits to all eligible tax filers, regardless of whether or not they earned sufficient income to owe tax. Refundable credits then, are a form of negative income tax. Rather than the tax filer paying the state, the state pays the tax filer.

An awareness of the use of tax expenditures to meet social policy objectives is relatively recent. Ken Battle observed that, in 1976, the National Council of Welfare introduced Canadians to the idea of tax expenditures for social welfare in a report entitled the *Hidden Welfare State*. The Council's claim that tax expenditures were as relevant to social policy as direct spending was regarded as heretical, but has subsequently become relatively common knowledge (Battle, p.1220). Indeed, the concept is quite familiar to low and middle income earning Canadians, who have received the Child Tax Benefit and the Goods and Services Tax (GST) credit on the basis of their tax returns for more than a decade. And of course, it is almost impossible for Canadians and Americans to be unaware of the tax incentives surrounding Registered Retirement Savings Programs (RRSPs) and Individual Retirement Accounts (IRAs), particularly as the annual contribution deadline approaches.

What is perhaps less commonly understood, however, is the degree to which tax expenditures address the complexity of social policy development and delivery in the post-welfare or neoliberal era. Spending reductions to directly funded social programs were common features of budgets in the 1980s and 1990s. While the need to eliminate deficits and reduce debts was offered as the most neutral justification for the cuts to social services, moral panic surrounding welfare dependency, a desire to diminish the policy influence of 'special interests', and the decision to address increasing trade competitiveness through flexible labor markets were also key justifications for austerity in the realm of social provision. Further, the failed process of constitutional renewal in Canada and the intense ideological divisions of the post-1994 U.S. Congress imposed significant institutional challenges to social policy making. Carefully designed tax expenditures were advanced as the magic formula to reduce social outlays and encourage individual responsibility for social risk, enforce labour force attachment, and diminish political contestation.

Tax Expenditures and Austerity

Tax expenditures initially figured in the budget restraint debate as items worthy of elimination. Their proponents, however, argued that tax expenditures could be used to retain the state's legitimacy as a provider of social benefits, even if these were less generous and more restricted, and to reduce administrative costs by limiting the provision of directly funded programs. When Surrey originally drew attention to tax expenditures, his concern was that they represented a sizeable and largely uncontrollable drain on the public treasury (Howard, p.104). Indeed, when deductions are designed as open-ended entitlements, the government foregoes its capacity to control spending, making such expenditures antithetical to an agenda of restraint. In Canada this open-ended design is uncommon, but the U.S. has proven more tolerant of such deductions. The American Home Mortgage Interest deduction is, perhaps, the most flagrant example. In the case of this tax expenditure, the larger the mortgage (and, generally, the home), the larger the deduction. In fact, the U.S. spends more than twice as much on the Home Mortgage Interest deduction as it does on directly funded housing programs (Ibid, p.28).

Currently, however, the interest surrounding tax expenditures emerges from their capacity to reduce social spending. Recent tax expenditure initiatives have been much more carefully targeted, designed with limits on spending or contributions and elimination or phase-outs related to income levels. In Canada, for example, the replacement of the universal Family Allowance and directly funded child benefits by the Child Tax Benefit, represented, even in the CTB's most generous year (1996), a $5.1 billion reduction from the high water mark of the directly funded programs (Battle, p.1226).[2] Further, as public contributions to pension programs and post secondary education have diminished, tax incentives for private savings have increased. The RRSP and Registered Education Savings Plan are Canadian examples of this phenomenon while Individual Retirement Accounts, which also include provisions for education savings, are American examples.

Augmenting their ability to deliver the message of austerity is the capacity of tax expenditures to convey the impression that they do not involve government spending (Block and Maslove, 1994, p.181). For most taxpayers, the fact that one receives a tax credit or deduction does not lead to the conclusion that the state has foregone revenue in order to make that tax break available. Instead, such tax breaks appear as a brief and targeted respite from the state's desire to lay claim to hard-earned wages. Hence, the demise of directly funded programs and the rise in tax expenditures appear as tax cuts and incentives to pursue our particular needs through the market. It is not immediately evident that, in enabling market provision, tax expenditures not only represent public spending but also redistribute foregone public revenues in the service of private profit.

Tax Expenditures and Neoliberal Ideology

The use of tax expenditures to convey the message of austerity points to a broader function of tax expenditures in an era of globalization; the articulation of neoliberal ideology. As the previous discussion suggests, tax expenditures are readily marshaled in the service of smaller government and in the promotion of private provision. Moreover, because of their administration through income taxation, tax expenditures convey a clear message that entitlement to tax benefits results from the process of earning income. While both Canadian and American tax expenditures include refundable credits, the fact that one's entitlement to those credits can only be enjoyed upon filing a tax return communicates the idea that paid work is a requirement for access to social entitlements. However, if the chief means of publicizing those credits is also through the process of tax filing, low wage earners and, in the Canadian case, social assistance recipients who neglect to file, may not receive the benefits to which they are entitled.

Interestingly, the most heralded recent social policy innovations in the U.S. and Canada are tax expenditures designed to benefit the working poor. In Canada, the National Child Benefit (NCB) is an additional component of the Canada Child Tax Benefit, paid to working parents and designed to address the phenomenon of the 'welfare wall'. The 'welfare wall' is constituted by disincentives to employment arising from the costs that people must incur when they make the shift from social assistance to paid employment (Battle, p.1233). In tying the refundable tax credit to earned income, the National Child Benefit represents public support for both wage earning and low wage employment. However, the dubious sanctioning of low wage employers is overlooked in favour of the allegedly greater good attributed to promoting independence from public support through labour force participation. Indeed, the Department of Finance explicitly articulated this rationale in outlining its objectives for the NCB, stating that the NCB was designed 'to promote attachment to the workforce resulting in fewer families having to rely on social assistance – by ensuring that families will always be better off as a result of finding work....' (Canada, Department of Finance, cited in Battle, p.1233).

The rationale supporting the American Earned Income Tax Credit is similar. As the directly funded welfare program, Aid to Families with Dependent Children (AFDC), became the focus of growing criticism for its alleged promotion of single parent families and generational poverty, the EITC was heralded as a much needed realignment of social policy priorities. In short, the EITC was consistent with basic American values (Howard, p.140). It promoted the work ethic while the AFDC, in paying benefits in the absence of labour force attachment, was seen as undermining that ethic.

This promotion of labour force participation has been particularly important for retaining the support of Southern politicians. As a region that has relied upon a low-wage economy in order to attract investment, Southern representatives have a well-established practice of resisting social policies that might weaken labour force attachment. Indeed, as John Myles and Paul Pierson have observed, the need to sustain its low wage, non-unionized workforce has been so significant that Southern politicians have historically opposed welfare policy measures that would actually deliver a disproportionate benefit to the South (Myles and Pierson, 1997, Online, Academic Search Elite, p.11). Ensuring the availability of an immiserated labour force was deemed more important than offering poor southerners some respite from poverty. The restricted availability of the EITC to families with waged income has thus been appealing to Congressional representatives from the south.

The targeting of the NCB and the EITC to low waged workers might also be read as a means to compensate at least some of the people who bear the costs of progress in capitalist societies (Titmuss, 1994, p.94). In general terms, social programs have been justified as a means to ensure that economically marginalized citizens continue to support a system that provides them with only limited opportunities. To the extent that the working poor have traditionally been neglected in favour of both the more destitute and middle income earners, the NCB and EITC may contribute to 'blue collar buy in'. Indeed, this observation is supported by the decision to expand the EITC in response to the 'discovery' of the working poor as a political constituency with sufficient strength to determine the electoral outcome in several swing jurisdictions (Howard, p.142). Howard cites the findings of pollster Stanley Greenberg who observed that the working poor were 'frustrated about doing everything right in terms of work and family and still being unable to afford a house, child care or health insurance or to save for retirement' (Greenberg, 1986, cited in Howard, p.142). As opposition to globalization increases and to the extent that the Canadian and American federal states continue to support enhanced access to international markets and global investment opportunities, popular resistance, particularly from those for whom globalization poses the greatest threat, will have to be addressed.

The fact that one's entitlement to these benefits is determined on the basis of a tax return also contributes to the appeal of a tax expenditure policy design for low income earners. It represents a real improvement over the invasive application process that characterized Fordist, means-tested programs (Harder, 2000). In both the U.S. and Canada, legislators, academics and anti-poverty advocates have supported tax credits as a means to ensure social provision in a post-Keynesian era. Directly funded programs have not fared well under the pressures of austerity, but since credits can be targeted to the poor, resources will not be 'wasted' in universal programs that provide benefits to everyone, including those who could afford to pay for them in the absence of public support (Donnelly, Welch and Young, 1999, p.88; Miller, 2000).[3] Additionally, Canada's National Anti-Poverty Organization (NAPO), while preferring direct spending to tax credits, has also argued that, if the government insists on pursuing tax reductions, it should ensure that low-income Canadians are the priority. NAPO (1999) identified increasing the Goods and Services tax credit as one means through which to deliver such a tax reduction. However, encasing social provisions within a tax expenditure design may not be a particularly efficient means to convey the message of social inclusion, since the degree to which these programs will be appreciated as government-provided relief for low-income is uncertain. Instead, low income people are more likely to see a tax refund as an incentive to purchase the services that they require from private providers, thus finding themselves encouraged to rely on a market system that contributed to their impoverishment in the first place.

At the other end of the income scale, tax expenditures have been used to promote savings and investment and, again, to reward economic activity that is socially desirable and supportive of globalization's demands. Although the design of indirect spending programs has become increasingly concerned with limiting the extent of the benefits that can be enjoyed through tax expenditures, it is nonetheless true that the more affluent benefit from tax expenditures to a much higher degree than the less well off. In the U.S., for example, Howard found that over 85 per cent of the benefits for home mortgage interest, real estate taxes and charitable donations went to people earning more than $50,000 per year, with the highest portion of that percentage earning more than $100,000 per year (Howard, pp.28, 32). In Canada, despite the fact that RRSP contributions represent the single largest tax expenditure, only one third of eligible Canadians contributed in 1997 (Donnelly, Welch and Young, p.91). Further and on the basis of 1992 data, Barbara Austin calculated that tax filers earning more than $100,000 contributed 44 times as much to an RRSP as tax filers earning under $25,000. When marginal tax rates are factored in, high income earners enjoyed 75 times the benefit received by low income earners (Young, p.46).

Just as tax expenditures targeted to low income earners can be viewed as supporting 'blue collar buy in', tax expenditures benefiting the well-to-do can also be understood as a means to ensure the continued support of the affluent for the state's social function. Indeed, the necessity of support from this constituency is substantially more imperative than the support of the poor, since they exert direct control over the levers of economic and political power. It is not surprising then, that the benefits of many tax expenditures are delivered in inverse relationship to financial need (Ibid., p.47).[4] In garnering support from this constituency, however, policy makers must balance their obligations to ensure social well-being with the business community's assertion of the need for less government and lower taxes. By providing tax relief for specific behaviours such as retirement savings or charitable giving, the state is able to sustain its role in providing for collective well-being, even if its capacity to ensure the quality and efficiency of the services is diminished. An unfortunate consequence of this outcome, however, is that as tax expenditures and tax reductions increase, the revenues available to fund programs for the poor diminish. As a result low income Canadians and Americans find themselves doubly compelled to rely on their own, meagre resources.

This encouragement of self reliance or at least private provision and its negative consequences for publicly supported social programs is also apparent in the U.S. government's use of tax expenditures to support employer provided benefit programs. Rather than implementing a public health insurance program, a national childcare program or a robust public pension program, the U.S. has chosen instead to rely on private insurance schemes. In fact, employer provided pension and benefit plans and employer contributions for medical insurance premiums and medicare constituted the two largest U.S. tax expenditures in 2000 (Saxton, 1999).

According to the terms of these tax expenditures, employers receive tax deductions in return for the benefit packages they provide to their workers. In the U.S., as in other Anglo-American democracies, however, the number of people employed under conditions of standard employment is decreasing. In addition to the reduction in wages that this flexibilization of the labour force has entailed, it has also reduced the availability of benefit packages. As a result, only the most privileged workers – those working for large and successful employers – receive the social protection that these packages afford.

While the benefits of working for a large employer are obvious and hence provide an incentive for citizens to obtain the necessary training to pursue employment in these firms, the lack of good jobs effectively renders such an incentive meaningless. Indeed, the dependent relationship between the employee and employer, already existing as a result of the wage relation, is further entrenched by such benefit programs. Workers may feel unable to criticize employment practices or resist harassment for fear of losing not only their jobs but also their health benefits and pension contributions. On the other hand, to the extent that sufficient numbers of middle and upper middle class voters are, in fact, covered under private insurance schemes, the pressure on the U.S. government to implement a public program is dissipated and the opportunities for private health service providers are sustained.

The role of tax expenditures in exacerbating dependency on private sources of provision is not restricted to employee benefit programs. In fact, the most extreme reinforcement of dependency is exacted through the use of family income as the basis of entitlement for tax expenditures. In the U.S. the use of family income is the norm, since the determination of personal income tax liability is based on a system of joint filing in which husband and wife couples are taxed as a single unit of income. Although American couples have the option of filing separately, this option is rarely worthwhile (Zelenak, 2000, p.12). In Canada, by contrast, the individual serves as the basis of taxation, with eligibility for particular tax expenditures, such as the CCTB and the Child Care expense deduction, being based upon family income.

The presumption of income pooling within families is not new to social policy design, but it has been the subject of considerable debate (McCaffrey, 1997, p. 4; Ontario Fair Tax Commission, 1993, p.263; Zelenak, p.17).[5] Critics have argued that, while most individuals do live in multi-member households, at least in part because of the economic benefits that are thus derived, the financial relationships that attend collective living arrangements are as distinct as the people who form them. Moreover, even in situations in which income is shared, it is not necessarily the case that both parties have equal control over the spending decisions, with women and their generally weaker earnings capacity bearing the brunt of this inequality (Himmelweit, 2000, p.3).

In fact, the use of family income to determine tax expenditure eligibility is a means for the state to reduce social outlays. This reduction is justified through the presumption that people involved in intimate relationships have access to more financial resources than what they earn individually. In the case of the Canadian child care expense deduction, for example, it is the parent with the lesser income who must claim the deduction (Canada, Customs and Revenue, 1997). Because tax deductions provide greater benefits to people in higher income brackets, the requirement that the lesser earner claim the expenditure is likely to result in a smaller benefit. However, this diminished benefit can be justified because additional financial resources are presumed to be available to the lesser income earner from the higher income earner. Since women generally earn less money than men, this means that while the state recognizes that women need help with childcare expenses in order to participate in the paid labour force, they should also expect to rely upon their better-paid partners.

The reduction in social resources that have resulted from the state's presumptions surrounding appropriate relationships is understandable, if troubling , in the context of the imposition of financial discipline on the public accounts. More worrisome from the perspective of a robust conception of citizenship is the erasure of autonomy and self-reliance that occurs when the subject of discussion shifts away from the state and the market to the family. While feminist theorists have drawn our attention to the state of *interdependence* upon which the autonomous liberal individual relies, they have also underscored the fact that marginalized groups have been systematically prevented from enjoying even the approximations of liberal individualism to which more privileged groups have laid claim (Pateman, 1988). The fact that tax expenditures help to obscure and even deny these aspirations for autonomy while claiming to provide the resources for their realization is particularly disturbing.

At the same time that tax expenditures with social purposes promote the neoliberal values of self (or familial)-reliance, hard work and smaller government, they also encourage citizens to manage social risk through the integration of their private savings into global financial capital markets (Harmes, 2001).[6] The fact that national governments have determined that individuals alone, or as participants in private benefit plans, can, and indeed should assume this level of risk in securing their future well-being, attests to the vigour with which neoliberal ideology has been embraced. And just as employer benefit plans help to circumvent pressures for public programs, reliance on healthy rates of return on investments for social risk undermine the potential progressive uses to which these pools of capital might be put. As Wally Seccombe (1997) has wryly suggested, 'try discussing with one's relatively affluent and financially secure academic colleagues whether the pension fund of your professional association ought to have investment criteria that might detract somewhat from the objective of risk adjusted profit maximization and see how people's insecurity concerning their family's financial future comes into play' (Seccombe, p.10).

Tax expenditures serve austerity objectives and to reflect many facets of neoliberal ideology, they have also proven to be particularly capable of garnering support from disparate parties who are otherwise disinclined to co-operate and to successfully traverse through arcane institutional structures. The success of the EITC in eliciting support from southerners has already been discussed, but it has also managed to unite representatives across partisan boundaries. This is a particularly impressive feat in the context of social policy, in which the vicious rhetoric surrounding the Republican 'Contract with America' is only the most obvious example of the obstacles officials confront in the process of consensus building. In fact, Howard argues that it is such obstacles to the development of directly funded social programs, which unintentionally promote the development of indirect programs (Howard, p.10). Perhaps the most persuasive explanation for the success of the EITC and other tax expenditures in brokering partisan unity is the fact that the number of representatives who might resist them is restricted. The Senate Finance Committee and the House Ways and Means Committee have exclusive jurisdiction over tax expenditures (Ibid.). Further, tax expenditures often pass through Congress as components of broader legislative measures. Rather than being the focus of an entire bill and hence destined to attract dissent, tax expenditures may simply be line items, buried in complex and potentially unrelated bills that have already succeeded in forging the required consensus. Indeed, this was the case for the EITC. Having failed to pass in 1972, 1973 and 1974, it was successful in 1975 when it was included with legislation designed to stimulate the economy in the aftermath of the OPEC oil shock (Ibid., p.70).

While passing legislation in Canada is much less arduous than the American process, the decentralized character of the Canadian federation places its own unique institutional barriers in the path of indirectly funded social programs. The Canadian division of powers assigns responsibility for social programs to the provinces and responsibility for direct (income) taxation to both the federal and provincial governments. Although the federal government has long played a role in social policy, new initiatives have frequently been resisted by Quebec on constitutional and nationalist grounds. And since the 1970s, federal incursions into provincial jurisdiction have also attracted suspicion from the western provinces, particularly Alberta. Further, with the implementation of the Canada Health and Social Transfer in 1996, the federal government undermined whatever provincial goodwill regarding social policy it still retained.

In the current, post-deficit and post (inter?) referendum period, the federal-provincial social policy relationship has been re-established in the Social Union Framework Agreement. Interestingly, it is an indirectly funded social program, the CCTB, which has been the first product of this agreement (to which Quebec is not a party). The federal government's objective with regard to the CCTB is to assume full responsibility for formerly provincially provided welfare benefits to children. According to the terms of the agreement, the savings that will accrue to the provinces as a result of this shift in child benefits is to be reinvested in other programs and services for low-income families with children (Battle, p.33). The tax expenditure design of the CCTB has undoubtedly been central in effecting this policy development as it provides the federal government with the authority to take action, even in the absence of provincial compliance. Provincial willingness to sign on to the Social Union Framework Agreement and the CCTB in particular, however, was more or less assured in the aftermath of significant reduction in federal social transfers that resulted from the CHST (Lazar, 2000).

In both the Canadian and American cases, a significant virtue of the tax expenditure mode of social policy delivery is the extent to which it avoids social conflict. Unlike the directly-funded programs of the Fordist welfare state whose promises of equality and inclusiveness attracted both criticism and demands for expansion from a growing array of marginalized social groups, tax delivered social benefits have been relatively immune from political debate. In part, this is because of the institutional structures through which they are devised and implemented.

The fact that American legislative debate concerning tax expenditures is largely limited to two committees and that, in Canada, federal-provincial social policy negotiations occur through the closed and secretive processes of executive federalism contributes to the limiting of opportunities for public input. But even more immediately, the complexity of the tax code and a commonplace belief that taxation issues are strictly technical contributes to a lack of understanding among social activists and the public generally regarding the explicitly normative purposes of tax expenditures.

Conclusion

Although tax expenditures are not an explicit result of globalization, they have several features that recommend their use as a mode of delivery for neoliberal social policy. With an appropriate design, they can convey the appearance of public provision even as that provision diminishes. They can indicate the importance of pursuing low wage employment over reliance on public resources as the preferred response of both the state and the market under conditions of increasing competitiveness. They can offer a 'middle ground' in normative debates surrounding the objectives and subjects of social policy. But they are not without their weaknesses. Their complexity limits public debate. In addition, they obscure an inherent tension in their advocacy of liberal individualism – the degree to which the allegedly autonomous individual is, in fact, reliant on the resources of others.

Among the central criticisms of the Fordist welfare state launched by proponents of the ideological right was the extent to which postwar social programs offered a hand out rather than a hand up. In reforming social policy, the right's objective has been to diminish the size of the state, increase the freedom of the market and reassert the virtues of individual liberty. In this way, it is imagined that the socially and economically marginalized will be compelled to pull themselves up by their bootstraps, realize the values of industriousness and thrift, and thereby find themselves worthy of capitalism's grace. For those who already enjoy prosperity, their hard work is rewarded even as the safety net that might absorb some of the shock of a fall from grace is removed.

Social programs delivered through tax expenditures thus convey an array of disciplinary techniques designed to both instill neoliberal values in citizens and offset neoliberalism's worst effects. Yet because of their complexity and opaqueness, the possibility of debating the merits of the neoliberal citizenship that tax expenditures are designed to encourage is largely foreclosed. Social policy through tax expenditures ultimately presents us with the thinnest of entitlements and the weakest of expectations from the governments we elect. While this may more easily integrate us into the global economy, it does little to ensure that we can truly succeed in its tortuous currents.

Notes

1 Growth of tax expenditures = 4.3 per cent; growth of direct expenditures = 3.2 per cent, see Howard p. 35.

2 The Child Tax Benefit was subsequently redesigned as the Canada Child Tax Benefit (CCTB) and is envisioned as the chief program for the alleviation of child poverty. Under the terms of the Social Union Framework Agreement, the CCTB will be substantially expanded and will eventually replace provincial income supports for families with children.

3 This view is discussed with regard to post-secondary education in Donnelly, Welch and Young, 1999, and with regard to the implementation of a public health care system in the U.S. in Miller, 2000.

4 Claire Young makes this point with regard to the hierarchy of Canadian pension provisions.

5 In Canada, the definition of family status has been extended to include first heterosexual, common-law couples and, as of the 2000 tax year, same-sex couples. This extension has been made at the behest of people whose familial arrangements fall outside of the married, heterosexual norm that has historically underscored public policy. However, it is not clear whether their inclusion is the product of a successful claim for justice or the state's desire to reduce social spending. Given the conservative character of the U.S. Congress, the extension of the married designation to common-law heterosexual couples has not occurred, and the further extension to same-sex couples seems a long ways off indeed. Even the possibility of reduced social welfare costs seems unlikely to bend Congress' commitment to the traditional family.

6 For a fascinating discussion of the means through which increasing numbers of citizens are being drawn into the dynamics of financial capital, see Harmes.

References

Battle, K. (1999), 'Child Benefit Reform: A Case Study in Tax-Transfer Integration', *Canadian Tax Journal*, Vol. 47, pp. 1219-1257.

Block, S. and Maslove, A. (1994), 'Ontario Tax Expenditures', in A. Maslove (ed), *Taxes as Instruments of Public Policy*, University of Toronto Press, Toronto.

Brown, W. (1995), 'Liberalism's Family Values', in *States of Injury: Power and Freedom in Late Modernity*, Princeton University Press, Princeton.

Canada, Customs and Revenue Agency (1997), 'Interpretation Bulletin 495R2', 13 January.

Canada, Department of Finance (1997), *Working Together Towards a National Child Benefit System*.

Donnelly, Maureen, Welch, Robert and Young, Allister (1999), 'Registered Education Savings Plans: A Tax Incentive Response to Higher Education Access', *Canadian Tax Journal*, Vol. 1, pp. 81-107.

Greenberg, S. (1986), 'Plain Speaking: Democrats State Their Minds', *Public Opinion*, Vol. 9, Summer, pp. 44-50.

Harder, L. (2000), 'Une politique sociale à l'image de la condition postmoderne: Quelques observations préliminaires', *Canadian Review of Social Policy*, Fall.

Harmes, Adam (2001), 'Mass Investment Culture', *New Left Review*, Vol. 9, May/June, pp. 103-24.

Himmelweit, Susan (2000), 'The Need for Gender Impact Analysis', UNISON, UK, 29 November.

Howard, C. (1997), *The Hidden Welfare State: Tax Expenditures and Social Policy in the United States*, Princeton University Press, Princeton.

Jackson, A. (2001), 'Can There Be a "Second Way" in the Third Millennium?', *Studies in Political Economy*, Vol. 65, Summer, pp. 39-64.

Lazar, H. (2000), 'The Social Union Framework Agreement and the Future of Fiscal Federalism', in H. Lazar (ed), *Canada: The State of the Federation*, Institute of Intergovernmental Relations, Queen's University, Kingston, ON.

McCaffrey, Edward (1997), *Taxing Women*, University of Chicago Press, Chicago.

Miller, Matthew (2000), 'Health Care: A Bolt of Civic Hope', *Atlantic Monthly*, October, pp. 77-87.

Myles, John and Pierson, Paul (1997), 'Friedman's Revenge: The Reform of "Liberal" Welfare States in Canada and the United States', *Politics and Society*, Vol. 25, December, pp. 443-473.

NAPO (National Anti-Poverty Organization) (1999), 'Submission to the Standing Committee on Finance: Canada at the Millennium: Strengthening our Fundamental Freedoms', Ottawa, ON.

Olsen, Gregg (2001), 'A New Convergence? Inequality and Social Policy in Canada, Sweden and the U.S. in an Era of Increasing Globalization', Conference Paper presented at the 10th Biennial Social Welfare Policy Conference, June 18.

Ontario Fair Tax Commission (1993), *Fair Taxation in a Changing World*, University of Toronto Press, Toronto.

Pateman, C. (1988), *The Sexual Contract*, Polity, Cambridge.

Ruggeri, G.C. and Yu, W. (1999), 'The Growth of Direct and Indirect Transfers to Persons in Canada: 1988-1996', *Canadian Tax Journal*, Vol. 47, pp. 544-61.

Saxton, J. (1999), 'Tax Expenditures: A Review and Analysis', Joint Economic Committee Study, United States Congress, August.

Seccombe, W. (1997), 'Working-Class Families Meet Capital in Cyberspace', Seminar Paper for Department of Political Science, York University, Toronto, January.

Titmuss, R. (1994), 'Essays on "The Welfare State"', in F. Twine, *Citizenship and Social Rights: The Interdependence of Self and Society*, Sage, London.

Young, C. (2000), *Women, Tax and Social Programs: The Gendered Impact of Funding Social Programs Through the Tax System*, Status of Women Canada, Ottawa, October.

Zelenak, Lawrence (2000), 'Doing Something About Marriage Penalties: A Guide for the Perplexed', *Tax Law Review*, Vol. 54, Spring, pp. 1-76.

Chapter 6

National Politics and Globalization: Varieties of Neoliberal Youth Labour Market Policy Under Thatcher and Blair

Nigel Boyle and Ravi Roy

The 1981 Youth Training Scheme was the principal response to the labour market crisis in the first Thatcher administration. The Blair administration's 'New Deal for a Lost Generation' is the 'third way' policy flagship. This chapter explores both the neoliberal policy paradigm that underlay these initiatives and the coalitions the two governments had to forge in order to implement them at the subsystem level. In both cases, there were alternative neoliberal policy options available. The triumph of an interventionist neoliberalism in 1981 and a welfare-to-work neoliberalism in 1997-98 resulted from the construction of advocacy coalitions that neutralized opposition without compromising core neoliberal beliefs. Policy change was not driven by exogenous economic pressures. Rather, ideas about national competitiveness among certain Thatcherite actors in 1981-83 and New Labour actors in 1995-98 were crucial. This analysis suggests that much of the globalization literature has overlooked sub-system level factors that have a decisive role in shaping policy.

Global Turbulence and British Labour Market Policy: A Policy Sub-System Approach

Three sets of arguments about the impact of global turbulence on national level policy actors have been advanced. The first is that the international integration of markets and capital mobility has dramatically eroded national autonomy: the end of the nation-state is at hand as international markets become the effective economic policy maker, with governments reduced to a vestigial, dignified role.[1] A second argument is that although states may still matter their options are narrowed to a single, neoliberal path: 'Governments lose some level of autonomy over policy because the "invisible hand" of capital movements rewards those states that pursue capital-friendly policies and punishes those states that favour other factors of production ... certain policy options will no longer be available in a world of increasing economic integration' (Hallerberg and Clark, 1997, p.2). This argument often implies that the state has lost its importance as a shaper of economic policy or that globalization if not forcing a retreat of the state, is resituating it 'into a subordinate relationship with global economic forces' (Falk, 1996, p.15). A third argument, stressing different national 'paths', argues that whilst states matter and alternatives to neoliberalism are still viable, globalization predetermines a particular neoliberal developmental trajectory in the 'Anglo-American' or 'liberal' world of welfare capitalism.[2]

This chapter challenges all of these views, making the case that domestic-level factors at the sub-system level allow for considerable scope for policy innovation. The argument that globalization simply means 'less state' has been widely challenged. Philip Cerny has argued that economic globalization has led not to a decline of state intervention but rather to an increase in intervention and regulation in order to promote competitiveness and marketization (Cerny, 2000, p.122). For Cerny this involves microeconomic intervention rather than macroeconomic intervention, responsiveness to international markets, and a focus on enterprise, innovation and profits rather than social cohesion. Active labour market policy targeting Britain's youth unemployed under Thatcher and Blair provides a stark example of a major increase in the level of state intervention in the context of global turbulence. The Thatcher case is particularly significant here as it is a dramatically counter-intuitive form of interventionism. Mrs. Thatcher's neoliberal labour market ideology, in conjunction with a youth labour market unemployment crisis in 1981, yielded a radical policy initiative – the Youth Training Scheme (YTS) – that was based on a sub-system coalition between 'Thatcherites' and interventionist elements of the 'corporatist' Manpower Services Commission (MSC). Propagating the 'deep core' policy paradigm that youth had to be made to adapt to changing market forces, the Thatcherites nonetheless were able to win the support of MSC administrators and business and union 'stakeholders' for a strategy that committed the government to substantial public expenditures and an activist agenda. Although officials and business and union leaders within the MSC shared a reformist perspective about the youth labour market that was decidedly 'Rhenish' – looking to the German model of high quality apprenticeships within a 'social partners' ideational framework – they were manipulated into overseeing a policy that effected a very different 'flexibilist' model.

Regarding the 'we are all neoliberals now' thesis, Geoff Garrett (1998) has argued that globalization, far from mandating one-size-fits-all neoliberalism, leaves the social democratic alternative as viable as ever. This chapter cannot test this thesis because Tony Blair's 'New Labour' never contemplated a 'Rhenish' alternative, let alone a social democratic one. What the chapter does demonstrate is that policy change did not consist of a centre-left government being forced to abandon partisan preferences to toe an exogenously determined line. There is a striking paradigmatic continuity in the youth labour market policies pursued by the Thatcher governments (1979-90) and the Blair government (1997-2001). Primacy is accorded to market forces and policy intervention is predicated on the idea of promoting flexibility and adaptation to promote national competitiveness. Cerny's notion of the 'competition state' certainly applies. There is a strong rhetorical continuity in the British case that distinguishes it from the 'Rhenish' or European model, and policy borrowing from the US was a prominent feature of policy in both the late 1980s and late 1990s. The Labour government elected in 1997, starting from '*New Deal for a Lost Generation*', a policy document issued in opposition in 1996, was able to craft a policy once in power that maintained the 'deep core' normative belief about the necessity of youth to adapt to the labour market (and not vice versa) whilst forging a coalition out of 'New Labour' modernizers and the training policy network of 'Training and Enterprise Councils' (TECs) that had been bequeathed them by the Thatcher and Major governments. The heresthetics[3] of policy change, manipulation of the framing of issues by political leaders in order to deconstruct alternative coalitions and construct a new winning coalition, is particularly important in the Blair case.

The rhetorical continuity and the broad neoliberal policy paradigm the Thatcher and Blair governments shared tend to overshadow a much over-looked feature of policymaking at the sub-system level: that there are *competing varieties of neoliberalism.* This chapter challenges the idea that there was a single, predetermined neoliberal path in the British case.[4] Sub-system contestation yields both remarkable *programmatic innovation* and counter-intuitive policy. The Thatcher government's Youth Training Scheme in the 1981-89 period and the Blair government's New Deal in 1997-2001 were flagship initiatives, derived from distinct partisan preferences. They were accomplished through the framing of the issue of youth unemployment to create a winning coalition within the policy subsystem. Whilst international forces may constrain policy choices, and may hasten the pace of policy change, they provide an incomplete causal explanation for the substance and direction of policy outcomes in these cases. The argument is that not only did the Thatcher and Blair policies differ from one another; each case involved a government opting for a particular neoliberal alternative at the expense of others.

The rest of the chapter is organized into four parts. First, we introduce the 'Advocacy Coalition Framework' that will be used to elucidate policy change at the sub-system level. Second, we present an analysis of the development of the Youth Training Scheme 1981-89 including an analysis of the evolution of YTS towards a work-welfare program in the 1985-9 period. Third, we present an analysis of the development of the 'New Deal' 1995-2000. In the concluding section of the chapter, we review the utility of our approach in explaining continuity and change in British labour market policy 1979-2000.

Policy Innovation and Advocacy Coalitions

The Advocacy Coalition Framework (Sabatier and Pelkey; 1987, p.237; Sabatier and Jenkins Smith, 1993) provides an analytic framework for examining policy innovation. It allows us to explain differences between Thatcher and Blair but also specify in each case how the particular change came about. The framework views policy subsystems as central in bringing about policy change (Sabatier, 1993, pp.16-17). A policy subsystem encompasses a large and diverse set of actors that attempt to translate their beliefs pertaining to a particular political issue or set of issues into governmental policies and programs (Ibid.). Given the number of actors involved in an issue like labour market policy, one must develop some way of aggregating groups of actors into smaller and theoretically useful categories (Ibid., p.25). 'Advocacy coalitions are composed of elite actors from a variety of institutions – interest groups, agency officials, legislators, executive overseers, intellectuals – who share a general set of normative and causal beliefs concerning the policy area' (Sabatier and Pelkey; 1987). According to Sabatier, most subsystems contain only a few politically significant advocacy coalitions, usually ranging from 'two to four important coalitions – the number being limited by all the factors that push actors to coalesce if they are to form effective coalitions' (Ibid., p.26).

The 'Advocacy Coalition Framework' (ACF) sees the policy process and policy change as involving competing coalitions of policy actors[5] within sub-systems mediated by policy brokers.[6] Coalitions form around different 'policy core' ideas: paradigms.[7] This approach highlights paradigm politics as core paradigmatic values provide the glue for competing coalitions. Theoretically, therefore, the ACF plays a crucial role in linking policy paradigms and policy networks. Learning (from feedback) is particularly important for secondary aspects of policy, areas beyond paradigm cores over which 'puzzling' (Hall, 1986, p.18) contestation can take place. The ACF also provides a clear definition of 'policy paradigm': the 'deep core' revolves around a central value. Secondary aspects of a policy paradigm may give rise to significant differences between actors who share the same core: differences over the seriousness of problems, preferences regarding regulations or budgets or the design of specific institutions.

The Youth Training Scheme: Initiative and Implementation 1981-89

> We all know that there is no prospect of getting unemployment down to acceptable levels within the next few years (consequently) we must show that we have some political imagination, that we are willing to salvage something – albeit second best – from the sheer waste involved (Prime Minister's Central Policy Review Staff Report, February 1981).

Despite coming to power in 1979 disliking what little there was of Active Labour Market Policy (ALMP)[8] in Britain, the 1979-90 Thatcher governments developed a set of ALMP programs[9] that involved a quintupling of expenditures. By the late 1980s, over one million people a year were occupied on Manpower

Services Commission (MSC) schemes. This spending came close to rivalling that on 'passive' unemployment and welfare programs, and was high in comparative perspective. ALMP during 1979-90 was the most spectacular, and counter-intuitive, aspect of Thatcherite labour market policy.

ALMP underwent a 'qualitative' paradigm shift under the Thatcher governments. The pre-1979 ALMP paradigm, which had been corporatist but essentially non-interventionist, was shattered between 1979-81 whilst being contested by a new set of 'flexibilist' neoliberal ideas promoted by the Thatcher government and its supporters. ALMP 1979-90 involved a prolonged struggle between the MSC's 'developmentalist' or 'Rhenish' alternative and that of the Thatcherites. The MSC's house philosophy was based on an analysis that saw Britain's relative economic decline as being rooted in a flawed social ethic, a cultural constraint on economic modernization, and a constraint that had to be challenged. The key actors involved in the development of MSC ideas and programs shared these views.[10] The MSC saw its task as involving the transformation of entrenched social values that separated education from training and detached education from questions of economic development. This 'new vocationalism' regarding education was to be accompanied by an effort to change the national psyche regarding wealth creation (what would become, in Thatcherite rhetoric 'the enterprise culture', now embraced by New Labour) (Brown, 2001).

Mass unemployment allowed the MSC to build a fire-fighting empire on the basis of its ability to 'get things done', but it had to tailor its paradigm to suit the ideological predilections of the government. In doing so, different aspects of its paradigm had different sorts of attractions. Whereas the Thatcher government's rhetoric increasingly came to emphasize 'the enterprise culture', with a stress on maximum feasible competitive flexibility ('pricing people into jobs'), the MSC's house philosophy was rooted in a desire to end the distinction between mental and manual labour, increasing qualitative flexibility. The two versions of the paradigm are set out in the simultaneously produced 'New Training Initiative' documents by the government and the MSC (1981ab). They shared the same paradigm, and were induced by the common realization of the political and institutional opportunities available, but their versions of the paradigm were distinct: parallel, they would never meet. The critical distinction between the two variants of the new paradigm concerned the question of 'compulsion': should people be forced into training programs, on pain of loss of benefits, or should training be entirely voluntary? This distinction came to have considerable resonance in all cases of ALMP in the 1980s.

The Youth Training Scheme initiative of 1981 involved the introduction of a comprehensive post-educational training system and a paradigm-breaking shift to a paradigm focused on labour flexibility. With other political priorities driving macroeconomic policy, ALMP bore the brunt of labour market problems in the 1980s. In order of their immediacy these problems were: (i) the administrative and financial strains consequent on mass unemployment; (ii) the collapse of the apprenticeship system in the 1980-82 recession; (iii) the 'Low Skill Equilibrium' (Finegold and Soskice 1987, p.4) afflicting Britain vis-à-vis competitors. The

1975-76 and 1979-82 surges in unemployment hit youth especially hard. Youth unemployment was thus a more acute crisis, especially because of its social and political consequences (punk in 1976, urban rioting in 1981).

The Youth Training Scheme was proposed in a May 1981 MSC consultative document, (1981a) accepted by the government in 1982, and became fully operational in 1983. It involved the government committing £1 billion per year for 460,000 12-month trainee places. Trainee allowances were set at £25 per week and this, together with all training costs was to be paid by the Exchequer. Participation in the scheme was voluntary (unemployed youth were not obliged to join). The proposal stated 'we must move towards a position where all young people under the age of 18 have the opportunity either of continuing in full time education or of entering training or a period of planned work experience combining work-related training and education' (Ibid., para 23). The document's key assumptions were that policy change should be dictated by the needs of the economy (rather than the educational needs of the individual) (Ibid., para 27); that the need was for a more versatile, multi-skilled workforce (Ibid., para 26); and that though the provision might 'reduce the vulnerability of individuals to unemployment', the reforms were designed to improve training and only indirectly to reduce unemployment (Ibid., para 30). Given the government's earlier laissez faire views about training this was a remarkable policy departure. However, there was no certainty that the government would act on the MSC recommendations.

Two events changed circumstances drastically. The nationwide riots of July 1981 (*Financial Times*, 13 July 1981) brought the issue of youth unemployment to a head, whilst Mrs. Thatcher's September 1981 purge of the cabinet 'wets' saw arch Thatcherite Norman Tebbit replace the 'corporatist' James Prior as Minister for Employment. Many individual unions opposed the Trades Union Congress (TUC)'s strongly supportive line, and many voluntary organizations were similarly concerned. However, even among opponents, the consensus was that it was better to work within it for improvements.[11] Above all, the MSC derived enormous power through what might be termed the 'oasis effect': anyone interested in spending programs knew that it alone was in a position to get the funding.[12]

Despite the government's distaste for the TUC and its contemporaneous efforts to 'disestablish' the unions in other policy subsystems, the government had no alternative to working with the TUC on the Commission itself and allowing the unions at the level of the Area Manpower Boards an effective veto over the use made of MSC schemes locally. TUC cooperation was seen as especially vital in developing YTS, as the government feared that if the TUC opposed it so would large numbers of private employers who had much less to gain from the scheme than they had to lose in needless conflict with the unions (Young, 1990, p.138).[13] The small business lobby had no influence in forming YTS. Not only was the TUC able to ignore opposition from some left wing unions and union factions,[14] it was also perfectly willing to side with the Confederation of British Industry (CBI) and 'double-team' the voluntary sector, whose co-operation in delivering many YTS places was important, (Young, p.78) in internal MSC politics.

In addition to assembling a broad 'advocacy coalition', the MSC was remarkably effective in the rapid formulation and implementation of policy. Among policy makers, it swiftly acquired the reputation of having the 'ability to get things done'.[15] David Young, first as MSC chair then later as DE Secretary of State, was forever tagged with a quote from Mrs. Thatcher that 'other people come to me with their problems, David comes with solutions' (*Financial Times*, 5 April 1986). In 1986-88, the MSC empire's spectacular growth reached its zenith in this period, but its 'Rhenish' version of the paradigm was emasculated as ALMP itself became more closely linked with the benefits system.

> We will now guarantee a place on the YTS to every school leaver under 18 who is not going directly into a job.... We will take steps to ensure that those under 18 who deliberately choose to remain unemployed are not eligible for benefit.... We will improve the Community Programme [the main program focused on the long term unemployed] to make it full time and better able to help those with families. We shall pay those working on the programme an allowance giving a premium over and above their social security payments' (1987 Conservative Party Manifesto).[16]

After re-election on this manifesto in 1987, the government announced its plans for a new 'Employment Training' (ET) program, the central element of an incipient workfare system.[17] Together with a 'guarantee' of an ET place being made to all those aged 18-24 (and it was hoped that this would be extended to all the unemployed after a while), introduction of compulsion and the tightening of eligibility rules, made refusal of an ET place likely to result in benefit loss. There was a training component in the new scheme and great stress was put on motivational 'personal action plans'. But this was not the MSC's 'Rhenish' House Philosophy. Much of the most important meat put on the skeletal ET originated outside the MSC: the Restart initiative had been the brainchild of David Young in his time as Employment Secretary (Young, p.165); and the main 'ideas merchant' influential in the development and ancillary reforms was not Geoffrey Holland but Kay Stratton, an American advisor brought into the DE by new Employment Secretary Fowler. A former Massachusetts Secretary of Economic Affairs for Employment and Training, Stratton was parachuted into the DE to promote school compacts, local training councils and a workfare system (Fowler, pp.298-299).

Despite the TUC's desperate effort to cling on to the last vestige of corporatist policymaking, a revolt by member unions forced the TUC to withdraw support for ET in September 1987. As threatened, the Government moved immediately to abolish the MSC and all tripartite mechanisms in ALMP.[18] It was only after the TUC's forced withdrawal from ET and the abolition of the MSC that the pattern regarding business involvement in ET (and thus in post-MSC ALMP) became clear. The fireworks over the TUC's role had obscured the fact that the CBI had become marginalized.[19] Since then the government had been fishing for ideas on alternative ways of involving employers in youth and adult training, initially considering an expanded role for chambers of commerce (*Financial Times*,

20 May 1985). The MSC prepared plans for a network of employers groups (which were to become the Training and Enterprise Councils) in the summer of 1986.[20]

Through the ET initiative the government attempted to reform the societal actors with which it had to deal in the ALMP policy network. This involved abandoning the last vestiges of macro-corporatism and attempting to foster a more localized micro-level clientelism: the new TECs received the bulk of ALMP revenues from government; their chairpersons communicated directly with the Employment Secretary; and their membership was skewed towards smaller, service sector, and politically 'Thatcherite' employers (*Financial Times*, Report by Apex Trust, 2 May 1991). This new, neoliberal advocacy coalition marginalized the MSC-based coalition that had predominated since 1981. The Labour Party and the unions continued to articulate the 'Rhenish' alternative in impotent opposition. However, by the time the Labour party looked like returning to power it had explicitly abandoned this alternative and adapted a new, neoliberal policy.

New Labour, New Liberalism, New Deal[21]

> New Labour is a party of ideas and ideals but not of outdated ideology...we have liberated these values from outdated dogma or doctrine, and we have applied these values to the modern world. I want a country in which people get on, do well, make a success of their lives....We will give under-25's opportunities for work, education and training. Four options will be on offer. Rights and responsibilities must go hand in hand, without a fifth option of life on full benefit (Labour Party Manifesto, 1997, *Britain will be better with New Labour*).

Tony Blair's emergence as Labour leader in 1994 precipitated an ideological refoundation of the party. Although 'third way' rhetoric usually stressed that New Labour was transcending traditional social democracy, a paradigmatic shift affecting all aspects of economic and social policy was undertaken that abandoned core social democratic goals. The 1997 manifesto guaranteed a conservative macroeconomic stance (which turned out to include central bank independence), a commitment not to raise income tax, and a promise to serve the interests of business interests. Labour market policy involved retaining the main institutional architecture created by the Thatcher governments and the commitment to get a quarter of a million young people off benefit and into work. This stance reflected both the policy review launched in 1987 after three crushing electoral defeats, and the 1994-7 founding of 'New Labour', heavily influenced by the example of the Clinton administration in the US.

Although Labour adhered to the 'Rhenish' model in the 1976-87 period, after the 1987 defeat the Party embarked on a two-year policy review during which it began to accept two important modifications to its traditional welfare collectivist position. First, there was the formal acknowledgement that the role of the state should be limited.[22] In economic terms, Labour had seemingly abandoned its belief that the state should attempt to manipulate economic outcomes. The only form of intervention now considered feasible was 'market management' through medium-term supply-side policies, the aim being to promote long-term economic stability above all else. Second, this recognition of the 'efficiency and realism that markets can provide' found an echo in the acceptance of individual liberty and responsibility as opposed to social equality as the primary goal of social policy. The 1992 Labour party manifesto, *Meet the Challenge, Make the Change*, made it clear that citizens that citizens 'had to take responsibility for their own lives and fulfill their obligations to others'.

If Labour under Neil Kinnock's leadership had begun the process of moving towards a post-welfare ideology on broadly Schumpeterian lines (Ellison, 1997, pp.34-56), further changes were in store. The Commission on Social Justice (CSJ) appointed in the wake of the 1992 election defeat, together with both changes in ideology and Party structure which followed Tony Blair's election as leader in 1994, were the two most significant stages on the way to what may be called the Party's present 'Social Schumpeterian' stance (Ibid.). In its final report, the Commission on Social Justice (CSJ) advocated a series of policy options that where intended to provide the basis for a conception of citizenship grounded in responsibilities as well as rights. Employment flexibility was established as a core policy value. The CSJ sought to create a new welfare ethic that was based on providing certain individual rights and responsibilities, particularly to work where work is available. However, even the CSJ's renovated social democracy was jettisoned as soon as Blair became Labour party leader.

Blairism is rooted in the notion of individual rights being inextricably linked to individual responsibility. New Labour 'modernizers' believed that labour market policy would be designed in accordance with these core beliefs. The Blair government sought to establish tight eligibility criteria with time limits on traditional welfare benefit in an effort to dramatically reduce 'welfare dependency'. This core policy belief was supported by think tanks[23] such as the Demos Institute founded in 1993, and allied scholars such as Anthony Giddens. The influence of Demos and its neoliberal ideas is evidenced by the appointment of Geoff Mulgan (co-founder of the Demos) to head Number 10's Social Exclusion Unit in 1997 (Ibid.).

The US model looms large at this point for Tony Blair, Gordon Brown and the New Labour modernizers. Shared neoliberal ideas regarding the need to reform labour markets in order to make them more internationally competitive was rooted in the common struggles experienced by both the Labour and Democratic Parties in the era of globalization. Whereas in 1990 political strategists and electoral commentators were asking what the Democratic Party could learn from its British counterpart (King and Wickham-Jones, 1999, p.64) by 1993 the US was the model (Ibid.). The election of Bill Clinton in 1992 was the crucial breakthrough for Democratic Leadership Council (DLC) 'New Democrats'. Clinton championed the cause of economic growth through entrepreneurial initiative over government-led redistribution and strongly advocated substituting a policy of 'workfare' in place of traditional welfare dependency (Ibid.). New Labour had strong intellectual ties with key figures in the Clinton Administration. Ed Balls, the special adviser to Gordon Brown who was most intimately involved in creating New Deal, studied under Larry Summers (Secretary of the Treasury) and Lawrence Katz, (who served under Robert Reich in the Department of Labour), whilst at Harvard. They co-authored a paper that analyzed British unemployment by region and skill and concluded that long term unemployment was largely the result of 'skill mismatches and a loss of the culture of work...'(Ibid.). Ed Balls points out that both the Clinton and Blair governments' welfare reform strategies have been forged in accordance with this basic logic.[24] Gordon Brown frequently met senior officials in the Clinton administration (such as then US Deputy Treasury Secretary Larry Summers and Hilary Clinton) to discuss fundamental aspects of economic policy strategy, often placing the issue of welfare and employment at the top of the list ('New Labour's Gurus: The American Connection', 1997, p.63).

The New Deal initiative was part of a broader strategy aimed at fostering a partnership between individuals and government through a labour market paradigm based on the principle of helping individuals move from welfare-to-work.[25] As shadow Chancellor, Gordon Brown sought to aggressively promote this agenda by raising more money for youth training by placing austere limits on welfare benefits for the long-term unemployed.[26] Brown set out the main elements of New Deal in a 1995 speech. The policy document, entitled 'New Deal for a Lost Generation', was presented on May 16, 1996.[27] A one-off Windfall Tax that would fall on privatized utilities would pay for the scheme ('Labour's Training Policy', 1996, pp.58-59).

Corporatist labour market institutions central to the 'Rhenish' model and to the MSC in the 1980's were seen by the Blair government as too rigid and interventionist to deal with dynamically changing labour market conditions. Most importantly, their corporatist genealogy was embedded in the traditional welfare state apparatus that had become too expensive and, therefore, unsupportable given new fiscal imperatives (Driver and Martell, n.d., p.63). The Blair government believed that bringing about monetary and fiscal stability would draw increased investment that would in turn produce higher growth and productivity.[28] For Blair and his followers, this meant keeping levels of taxation and spending to relatively low levels in order to control inflation (Driver and Martell, pp.41-42).

In 1997, having served less than six months in office, Brown and Blair sought £3.1 billion to address youth unemployment ('New Deal Special Report', 1998, pp.52-58). In 1998 Employment Minister Andrew Smith issued a classically Blairite speech that formally launched New Deal into action (Ibid.). It entailed a complex set of arrangements that involve inter-agency involvement for the program's implementation. Ministers directly involved with New Deal were determined that scheme should not be run exclusively by the Education Service, in an effort to curb its direct power over the distribution of benefits ('Jobs for the Boys and Girls', 1998, pp.22-23). The result is a complex pattern of arrangements in each of the 136 Education Service districts. It is important to emphasize that each district possesses its own unique institutional arrangements that involve various public-private, cooperatives, which is viewed a critical for ensuring the flexibility required to respond to regional needs.[29]

New Deal was meant to be fundamentally different because it is based on local partnerships between employers, local authorities, training providers, Training and Enterprise Councils (TECs), Local Enterprise Companies, Jobcentres, environment groups, voluntary organizations and others. The Training and Enterprise Councils inherited by the Blair government were utilized during the first two years of New Deal, but were then abolished as the government found the flexible mixture of different local agencies preferable to the employer-dominated TECs. Thus these relics of 1980s Thatcherism went the way of the relics of 1970's corporatism before them. Initially they assisted in winning the support of employers who might otherwise have refused cooperation that was deemed necessary for the success of the initiative. Once the advocacy coalition had facilitated the initiative these institutions were superfluous to New Labour.

Conclusion

Using Thatcher's YTS and Blair's New Deal youth strategy as units of study, this chapter demonstrates that the paradigm shift in labour market policy was based upon a qualitative shift from a core belief that governments can and (in cases of structural unemployment) should intervene in the labour market, to a core belief that market mechanisms should determine the structure of labour markets. The broad underlying ideas each government embraced were remarkably similar, though framed for different audiences. Each initiative relied upon governments that were able to build broad support among potential ideational allies in the policy subsystem for their agenda.

We explain both radical policy innovation and the continuities of labour market policy in Britain by borrowing key insights from the Advocacy Coalition Framework (ACF). In the case of YTS from 1981 to 1985 the labour market policy subsystem was comprised of four important groups including: *i)* traditional corporatists in the MSC, *ii)* new MSC interventionists, *iii)* Thatcherite interventionists, and *iv)* ultra marketeers. YTS was jointly supported by new MSC interventionists along with Thatcherite interventionists. The two groups shared a common policy belief in the need for an interventionist strategy of job training that would encourage the move to more flexible markets. The emergence of work-welfare in the 1985-89 period involved the triumph of policy ideas imported from the US and the demise of the 'Rhenish' approach favoured by MSC interventionists. The Fowler/Stratton line displaced the Holland/Young/Nicholson approach. This shift also involved the dismantling of the MSC itself. With its abolition the newly dominant Thatcherite paradigm, and its supportive coalition now institutionally lodged in the new Training Enterprise Councils, was ascendant. The period of the Major government 1990-97 witnessed the dominance of

Thatcherite interventionists now ensconced in the TEC network: employer-dominated but dependent on central government for resources and direction (a meso-level version of the 'free economy and the strong state').

Tony Blair's ideological refoundation of the Labour party in concrete policy terms involved the marginalization of the 'Rhenish'/corporatist synthesis. In terms of rhetoric the importance of education and training for social and economic progress was maintained: 'equal opportunity in the enterprise culture'. However, the ideas emanating from the new Blairite think tanks such as Demos, increasingly influenced by the experience of the Clinton administration with 'welfare reform', involved an acceptance of the neoliberal premises already guiding active labour market policy – stressing the responsibility of the unemployed to render themselves employable, the primacy of private sector employment, and the proactive role of government in using the benefit system to 'move people into work'. Union and other 'stakeholders' were marginal in this development. The 'New Deal' initiative brewed primarily by Gordon Brown in 1995-6, could therefore look to the TEC network for its implementation. The Blairite modernizers were distinct from the TEC 'flexibilizers' in stressing individual responsibility over the needs of business. This stance demanded a much finer tailoring of policy to meet local requirements and the needs of different categories of the unemployed.

This chapter has explored both the neoliberal policy paradigm that underlay policy initiatives and the coalitions governments had to forge in order to implement them at the subsystem level. It is found that in both cases there were alternative neoliberal policy options. There are different varieties of neoliberalism. The triumph of an interventionist neoliberalism in 1981 (at the expense of both the 'Rhenish' and laissez faire alternatives) and a welfare-to-work neoliberalism in 1997-8 (at the expense of the employer-dominated status quo and any sort of revived corporatism) resulted from the construction of advocacy coalitions that neutralized opposition without compromising core neoliberal beliefs.

Notes

1 For a popular version of this, see Ohmae, 1993. Among political scientists those working on capital mobility often make the strongest claims, see Andrews and Willett, 1997, pp. 479-511 and Kurzer, 1993.

2 Identifying the extent and determinants of policy continuities in Britain has been a major preoccupation of much of the literature on both the Thatcher and Blair administrations. Four sets of factors have been identified as influencing these initiatives and continuities/discontinuities with the past: ideological shifts, Pierson, 1994; incremental development, Riddell, 1992; long-standing policy legacies, King, 1995; and problem-driven circumstances (temporal sorting models). In the comparative literature the work of Esping-Andersen, 1990, has influenced a generation of comparativists, for example those in Hall and Soskice 2002.

3 Heresthetics is the art and science of political manipulation. Heresthetics involves the strategic manipulation of issues to bolster one policy coalition and fracture rival coalitions, see Riker, 1986.

4 An interesting counter example is the neoliberal celtic tiger. Since 1987 the Irish Training and Employment agency FÁS has pursued policy radically at odds with both Thatcher and Blair's Britain: a 'competition state'; a 'globalized' economic strategy; but a deeply entrenched model of 'social partnership', see Boyle, 2002.

5 Actors' organizational affiliation is not primordial; members of different coalitions come from different organizations.

6 Coalitions may attempt to map their goals into policy by, among other means, 'venue shopping'.

7 These are distinct from system-level 'deep core' beliefs, more broadly applicable and less directly relevant to the policy domain.

8 'Active' labour market policies (ALMP) involve government action to shape the demand for labour by creating jobs and/or increase the supply and quality of labour through training programs.

9 41 between 1979 and 1990.

10 Geoffrey Holland was an early planner of the Training Services Agency and he subsequently became director of the MSC and, after its abolition, permanent secretary at the Department of Employment. In an interview with Peter Hennessy (1988), *Independent*, 2 February, he aligned himself directly with the cultural constraint thesis.

11 Youthaid made recommendations along these lines, see THES, 15 April 1983.

12 Bryan Nicholson (MSC Chairman 1984-6) stressed this point, comparing the MSC to the University Grants Commission in the 1960s after the Robbins Report, interview 18 November 1987.

13 Lord Young stresses this view on the pusillanimity of employers and the resultant fear for the implementability of YTS.

14 This proved to be an enduring capacity: even when the government began violating tripartite norms in the later 1980s the TUC had little difficulty in by-passing union dissent.

15 A phrase used by one of the TUC Commissioners in evidence to the a House of Commons Employment Committee, 1981-2 (HC 221, *The Work of the Department of Employment Group*, HC 348-i. (HMSO).

16 Conservative Party Manifesto (1987), 'The Next Moves Forward'.

17 Another element was the 'Restart' scheme. Its perceived success (stressed by both Young, p. 174 and Fowler, p. 187) did much to set the terms of the debate over the extent of work-shyness on the part of the unemployed.

18 The government announced this on 15 September 1988, *Financial Times*, September 16 1988, and carried this through, despite last minute pleas by the TUC, in its December 1988 White Paper, *Employment for the 1990s*, Cmnd 540, HMSO.

19 The CBI had not shown much interest in the long term unemployed. The government's marginalization of the CBI coincided with the CBI developing a much more sustained interest in training issues beyond the issue of subsidies for costs, see *Towards a Skills Revolution*, 1990.

20 MSC chairman Bryan Nicholson being instrumental here; see *Financial Times*, 31 July 1986, and 11 August 1986.

21 According to a textual analysis of 53 of Tony Blair's speeches 'New Deal' (70 instances) was second only to 'New Labour' (72 instances) as the most frequently used phrase, see Fairclough, 2000; and *The Guardian*, 3 March 2000.

22 Neil Kinnock commenting in the Review's main published document that 'there is a limit to what the modern state can do'.

23 Interview with Richard Warner, General Manager, *Demos Institute*, 18 July 1999.

24 Interview with Ed Balls, Special Adviser to the Chancellor of the Exchequer, HM Treasury, 18 November 1998.

25 Interview with Mr. Bill Wells, DFEE, 26 July 1999.

26 Interview with Luke Bruce, The Labour Party Policy Unit, Milbank Tower, 21 July 1999.

27 Interview with Andrew Maugham, Special Adviser to the Secretary of State for Social Security, 27 July 1999.

28 Interview with Andrew Kilpatrick, Head of Macroeconomic and Fiscal Policy, HM Treasury, 16 November 1998.

29 Interview with Mr. Bill Wells, DFEE, 26 July 1999.

References

Andrews, David and Willett, Thomas (1997), 'Financial Interdependence and the State: International Monetary Relations at Century's End,' *International Organization*, Vol. 51, pp. 479-511.

Boyle, Nigel (2002), 'Employment Programs in Ireland 1987-1999: National, Sub-national and Supra-national Governance in a Globalized Political Economy', presented at the International Studies Association Conference, New Orleans, 23 March.

Brown, Gordon (2001), *Wall Street Journal*, 14 June.

Cerny, Philip G. (2000), 'Restructuring the Political Arena: Globalization and the Paradoxes of the Competition State', in Randall D. Germain (ed), *Globalization and its Critics: Perspectives from Political Economy*, Macmillan - now Palgrave, Basingstoke.

Conservative Party Manifesto (1987), 'The Next Moves Forward'.

Driver S. and Martell, L. (n.d.), *New Labour: Politics After Thatcherism*, Polity Press, Cambridge, p. 63.

Ellison, N. (1997), 'From Welfare State to Post-Welfare Society: Labour's Social Policy in Historical and Contemporary Perspective', in B. Brivati and T. Bale (eds), *New Labour In Power: Precedents and Prospects*, Routledge, London, pp. 34-56.

Esping-Andersen, Gosta (1990), *The Three Worlds of Welfare Capitalism*, Princeton University Press, Princeton.

Finegold D. and Soskice, D. (1987), 'The Failure of Training in Britain: Analysis and Prescription', *Oxford Review of Economic Policy*, Vol. III, p.4.

Fairclough, Norman (2000), *New Labour, New Language*, Routledge, London.

Falk, Richard (1996), 'An Inquiry into the Political Economy of World Order', *New Political Economy*, Vol. 1, No. 1, p. 15.

Fowler, Norman (1991), Ministers Decide: A Personal Memoir of the Thatcher Years, Chapmans, London.Garrett, Geoffrey (1998), *Partisan Politics in the Global Economy*, Cambridge University Press, Cambridge.

Hall, P. A. (1986), *Governing the Economy*, Polity Press, Cambridge.

Hall, Peter and Soskice, David (eds) (2002), *Varieties of Capitalism: The Institutional Foundations of Comparative Advantage*, Oxford University Press, Oxford.

Hallerberg, Mark and Clark, William Roberts (1997), 'How Should Political Scientists Measure Capital Mobility? A Review,' paper prepared for presentation at the 1997 Annual Meeting of the American Political Science Association, Washington, D.C., 28-31 August.

'Jobs for the Boys and Girls', *New Statesman*, 13 February 1998, pp. 22-23.

King, D. (1995), *Actively Seeking Work*, Oxford University Press, Oxford.

King D. and Wickham-Jones, M. (1999), 'From Clinton to Blair: The Democratic Party Origins of Welfare to Work', *Political Quarterly*, Vol. 70.

Kurzer, Paulette (1993), *Business and Banking*, Cornell, Ithaca.

'Labour's Training Policy' (1996), *The Economist*, 18 May, pp. 58-59.

MSC (Manpower Services Commission) (1981a), *A New Training Initiative: A Consultative Document*, MSC, Sheffield, May.

MSC (Manpower Services Commission) (1981b), *A New Training Initiative: A Consultative Document*, MSC, London, May.

'New Deal Special Report' (1998), *New Statesman*, 3 April, pp.52-58.

'New Labour's Gurus: The American Connection' (1997), *The Economist*, 8 November, p.63.

Ohmae, Kenichi (1993), *The End of the Nation State: the Rise of Regional Economies*, Free Press, New York.

Pierson, P. (1994), *Dismantling the Welfare State*, Cambridge University Press, New York.

Riddell P. (1992), *The Thatcher Era and its Legacy*, Blackwell, Oxford.

Riker, W. (1986), *The Art of Political Manipulation*, Yale University Press, New York.

Sabatier, P. A. (1993), 'Policy Change Over a Decade or More,' in P.A. Sabatier and H. C. Jenkins Smith, *Policy Change and Learning: An Advocacy Coalition Approach*, Westview Press, Boulder.

Sabatier, P. and Pelkey, N. (1987), 'Incorporating Multiple Actors and Guidance Instruments into Models of Regulatory Policymaking: An Advocacy Coalition Framework', *Administration and Society*, Vol. XIX.

Towards a Skills Revolution (1990), CBI, London, July.

Young, Lord (1990), *The Enterprise Years: A Businessman in the Cabinet*, Headline, London.

Part II

Strategies for Dealing with Global Turbulence

Chapter 7

Contesting Neoliberalism: The Political Economy of Transnational Protest[1]

Jeffrey M. Ayres

Contesting Neoliberalism: The Political Economy of Transnational Protest

For over a century popular sector groups exercised power by drawing upon a repertoire of protest tactics rooted in the nation-state. Lately, however, popular contention has undergone noticeable transnational innovations, responding especially to the implementation of neoliberal policy initiatives over the past decade. Yet, while neoliberalism and its concomitant discontents have become a percolating reality for many years, not until the 'battle of Seattle' at the 1999 World Trade Organization (WTO) meetings did studies of the growing trend of protest became an especially fashionable issue for analysis. In fact, since the WTO meetings, an explosion of commentaries have emerged, including more popularly accessible renditions by engaged activists, complemented increasingly by more systematic attempts to assess the aftermath of Seattle.[2] Those working in the political economy tradition should also contribute to this debate, and can do so by profitably borrowing from recent advances in social movement research. For, the challenges posed by neoliberal globalization, and the stakes involved in the current trend of transnational resistance, are intimately tied to the structure and processes of exercising power and distributing wealth in this interdependent global economy. Only now, events demand that in addition to focusing on such traditional political economy concerns as the relationships between labour and capital, and between the state and the market, those new non-state actors, social movements and international institutions prominently involved in this contemporary power struggle deserve attention as well.

The Repertoire of Contentious Politics

Contentious politics can be defined as 'collective activity on the part of claimants or those who claim to represent them relying at least in part on non-institutionalized forms of interaction with elites, opponents or the state' (Tarrow, 1996, p.874). The specific set of tactics available to actors making such oppositional claims at a particular historical moment can be referred to as the repertoire of collective action (Tilly, 1977, pp.479-504; Tilly and Tilly, 1981).[3] The repertoire concept can help provide a framework for understanding how neoliberal policies have encouraged an array of new transnational tactical claims-making, in new forms and recurring with new variations.[4] It can also suggest that this period of transnational restructuring, exacerbated by the contradictions of neoliberalism, represents a pivotal moment, where the changed international and domestic political-economic environments have encouraged a tactical adaptation on the part of social actors collaborating in new ways in the pursuit of a shared interest: to contest the multiple and negative repercussions of the neoliberal model on aspects of the social, political, environmental and economic life in this new century.

The repertoire of contention over the stretch of history has included a dizzying array of possible tactics: from eighteenth century barricades, bread riots and inter-village brawls, to nineteenth century labour marches and electoral rallies, to twentieth century factory occupations, sit-ins and email petitioning. Each evolution in the forms of popular struggle has been linked to changes in capitalism and the state. For example, the development of the modern, increasingly urban-centred state and the advancement and spread of industrial capitalism by the early nineteenth-century encouraged the rise of new nationally-oriented social movements and mass-based labour unions, which now principally targeted the state. The rise of large-scale associations, including national political parties, and developments in national print media, buttressed these new protest innovations (Tarrow, 1998).

Nationally-oriented protest tactics persisted well into the post-World War Two era, during which time social and political conditions became more favourable to labour and other popular sector groups (Cameron and Drache, 1985).[5] A dramatic increase in the government's role in the economy, and the development of an array of social programs, including a more progressive tax system and the expansion of the social welfare system, coincided with these tactics. In the post-war years, incomes rose and working conditions improved, middle classes expanded, and a balance was struck between civil society, government and capital. These advances in working and living conditions evolved in no small part due to the efficacy of popular sector strategies directed at the state. The threat of mass protest, labour action, strikes, electoral pressure and collective bargaining processes kept the contested social compact in check, illustrating the degree to which popular sector groups had gained a degree of social and political regulation over capital. Moreover, policy gains achieved through national-level strategies were hardly limited to improvements in working conditions: the American civil rights movement and the women's movement achieved significant policy gains through protest tactics that had changed little for decades while continuing to target the state.

Global Economic Instability and the Neoliberal Turn

This social compact would be dramatically undercut by the increasingly instability and unpredictability that beset the world economy in the early 1970s. The deteriorating global economic position of the U.S., the twin, OPEC-induced oil shocks and the increase in international competitiveness from newly developing countries would presage a dramatic disruption in the balance of power between popular sector groups and capital. Employers and capital responded to these instabilities with a tactical shift in the prescription of neoliberal policies. These included an aggressive push for freer markets, increased mobility for capital and multinational corporations, privatization of government-provided services and deregulation of hard-won environmental, social, consumer and workplace protections. Corporations, governments and well-funded right-wing think tanks would market such initiatives as the only alternative to the less predictable environment. Moreover, the implementation of neoliberal policies over the following two decades would encourage a massive global restructuring of power relations, featuring an increased reliance on transnational strategies for capital and corporations in reaction to immobile and nationally rooted popular sector groups.

The power of transnational capital has been dramatically enhanced over the past two decades, due to its increased fluidity and speed of movement. Capital now disciplines governments from the industrialized North to the lesser-developed South: it exerts enormous budgetary influence through the structural adjustment programs of the International Monetary Fund (IMF), while similarly straight jacketing industrialized governments through bond rating agencies and stock markets. Border-hopping capital has been complemented by regional and multilateral efforts at trade and investment liberalization. The mid-1980s witnessed a successful push for a bilateral Canada-U.S. free trade agreement (CUSFTA), which was accompanied by advances in trade liberalization through the General Agreement on Tariffs and Trade (GATT) through the Uruguay Round beginning in 1986. Building on the CUSFTA in 1989 would be the North American Free Trade Agreement (NAFTA) in 1994, and the pinnacle of neoliberal achievement, the World Trade Organization (WTO) in 1995.

The new transnational strategies for capital and corporations have been fortuitously aided by the collapse of the Soviet Union and Eastern European communist regimes, and by the embrace of market economics by authoritarian China and Vietnam. The barriers that had once separated capitalist markets from command economies, and which had geographically constrained capital, disappeared by the 1990s. These barriers had in part forced capital into the post-war social compact, encouraging the trade-off of rising incomes and better working conditions for labour peace. The threat that the state socialist models represented also helped convince capital and employers to tolerate the social welfare state. Yet, neoliberalism as both a policy and an ideology has now gained significant strategic advantages by the collapse of the alternative, albeit undemocratic models and by the openness of these new markets to the exit strategy increasingly practiced by multinational corporations.

The neoliberal turn has created profoundly difficult conditions for those popular sector groups, including labour, whose efforts to regulate and humanize capital within national borders have been dramatically undercut (Panitch, 1986; McBride and Shields, 1997; Higgott and Deretek, 1999, pp.483-498; Ross, 2000, pp.78-91).[6] Working people around the world have been hard hit, experiencing varying degrees of stagnant if not declining wages, an exacerbation of income inequality and increased insecurity over possible future job losses, through outsourcing, privatization or factory closure. The distributional effects of neoliberalism have been well-documented, as have the profound social conflicts and tensions arising out of the continued exacerbation of income inequality both within and between countries (Rodrik, 1997).[7] The distributional problem and its attendant conflicts are by no means limited to the industrialized North; the IMF's structural adjustment policies have reduced worker power, incomes and opportunities in the developing South, with the economic downturn of the late 1990s in East Asia hitting the lower classes especially hard (Mittelman, 2000; Scott, 2001; 'Seven Years Under NAFTA', 2001).[8]

Neoliberal policies have also increasingly influenced national budgetary planning and constrained state spending priorities. National social programs, interest rates and individual and corporate tax rates are frequently adjusted with an eye to creating an attractive political climate for foreign investment. This is particularly notable in light of the increased mobility of capital in search of immediate and higher returns on investment, which has reduced the effectiveness of national tax programs and increasingly shifted the tax burden from mobile capital to immobile workers. The loss of tax revenues has in turn had a trickle down effect: the pressure to downsize government and roll back the provision of social programs has affected local and regional governments, who are left to grapple with a host of social and environmental challenges on an ever dwindling budget.

These budgetary constraints have further hamstrung the abilities of governments to diffuse social tensions and conflicts exacerbated by economic restructuring. With budgets reduced and tax revenues depleted, the social programs that once served as critical buffers against widespread social unrest have become frayed. As a result, across Western Europe and North America, there has arisen increased insecurity and unrest amongst public sector workers faced with limited wage gains, benefit cutbacks and the privatization of government services.[9] The budgetary restraints implicit in the so-called 'Maastricht orthodoxy' that paved the way for the introduction of the European Union's common currency, the Euro, represented a case study in the tensions being fostered by the clash between governments bent on fiscal downsizing and workers struggling to maintain the limited protections earned in the post-war era.

It would be a mistake, however, to focus solely on workers and the decline of their bargaining power under neoliberalism. In fact, neoliberal policies have exacerbated existing forms of non-territorial marginalization, affecting a much broader constituency of groups destabilized by the assault on public sector resources and initiatives. Trade regimes such as NAFTA and the WTO have had a particularly destructive effect on women. Many women are disproportionately employed in those low-wage, semi-skilled positions frequently eliminated by the direct competition fostered from the introduction of lower wage countries into such trade agreements, or have witnessed critical government funding to their organizations reduced by budgetary cutbacks (Bashevkin, 2000, pp.109-127; Young, 2000, pp.315-327). Neoliberal initiatives have also upset environmental groups and disrupted the 'environmental compact' that had throughout the 1970s increasingly constrained capital with national environmental regulations. Environmentalists have been on the defensive on at least two fronts: regionally, against regimes such as NAFTA which invite the shifting of production to countries with lower environmental standards, or as witnesses to national parliaments increasing ineffectiveness against regulation-eroding decisions by the WTO.

In short, neoliberal initiatives over the past two decades have served as dramatic impediments to labour and popular sector power. Again, this is not to suggest that popular sector groups have failed to resist this strategy. Resistance to the antagonisms built into the neoliberal program, with its shift in income, power and wealth, has been widespread: from workers in the developing South protesting the social cutbacks implicit in the IMF's structural adjustment policies, to the Canadian and then more broadly North American groups that protested against the CUSFTA and NAFTA, to the French public sector workers demonstrating against the Maastricht Treaty, anecdotal evidence abounds of episodes of resistance to neoliberal policies.[10] Yet, it has become increasingly clear that this power shift has reduced the efficacy of national level strategies and protest tactics. The combination of mobile capital and multinational corporations that can quickly exercise the option to shift or outsource production overseas has undercut the threat of labour and other types of popular sector action, and limited the overall effectiveness of nationally-rooted forms of collective action.

Neoliberalism as a Locus of Transnational Dissent

In response to the debilitating effects of neoliberal capitalist restructuring, popular sector groups have been forced to make substantial innovations in their tactics. Notably, popular contention has lately taken on a transnational orientation, in forms of association, in tactics adopted, and in targets identified. Global economic restructuring has provoked changes in the size and character of groups mobilizing to counter capital's transnational shift in power and strategy. Recently, a variety of new and unorthodox alliances and coalitions have emerged, from transnational social movement organizations, cross-border coalitions, and cross-sector alliances between historically suspicious groups. This transnational innovation is related to the limits placed on national tactics by neoliberal conditioning, and popular sector groups have consciously rescripted their protest strategies to challenge the recent erosions in their power.

Transnational Associational Innovations

Organized labour, despite compelling challenges, has begun to cooperate much more extensively across national borders in recent years (Mazur, 2000, pp.79-93; Hathaway, 2000; Gordon and Turner, 2001). In fact, a growing number of cases of union solidarity, cross-border alliances, and parallel strikes have injected a sense of efficacy into transnational mobilizing. Elements of this new approach can be found in the efforts of such international labour organizations as the International Confederation of Free Trade Unions, which has mobilized to push for the inclusion of social clauses in trade agreements, and has attempted to reestablish social regulations at the national, regional and international levels (O'Brien, 2000, pp.533-555). In addition to developing cross-border labour solidarity, unions have also increasingly cultivated alliances with other popular sector groups. There has been an opening for such cross-sectoral alliances because of the overreach of neoliberal capital: the reorganization of social power has antagonized a broad swath of increasingly mobilized constituencies who have turned to transnational coalition-building and organizations for leverage. Environmental groups, women, indigenous peoples and students along with labour have developed a number of transnational alliances and coalitions to educate, strategize and challenge a variety of neoliberal initiatives.[11]

This popular transnational reorientation in scale and association is a particularly prominent feature in the ongoing campaigns against neoliberal trade and investment accords. The seeds for mobilizing in unorthodox, cross-sectoral and ultimately cross-border coalitions were sown partly in the anti-CUSFTA and anti-NAFTA campaigns of the late 1980s and early 1990s. During these campaigns, activists across North America gained experience, shared strategies, and diffused new forms of cross-border activism. While national campaigns in Canada, the U.S. and Mexico proved important for public education and arousing public opposition to these accords, the transnational associational innovations that emerged out of these campaigns would set the stage for a post-NAFTA context of wide-ranging contention against a variety of neoliberal policies.

A particular hotbed of cross-border alliance building has been the Maquiladora border region between the U.S. and Mexico. During the past ten years, thousands of corporations have moved to this region to exploit low wage labour conditions and lax or non-existent environmental and social standards. The Coalition for Justice in the Maquiladoras (CJM) is one of the more notable and longest lasting transnational coalitions targeting the resulting environmental degradation and worker exploitation in this area. Not restricted to traditional labour actors, the CJM draws from a broad, trinational base of Mexican, U.S. and Canadian unions, churches, human rights organizations, women's and environmental groups, and international solidarity actors to pressure corporations to adopt socially and environmentally responsible practices in the Maquila area (Kamel and Hoffman, 1999).[12] The CJM has for over ten years now employed over three dozen coordinated cross-border campaigns targeting specific corporations, educating workers, holding press conferences to bring unscrupulous corporate practices to public light, and documenting the facts of cases to give popular sector actors leverage for demanding reforms and law abidance (Williams, 1999, pp.139-166). It has also drafted a 'Maquiladora Standards of Conduct', which it seeks to apply to all U.S. companies operating in the area, encouraging them to promote a socially and environmentally safe workplace, and an adequate standard of living for workers in this area.

There are many other examples of cross-border alliance building that defy the restricted parameters of national level protest. In 1992, for example, the U.S. based United Electrical Workers (UE) worked with the Frente Auténtico del Trabajo (FAT), an autonomous Mexican federation, to form a 'Strategic Organizing Alliance'. The Alliance similarly targeted multinational corporations for publicity campaigns, and in 1996, assisted in the opening of CETLAC Worker's Center in Ciudad Juárez, Mexico's second largest border city in the Maquila region, which provides workers with workplace related education and legal assistance (Cook, 1997). The Echlin, now Dana Worker's Alliance is another important example of transnational unionism. Formed out of a 1996 U.S. meeting of groups of North American labour activists, the trinational Alliance consists of unions in different industries in Canada, the U.S. and Mexico representing workers in the Dana corporation, an Ohio-based auto parts manufacturer.[13] In 1997, the Alliance filed a trinational complaint under the NAFTA labour side agreement to the U.S. National Administrative Office challenging the violation of workers rights in Mexico, the weakening of safety and the health of workers and the Mexican government's support of union busting by Dana (Rosen, 1999, pp.37-39). The Alliance backed its NAO complaint with cross-border actions, solidarity activities at North American Dana workplaces, and trinational media campaigns (Dreiling, 1999). In 1998, after trinational hearings, the NAO ruled in favour of the Dana Alliance, ordering cabinet level consultations between the U.S. and Mexico to address the unsavoury corporate and state practices.

The transnational mobilization against the FTAA has also encouraged organizational innovations. Transnational social movement organizations, such as the Toronto-based Common Frontiers, and the Hemispheric Social Alliance (HSA), whose secretariat has been based in Mexico with the Red Mexicana de Acción Frente al Libre Comercio (RMALC), have played a pivotal role in coordinating collective action and in developing alternatives to hemispheric neoliberalism and corporate irresponsibility across the Americas. Both Common Frontiers and the HSA include as working partners dozens of hemispheric civil society groups opposed to the FTAA. Common Frontiers emerged out of the struggle in Canada against the CUSFTA, to initially provide North American groups with a resource base for mobilizing against NAFTA, while representatives of dozens of civil society groups created the HSA while massing at the 1998 People's Summit of the Americans in Santiago, Chile, an alternative event running parallel to the second America's heads of state summit. The transnational structure of both of these groups has helped activists draw upon hemispheric-wide constituencies for developing and editing the *Alternatives for the Americas* document, a social-developmental alternative to the proposed FTAA,[14] as well as for planning the alternative People's Summit at the 2001 Quebec City America's heads of state summit.

Shifts Towards Transnational Tactics

Beyond these organizational innovations, activists have often employed transnational tactics to contest neoliberal policy initiatives. Increasingly directed outside the state, these protests have been supported by innovations in communications technology. The development and public accessibility of the Internet as a new medium for communication, and the rapid speed with which it can globally transmit information, has made it an especially effective resource for activists challenging trade and investment regimes. From the Zapatistas rebellion against NAFTA and the Mexican government, to the collapse of the talks on the Multilateral Agreement on Investment (MAI), to the battle in the streets of Seattle over the WTO's millennial round, to the planning of the 2nd People's Summit of the Americas and the mobilization against the FTAA in Quebec City, the Internet has consistently caught state authorities, trade bureaucrats, and security forces off guard and provided activists with surprise leverage in their campaigns.[15]

The leaked release and subsequent web-page posting of a draft of the MAI in 1997 by activist groups in the U.S. and Canada proved to be a public relations fiasco for the MAI negotiators at the Organization for Economic Cooperation and Development, in Paris. The French government, which finally doomed the MAI when it pulled out of the talks by late summer 1998, credited civil society activists and their Internet campaign in particular for the failure of the negotiations.[16] In Quebec City, moreover, another leak, this time of the purported 'investor-state clause' of the FTAA put bureaucrats on the defensive. FTAA negotiators promised in response to release a text of the FTAA, but only after it had been translated into the four languages of participant countries. Ultimately, under pressure by the HSA and building media scrutiny, FTAA negotiators released a draft of the text in July 2001.

A number of new Internet tactics have helped activists strategize and make claims against proponents of economic restructuring. Web pages are certainly crucial sources of immediate information, as are the list serves and electronic discussion groups that have proliferated around successive summits of the MAI, the WTO, the IMF, the World Bank and the FTAA. Opportunities have abounded for new forms of electronic activism around these summits: individuals could participate in the construction of a 'Citizen's MAI' or find information on creating an 'MAI-free' zone in their local community, email petition members of the Canadian parliament to oppose the WTO millennial round at Council of Canadians Internet site or join a 'virtual sit-in' by logging on to the official WTO Internet site to jam access to the site by other information seekers during the WTO millennial round. If unable to physically participate in the official planned march against the FTAA, one could join in a 'People's March on the Internet,' in effect showing solidarity with the marchers in Quebec City. Activists can also join the

Spanish language e-mail list for the HSA, and gain access to news and unfolding strategy from coalitions in countries across the hemisphere.

Targeting Outside the State

Beyond exploiting the Internet, transnational protestors have increasingly targeted corporations, trade and investment regimes and international institutions, such as the World Bank and the IMF (Ayres, 2001, pp.55-69). Notable campaigns have proliferated against sweatshop and child labour practices favoured by corporations, and against the meeting-places of the corporate elites. Over the past several years, the annual meeting of business, bureaucratic and political elites at the World Economic Forum, at the Alpine ski resort in Davos, Switzerland, has become a target of protestors. In fact, following the collapsed millennial round talks at the meeting of the WTO in Seattle in 1999, elites have been on the run successively in Davos, Washington, DC, Prague, Melbourne, Nice, Quebec City and Genoa, Italy. This protest pattern suggests that the framework for collective action is shifting: whereas the national social movement, and the national constellation of tactics upon which it depended, thrived on the opportunities provided by the state and domestic actors, increasingly, international agencies and institutions are also structuring opportunities for transnational protest against neoliberalism.

The flowering of alternative transnational gatherings held parallel to the trade, investment or business forums has become a new feature of this expanded protest repertoire. Such counter summits or teach-ins have become important settings for activists from around the world to educate, network, strategize and develop alternatives to the treaties being negotiated at the official forums. They have also become opportunities to pressure government and business elites to include social and environmental concerns into these negotiation processes, and at times embarrass authorities with timely leaks from the official negotiations. So-called 'People's Summits' have been proliferating: from the 1997 meeting of the leaders of the Asia-Pacific Economic Cooperation forum in Vancouver, to the 'counter-Davos' World Social Forum, attended by 10,000 activists in Porto Alegre, Brazil in January 2001, to the recent Second People's Summit in Quebec City in April 2001, during the FTAA heads of state meetings.

These People's Summits have at times proven quite innovative. For example, over 1,000 civil society activists from the Western hemisphere attended a multi-sectoral meeting in Belo Horizonte, Brazil, in May 1997, just prior to the official summit of hemispheric trade ministers. Participants in this counter-meeting criticized the neoliberal character of the FTAA, and called for the expansion of the FTAA agenda to include social concerns such as labour and human rights, as well as sustainable environmental and development practices. Hemispheric activists followed-up this meeting in April 1998 with the first People's Summit of the Americas, held parallel to the second America's heads of state meeting in Santiago, Chile. During this meeting, also attended by over 1,000 hemispheric activists and featuring thematic panels addressing various social concerns, participants created the HSA and drafted the social-developmental blueprint to the FTAA, *Alternatives for the Americas*.[17]

The HSA also coordinated the second People's Summit just prior to the third America's heads of state meeting in Quebec City in April 2001. Despite concerns that such parallel forums sponsored by hemispheric groups might lack the efficacy of direct participation in official meetings, or that successive parallel meetings might 'conventionalize' the process, and dampen media and public attention (Legler, 2000), the People's Summit likely trumped the meetings of the heads of state. Well-covered by the Canadian media, the Summit scored public relations points for the release of a leaked draft copy of the FTAA's negotiating text on investment.[18] Moreover, the Canadian summit advisor publicly admitted that the activists at the People's Summit were winning the public relations war and had done a better job at communicating their message than had the official Summit of the Americas.[19]

The struggles of the last half of the 1990s have helped to rescript popular sector protest strategies to counter the reorganization of social power that has so benefited capital these past two decades. National level protest campaigns have certainly not ended; national protest and lobbying efforts have continued within states that have not lost their policymaking capacities under neoliberalism, just redirected their efforts to assist more efficiently capital and employers. Nonetheless, the broadened international reach of protests, as well as the partial shift in claims-making to the international level, have put neoliberal globalizing elites in an unaccustomed defensive posture.

The Resilience of the State

Despite these clear successes, there is little room for naiveté or false hopes in any analysis of the struggle for power between capitalist and popular sector forces. This is especially true in light of the even harsher climate for political protest, which has emerged in the wake of the terrorist attacks on the United States on September 11th, 2001. The U.S. war on terrorism has created new constraints that raise questions about the future efficacy of transnational protest. In particular, state actors have clearly been rescripting power strategies to contend with, co-opt and undercut recent popular sector transnational innovations. Thus, similar to the pre-New Deal era, when union leaders were persecuted on conspiracy charges, and unions and strikers faced state militias and federal troops, today, civil society actors have seen their new tactics and strategies undermined by repressive security measures.

The crackdown on dissent, of course, certainly predates September 11th, and perhaps the most obvious manifestation of this counteroffensive has been the limits placed on such constitutional civil liberties as the freedom of speech and freedom to peaceably assemble. The constraints being placed by authorities on the right to dissent have taken on a variety of forms, but the pattern has become so commonplace as to be nearly an expected counterpart to the summits of government and business elites. Obviously, the events at the WTO meetings in Seattle, in December 1999, brought the harsh crackdown on neoliberal protestors to the attention of a wider audience, especially in the United States. There, the violent reaction by heavily armoured and armed police against WTO protestors was supported by the mayor of Seattle's decision to declare a 20-block no-protest-zone in direct violation of the Constitution of the United States' protection of the right to peaceably and freely assemble. Yet, this well-publicized crackdown was not the first time that state authorities had violently quelled protests against neoliberal gatherings. For years popular sector groups protesting IMF structural adjustment policies in the developing world have been accustomed to violent and repressive tactics used by authorities in undemocratic regimes, and Canadians received a recent taste of harsh police tactics in Vancouver at the 1997 APEC meeting of heads of state.[20]

Since the WTO meetings in Seattle, however, there has continued to evolve a pattern of civil-liberties violating crackdowns on protestors across Western Europe and North America, in countries much less accustomed to the use of questionable, if not blatantly undemocratic police tactics. In April 2000, for instance, during the meetings of the IMF and the World Bank in Washington, DC, numerous law enforcement tactics curtailed the ability of critics of neoliberal globalization to mount mass demonstrations. Questionable tactics, many of which failed subsequently to stand up in a court of law, included: preemptive raids and closures of organizing spaces on the pretense of fire code violations; the targeting of movement leaders for arrest on trumped up charges of terrorism and bomb making; the demand for excessively high bails for nonviolent protestors; and excessive force in arresting and dispersing nonviolent protestors.

The security measures adopted at the April 2001 Quebec City FTAA heads of state meetings further highlighted changes in the state's responses to protestors. In downtown Quebec City, a tall fence, dubbed by critics as the 'wall of shame', physically cordoned off protestors from the FTAA meetings, as well as thousands of city residents who required passes to travel to and from their homes and workplaces. The ensuing clash in Quebec City also encouraged a broadening of police tactics against activists. Complementing the use of tear gas against nonviolent protestors, the preemptive arrests of movement leaders and the possible violation of the Canadian Charter of Rights and Freedoms protection of the right to peaceably assemble, was the police use of plastic bullets – tactics commonplace in areas wracked by civil war and armed conflict – but rare in instances of gatherings of nonviolent protestors against state policy initiatives. The death of a demonstrator, and the bloody, late-night raid and beating of sleeping protestors, by Italian riot police during the July 2001 G8 Summit in Genoa, Italy, only served to further magnify the increasingly reckless behavior of police during international gatherings, and sparked an outcry of alarm from European capitals over the use of unwarranted and repressive tactics.

Security forces have not been limited to the use of physically harsh tactics in their response to protestors. State and corporate power strategies have also been rescripted through heightened surveillance of protest leaders and groups critical of neoliberal policy initiatives. While Seattle's authorities were clearly caught off guard by the use of the latest communications technology, including the Internet and cell phones, the post-Seattle context has changed: extensive electronic surveillance of protest group list servers and email traffic by intelligence agencies and public relations firms is now commonplace.[21] The decision by the WTO secretariat to try and restart millennial round talks and hold its fall 2001 ministerial meeting in the Persian Gulf Emirate of Qatar – a regime unaccustomed to, and unprotective of, civil liberties – and a locale much less accessible to critics of neoliberal policies, fit well into the generalized pattern of promoting such trade and investment initiatives at the expense of popular sovereignty, transparency, and democratic accountability.

Conclusion

The political-economic context after the terrorist attacks on the United States is fluid and unpredictable. In particular, the possible regulation of global capital and the constraints of a potential global social compact are scenarios not looked kindly upon by neoliberalism's promoters. Moreover, the rapid response by the state to the innovations in protest repertoires further underscores the fact that structural pressures are driving the political process, in this case as neoliberal policy initiatives dressed as national political imperatives. Nonetheless, the extremism characteristic of these state responses only serves to highlight the legitimation crisis being experienced by the institutions and advocates of neoliberal globalization. The concern for the next several years, however, is that state responses to terrorism will be used in part as smokescreens for a renewed push for neoliberal policies, such as fast-track authority, the FTAA and the WTO millennial round, all of which are initiatives whose outcomes were much more seriously in doubt prior to September 11th.

Are these tactical innovations nonetheless indicative of a fundamental change in the way people contend for power and policy change? The recent period of transnational restructuring of protest tactics is certainly a pivotal moment for opponents of neoliberalism, with both national and transnational tactics in play. However, it is certainly far from clear that the innovations in popular sector strategies will be politically successful towards the goal of containing and regulating global corporations and capital. Moreover, while the framework for collective action has been shifting of late, national states, especially after September 11th, will most likely remain the key sites for political contestation and the likely arenas for future attempts to curtail the neoliberal agenda. Nonetheless, these ongoing protest efforts, which clearly seek to prevent the social, political and ecological aspects of life from becoming marginalized by economic forces, represent a developing and natural subject of investigation for students of political economy, who have always sought to bring similar disputes over the distribution of power and wealth to the forefront of their analyses. The built-in tensions, contradictions and power struggles around neoliberalism thus naturally invite a broadened political-economic approach to consider this period of instability and the social actors that are resisting the prevailing neoliberal order.

Notes

1 This paper was originally presented at the conference on Global Turbulence: Instability in National and International Political Economy, Simon Fraser University, Harbour Centre Campus, Vancouver, British Columbia, Canada, 19-20 July 2001. The author gratefully acknowledges the research and travel funding provided by the Canadian Studies Program of the University of Vermont, the Canadian Consulate General in Boston, Massachusetts, and travel funding from the organizers of the above conference. I would like to thank Marjorie Griffin Cohen, Sidney Tarrow and Richard Nimijean for helpful comments on earlier drafts.

2 For engaged activist viewpoints, see Danaher and Burbach, 2000; Clarke and Barlow, 2001; Starr, 2000; for emerging academic analyses, see Smith, 2001, pp.1-19; Lemire, 2000, pp.49-78.

3 The concept of the repertoire originated with the work of Charles Tilly.

4 A useful but limited start can be found in Piven and Cloward, 2000, pp.413-430.

5 The term 'popular sector' here refers to a broad cross-section of groups, including women, labour, farmers, native peoples, disabled and other racial and ethnic minority groups, which remain relatively marginalized from decision-making institutions and who have articulated a critical counter-discourse to a capitalist-oriented political economy.

6 The literature on the crisis facing workers and other popular sector groups has become too voluminous to cite fully.

7 Rodrik has focused particularly on the conflicts and 'severe tensions' that have resulted from the effects of continued economic integration on domestic wages in industrialized countries.

8 Mittelman's (2000b) work on the antagonistic effects of neoliberal globalization on Southern workers and the underclass is a particularly useful complement to the work done on the deindustrialization of the North. See also the recent report, 'Seven Years Under NAFTA' (2001), which documents in empirical detail the negative impact on wages, income and poverty in Mexico and the U.S. after seven years under NAFTA, available on-line.

9 The French strikes by public sector employees in the face of proposed budgetary cutbacks by the then Juppé government in the so-called winter of discontent in 1995, and the strikes by the Ontario teachers union that following spring, were clear examples of the pressures being felt by public sector workers.

10 For a view of the South, see Walton and Sedden, 1994; and for North American and European reactions, see Rodrik, 1997; Ayres, 1998.

11 On environmental resistance, see Patterson, 1999, pp. 129-145; Mittelman, 2000a, pp. 383-388; Pellow, 2001, pp. 47-67; for women, see Gabriel and MacDonald, 1993, pp. 535-562; indigenous resistance, see Cleaver, 1998, pp. 621-640; Schulz, 1998, pp. 587-616; for students, see Mandle, 2000, pp. 90-103.

12 The CJM, while not immune to the tensions that have arisen between actors from the three participating countries, has made great strides to increase the

participation of Mexican groups and provide a trinationally balanced infrastructure. Notably, since 1997, over fifty per cent of the CJM's board members have been representatives from Mexican civil society groups.

13 This ten-union Alliance includes the UE, the Teamsters, the Canadian Auto Workers and FAT.

14 Extensive information on Common Frontiers; Hemispheric Social Alliance; and *Alternatives for the Americas* document, available on-line.

15 On the Internet and the MAI, see Ayres, 1999, pp. 132-143; the WTO, see Smith, 2001; and the Zapatistas, see Cleaver, 1998.

16 See the French original of LaLumière, Catherine, Landau, Jean-Pierre, Glimet, Emmanuel (1998), *Rapport sur l'Accord muultilaterial sur l'investissement (AMI)*, which credits civil society groups and their cross border activism and communication for the demise of MAI talks, available online at Relations Internationales' Internet site.

17 The *Alternatives for the Americas* document, also available on-line, has gone through a number of drafts, drawing upon the expertise of activists particularly from Canada, the U.S. and Mexico. A conscious attempt has been made to translate it into English, Spanish, French and Portuguese.

18 Apparently similar to NAFTA's chapter 11 investment clause, the FTAA investment provision would empower corporations with the right to sue governments and challenge laws and social and environmental regulations that might undermine profits or curtail investment opportunities. See the Second Peoples' Summit of the Americas, available on-line, for the HSA press release on the leaked investment chapter.

19 'People's Summit Outscoring America's Summit: PM Advisor', available on-line on *CBC News* Internet site.

20 See Pue (2000) for analyses of the fallout from the conflict during the Vancouver APEC summit.

21 For examples, see the leaked analysis of dozens of the groups involved in the WTO protests, compiled by the U.S. Public Relations firm Burson Marsteller, including its cover letter to 'corporate clients', which warns of the 'potential ability of the emerging coalition of these groups to seriously impact broader, longer-term corporate interests', available on-line at *Scoop Headlines*, March 2000. Also see the Canadian Security Intelligence Service (2000), 'Anti-Globalization – A Spreading Phenomenon' Report #2000/08, *Perspectives*, August, on the Canadian Security Intelligence Service Internet site.

References

Ayres, J. (1998), *Defying Conventional Wisdom: Political Movements and Popular Contention Against North American Free Trade*, University of Toronto Press, Toronto.

Ayres, J. (1999), 'From the Streets to the Internet: The Cyber-Diffusion of Contention', *The Annals of the American Academy of Political and Social Science*, Vol. 566, pp. 132-143.

Ayres, J. (2001), 'Transnational Political Processes and Contention Against the Global Economy', *Mobilization*, Vol. 6, No. 1, pp. 55-69.

Bashevkin, S. (2000), 'In the Shadow of Free Trade: Nationalism, Feminism and Identity Politics in Contemporary Canada', *Journal of Canadian Studies*, Vol. 35, No. 2 pp. 109-127.

Cameron, D. and Drache, D. (eds) (1985), *The Other Macdonald Report: The Consensus on Canada's Future that the Macdonald Commission Left Out*, James Lorimer, Toronto.

Canadian Security Intelligence Service (2000), 'Anti-Globalization – A Spreading Phenomenon' Report #2000/08, *Perspectives*, August.

Clarke, T. and Barlow, M. (2001), *Global Showdown: How the New Activists are Fighting Global Corporate Rule*, Stoddard, Toronto.

Cleaver, H. (1998), 'The Zapatista Effect: The Internet and the Rise of an Alternative Political Fabric', *Columbia Journal of International Affairs*, Vol. 51, No. 2, pp. 621-640.

Cook, M. (1997), 'Regional Integration and Transnational Politics: Popular Sector Strategies in the NAFTA Era', in D. Chalmers et al. (eds), *The New Politics of Inequality in Latin America*, Oxford University Press, Oxford.

Danaher K. and Burbach R. (eds) (2000), *Globalize This! The Battle Against the World Trade Organization and Corporate Rule*, Common Courage Press, Monroe, Maine.

Dreiling, M. (1999), 'Unionism in Transnational America: Divergent Practices and Contending Visions in Labor's Fight with NAFTA', paper presented at the Meeting of the American Sociological Association.

Gabriel, C. and MacDonald, L. (1993), 'NAFTA, Women, and Organizing in Canada and Mexico: Forging a Feminist Internality', *Millennium,* Vol. 23, No. 3, pp. 535-562.

Gordon, M. and Turner, L. (2001), *Transnational Cooperation Among Labor Unions*, Cornell University Press, Ithaca, New York.

Hathaway, D. (2000), *Allies Across the Border: Mexico's 'Authentic Labor Front' and Global Solidarity*, South End Press, Cambridge, Massachusetts.

Higgott, R. and Deretek, R. (1999), 'Justice Unbound? Globalization, States and the Transformation of the Social Bond', *International Affairs*, Vol. 75, No. 3, pp. 483-498.

Kamel R. and Hoffman A. (eds) (1999), 'Cross Border Initiatives', in *The Maquiladora Reader: Cross-Border Organizing Since NAFTA*, American Friends Service Committee, Philadelphia, PA, Chapter Four.

LaLumière, Catherine, Landau, Jean-Pierre, Glimet, Emmanuel (1998), *Rapport sur l'Accord muultilaterial sur l'investissement (AMI)*, Relations Internationales, Ministère de l'Économie, des Finances et de l'Industrie.

Legler, T. (2000), 'Transnational Coalition-Building in the Americas: The Case of the Hemispheric Social Alliance', paper presented to the Summer Institute on 'Building the New Agenda: Hemispheric Integration and Social Cohesion', York University, Toronto, Canada.

Lemire, M. (2000), 'Mouvement social et mondialisation économique: de l'AMI au Cycle du millénaire de l'OMC', *Politique et Sociétés*, Vol. 19, No. 1, pp.49-78.

Mandle, J. (2000), 'The Student Anti-Sweatshop Movement: Limits and Potential', *The Annals of the American Academy of Political and Social Science*, Vol. 570, pp. 90-103.

Mazur, J. (2000), 'Labor's New Internationalism', *Foreign Affairs*, Vol. 79, No. 1, pp. 79-93.

McBride, S. and Shields, J. (1997), *Dismantling a Nation: The Transition to Corporate Rule in Canada*, Fernwood Publishing, Halifax.

Mittelman, J. (2000a), 'Environmental Resistance to Globalization', *Current History*, Vol. 99, pp. 383-388.

Mittelman, J. (2000b), *The Globalization Syndrome: Transformation and Resistance*, Princeton University Press, Princeton, New Jersey

O'Brien, R. (2000), 'Workers and World Order: the Tentative Transformation of the International Union Movement', *Review of International Studies,* Vol. 26, pp. 533-555.

Panitch, L. (1986), *Working Class Politics in Crisis*, Verso, London.

Patterson, M. (1999), 'Globalisation, Ecology and Resistance', *New Political Economy,* Vol. 4, No. 1, pp. 129-145.

Pellow, D. (2001), 'Environmental Justice and the Political Process: Movements, Corporations and the State', *The Sociological Quarterly*, Vol. 42, No. 1, pp. 47-67.

Piven, F. and Cloward, R. (2000), 'Power Repertoires and Globalization', *Politics and Society*, Vol. 28, No. 3, pp. 413-430.

Pue, W. (ed) (2000), *Pepper in Our Eyes: The APEC Affair,* UBC Press, Vancouver.

Rodrik, D. (1997), *Has Globalization Gone Too Far?*, Institute for International Economics, Washington, DC.

Rosen, F. (1999), 'The Underside of NAFTA: a Budding Cross-Border Resistance', *NACLA Report on the Americas*, Vol. 32, No. 4, pp. 37-39.

Ross, G. (2000), 'Labor Versus Globalization', *The Annals of the American Academy of Political and Social Science*, Vol. 570, pp. 78-91.

Schulz, M. (1998), 'Collective Action Across Borders: Opportunity Structures, Network Capacities, and Communicative Praxis in the Age of Advanced Capitalism', *Sociological Perspectives*, Vol. 41, No. 3, pp. 587-616.

Scott, B. (2001), 'The Great Divide in the Global Village', *Foreign Affairs*, Vol. 80, No. 1, pp. 160-177.

'Seven Years Under NAFTA' (2001), Institute for Policy Studies, Washington, DC.

Smith, J. (2001), 'Globalizing Resistance: the Battle of Seattle and the Future of Social Movements', *Mobilization*, Vol. 6, No. 1, pp. 1-19.

Starr, A. (2000), *Naming the Enemy: Anti-Corporate Movements Confront Globalization*, Zed Books, London and New York.

Tarrow, S. (1996), 'Social Movements in Contentious Politics: A Review Article', *American Political Science Review*, Vol. 90, No. 4.

Tarrow, S. (1998), *Power in Movement: Social Movements and Contentious Politics*, 2nd Ed, Cambridge University Press, New York/Cambridge.

Tilly, C. (1977), 'Getting It Together in Burgundy, 1675-1975', *Theory and Society*, Vol., 4, pp. 479-504.

Tilly, L. and Tilly C. (eds) (1981), *Class Conflict and Collective Action*, Sage, Beverly Hills, California.

Walton, J. and Sedden, D. (1994), *Free Markets and Food Riots: the Politics of Global Adjustment*, Blackwell, Cambridge, Massachusetts.

Williams, H. (1999), 'Mobile Capital and Transborder Labor Rights Mobilization', *Politics and Society*, Vol. 27, No. 1, pp. 139-166.

Young, B. (2000), 'The "Mistress" and the "Maid" in the Globalized Economy', in L. Panitch (ed), *Working Classes, Global Realities: The Socialist Register, 2001*, Merlin Press, London, pp. 315-327.

Chapter 8

Trade Unions and Competitive Nationalism: A House of Mirrors

Peter Graefe

Introduction

Labour movements and social democratic parties around the world have been wooed by the promise of progressive competitiveness strategies. These strategies promise to 'provide a reformed trade union movement, allied to a social democratic politics, with numerous opportunities to intervene in the economy, at a variety of levels, in support of traditional egalitarian concerns that at the same time support, rather than inhibit, economic efficiency' (Phillimore, 2000, p.559). Despite the breakdown of the post-war institutions of economic regulation and the renewed predominance of the capitalist mantras of free competition and free markets, unions and social democratic parties are considered capable of making capital an offer it cannot refuse: their cooperation, tied to enhanced representation on a variety of levels, can lead to a positive-sum class compromise based on creating a high-skills/innovatory growth path. According to Wright, the premise is that as long as capitalism is the only model on offer, 'a positive class compromise – if it is achievable – will generally constitute the most advantageous context for the improvement of the material interests and life circumstances of ordinary people' (Wright, 2000, p.958).

The appeal of progressive competitiveness is amplified in a context of minority nationalism. In a situation where nation-states are being hollowed out, minority nations can deploy regional competitiveness strategies as a means of asserting and maintaining their economic autonomy. There is a sense in which progressive competitiveness and minority nationalism exist in a virtuous circle: minority nationalism increases the supply of the extra-economic goods required for competitiveness (trust, culture, social partnership etc.), while the achievement of competitiveness reproduces a cross-class national consensus by allowing the majority to benefit and by compensating 'losers' (Keating, 1997a, p.32). The promise of this virtuous circle should only reinforce the appeal of what one can call 'competitive nationalism' for the labour movement and social democrats.

While competitive nationalism promises much to labour, it increasingly does so under false pretences. Reduced restraints to capital mobility and the strengthening hold of capitalist values on the popular imagination have reinforced business' bargaining power. The pressures of international competition, intensified by the mushrooming of competitiveness strategies, have likewise put the screws on businesses' willingness to make concessions and to shoulder higher wage and taxation costs (Keating, 1998, p.157). In these circumstances, institutions of social partnership and national consensus may serve to bind labour to an accumulation strategy that marginalizes its goals. Competitive nationalism can therefore become a 'house of mirrors' in two senses. First, progressive values are likely to be distorted beyond recognition when reflected in the mirror of competitiveness. Second, the linkage of nationalism with competitiveness reflects what the unions demanded, making it exceedingly difficult to step back from the flattering promises of competitive nationalism in order to establish an independent analysis and strategy.

As a preliminary effort to disentangle these knotty issues, this paper will survey the situation in Quebec, Canada, particularly with respect to the labour movement. In Quebec, the unions were key players in advancing the parameters of 'partnership' economic strategies, strategies strengthened and cemented by invoking the need for national consensus. In the process, however, they seem to have underestimated how the logic of competitiveness has redefined the national project much more in line with the interests of capital. In this context, the labour movement continues to be interpolated by progressive competitive strategies topped with institutions for forming a national consensus between major social actors, even as these strategies bring ever-thinner returns. The need to define an alternative political economy for the national project is left unfulfilled as the labour movement struggles to find the exit from this house of mirrors.

Minority Nationalism And Competitiveness

To start, it is useful to define the contested terms of nationalism and competitiveness. I follow Michael Keating in my use of the term 'minority nationalism' to refer to a national group within a broader nation-state that seeks wider forms of self-rule, self-expression and recognition, although not necessarily the full accoutrements of sovereign statehood (Keating, 1997b, p.35). 'Nations without states' is another shorthand used to describe this reality. These nationalisms, like those of their broader nation-states, can be considered as social constructions. Minority nationalist movements attempt to construct a coherent appeal by manipulating the cultural, political, economic and social dimensions of regional and national identity (1997a, p.24). Nationalism seeks to gather individuals together on the basis of a shared national identity, while subsuming or downplaying other bases of division, such as class or gender. The definition of minority nationalist identity is thus an act of power since it involves integrating conflicting groups into that identity, and assigning them different roles and positions based on their relative influence and strength.

Competitiveness is a more nebulous term, particularly as numerous variants have been proposed (static competitiveness, dynamic competitiveness, etc.). At a most basic level, in the context of the workings of a capitalist economy, the term refers to the ability of firms (or of the aggregate of firms within a particular economy) to survive by realizing a profit on the capital advanced in production. When promoted as a broader social goal, it is usually takes on a meaning closer to what David Coates labels 'structural competitiveness', namely: 'the ability of national economies to provide high and growing per capita incomes while exposed to foreign competition'. This second definition is more exacting since it judges competitiveness not only on the performance of firms, but also on the aggregate impact on incomes (and implicitly, although not necessarily directly, on living standards) (Coates, 2000, p.16).

The Decline of the Nation-State and the Rise of the Region

The linkage of minority nationalism and competitiveness occurs within the framework of the nation-state's decline and the rising economic potential of the regional scale. The story of the 'hollowing out' of the national state with its power being passed upwards (to supranational state institutions), downwards (to regional state institutions) and outwards (to market actors) is nearly a cliché. Nevertheless, one can characterize the post Second World War period of Atlantic Fordism as a period where the national scale of economic organization predominated, and where the national economy was seen as a natural and unproblematic object of economic management. The importance of the 'national' space for social organization was underlined by the close linkages between, and the significance of, notions of national economy, national society, national state, national citizenship and national society (Jessop, 2000, pp.337-38). Universal social programmes and regional development policies maintained or reinforced the territorial integration of the nation-state, and redefined the maps of citizenship and identity by stressing the national community over local or international ones (Jenson, 1995).

Strengthened international economic competition coupled with increased capital mobility has upset this pattern, by encouraging the rollback of the universalistic welfare state and the retooling of regional policy. Restructuring social policies to make them market reinforcing redefines eligibility away from universality, and thus dissolves the sense of shared citizenship at the level of the nation-state. This shift also erodes the nation-state's legitimacy since it shows its claim to be the engine of social justice and development to be unrealizable. This opens spaces for regions, and minority nations, to make countervailing claims about identity and the appropriate community for social solidarity (Brown, 1998, pp.9, 11; Jenson, p.103).

A similar story applies to regional policy. Under heightened international competition, states have moved resources out of territorial anti-disparity measures and into the aggressive restructuring of leading sectors. Hueglin speaks of 'a new public philosophy of disciplinarian austerity' where nation-states 'reclaim lost ground in the global economy arena by getting tough with [their] peripheries' (Hueglin, 1989, p.210; Keating, 1998, p.73). Once again, this opens spaces for regionalist or minority nationalist movements to pick up the slack and define the boundaries of their community as a relevant space for constructing a development model.

The creation of these spaces for regionalist or minority nationalist movements takes on increased interest, as regions become meaningful containers for dynamic, innovative and inclusive economic growth. The focus here is trained on the factors making regions essential scales of economic coordination. Storper, for instance, focuses on 'untraded dependencies', or region-specific assets in production such as conventions, informal rules and habits (Storper, 1997, pp.4-5). The regional innovation systems literature picks up on this thread to argue that economic development and the maintenance of high-end employment are increasingly dependent on the ability of regionally-specific economies to learn and innovate. Learning and innovation, in turn, rely on what could be considered as place-specific 'extra-economic' inputs such as: the existence of a thick matrix of institutions linking firms, research institutions and public infrastructure; networks for diffusing tacit knowledge; high levels of trust and 'social capital'; associative capacity and willingness to cooperate; and a shared culture (Cooke, 1997, pp.358-64; Braczyk and Heidenreich, 1998, pp.415-16, 433-35). Keating likewise picks up this thread in order to argue that regional competitiveness derives from the ability to exploit external economies of scale in industrial districts; accumulate social capital in terms of traditions of cooperation; and produce quality public goods (Keating, 1997a, p.31). These tendencies reinforce the prominence of the regional scale of the state due to its proximity to the milieu. Being closer to regional economic actors and institutions, it can adapt and respond quickly to support a reflexive and learning economy. Moreover, as intervention is geared to microeconomic and supply-side measures, the regional state finds itself about as well-equipped as the national one (Hollingsworth and Boyer, 1997, p.27).

These regional economies are not self-organizing, but depend on actors privileging the regional scale of development and forming a development coalition. Keating defines these coalitions as 'cross-class, place-based alliance[s] of social and political actors, dedicated to economic growth in specific localities' (Keating, 1998, p.144). To the extent that regional competitive success relies on harnessing partnership and social cooperation, these coalitions must make appeals that integrate a wide range of actors. Success on the terrain of development should in turn provide enough resources to compensate losers and thus reproduce the region's intangible factors of production and ensure continued support for the coalition. Keating captures the *promise* of these regional competitiveness strategies with his 'virtuous model of regional development':

> … there is a successful programme of economic development. Social integration is secured and marginalization avoided. Culture and identity are safeguarded.

The environment is conserved. These serve to create social capital and public goods, which in turn favour economic growth (Keating, 1997a, p.32).

Given this possibility for inclusive development, based in part on enhanced representation in decision-making for unions, it is not surprising that regionalism has had a left flavour since the 1960s. One response for labour movements faced with capital restructuring is to fall back on local-based forms of resistance (Keating, 1998, p.108). More pointedly, there are many areas of overlap between the political economy said to underlie the successful region, and supply-side social democratic strategies. Indeed, if one follows Rogers and Streeck (1994), only social democracy can create the 'productive solidarities' of association, skill, public goods, trust and good will that underlie quality strategies. High wages, low wage differentiation, as well as associative and democratic participation close off the low-wage production options while opening opportunities for significant productivity gains (Streeck, 1994; Wolfe, 1992). Regionalism promises to make development inclusive, both in terms of governance, and in the distribution of gains.

It is nevertheless important to raise some caveats. As Lovering underlines, the work on the competitiveness of regions walks a slippery line between description and prescription (Lovering, 1999, p.390). While changes in scales are occurring, and the importance of regional initiatives is growing, this change should not be exaggerated on two counts. First, for all the talk of the hollowing out of the national, it remains an important scale for state action. Jessop has underlined that the national state remains best equipped to deal with issues of territorial integration, social cohesion and social exclusion – hardly minor questions! This is not to ignore what Jessop terms the meta-governance roles of rule-setting, strategic information provision, hierarchic coordination, and attempts to alter the identities and interests of other actors (Jessop, pp.354-55).

Even disregarding this 'metagovernance' role, the nation-state's expenditure still has significant economic impact. Lovering notes that UK public spending in Wales contributed twice as much to gross job creation than did foreign direct investment, and had twenty-two times the impact of manufacturing (manufacturing being the purported centre of Wales' learning economy) (Lovering, p.382). More broadly, the success of microeconomic/supply-side regional strategies remains highly dependent on a supportive macroeconomic framework, and often on supportive nation-state level research infrastructures (Amin, 1999, p.376; Bradford, 1998, p.564; Vavakova and Wolfe, 1999, p.107, 125).

Second, while the national has been hollowed out, it is likely too early to declare regions as the prized locales for non-neoliberal growth strategies. The sustainability of regional strategies in the face of intense interregional competition is open to question, and their current significance may be a short-lived artefact of the absence of systemic regulation. If competition is such that only some localities can 'win', and this at the expense of most others, the resulting order is not likely to spur regional growth so much as to create a regional space for managing 'competitive austerity' (Albo, 1994, p.147, 157; Peck and Tickell, 1994, p.281-82, 298). The story of dynamic regions spurring innovative and inclusive development may be not be much more convincing than Lovering's counter story of 'the conservative and cautious nature of the construction of a market order in the context of suppressed growth, mediated through a reconstructed spatiality of the state' (Lovering, p.397).

Add Nationalism and Stir

Despite this useful dose of scepticism about the regionalization of economic development, it remains that regionally-based strategies continue to attract the interest of policy-makers and academic observers. For minority nationalist movements, they hold yet further attraction. The stress on the regional scale of governance promises to reinforce the relevance of economic units closely congruent with the boundaries of the minority community. More importantly, an economic policy that portrays the minority nation as pitted against a series of rival regional economies serves to strengthen the national identity at the expense of class-based ones by invoking territorial solidarity to overcome class conflict. The 'progressive' promise of competitiveness policy, namely that high quality jobs and public services can be maintained in spite of competition, is likewise attractive because it allows for the socially-inclusive form of development required to maintain a broad-based nationalist coalition (Keating, 1998, p.160).

At the same time, minority nationalism provides a number of elements to strengthen a regional competitiveness policy. Nationalism draws upon and enriches a shared culture, and thus provides a set of symbols and keys for organizing social relations, and for making sense of the minority nation's integration into the global economy (Keating, p.152; Latouche, 1993). Secondly, nationalism may well increase the density of institutions within a given regional space. Since minority nations are deprived access to many policy levers, they must undertake a great deal more organization outside the state. However, where minority nations control powerful regional governments, the process of competitive state-building may have similar results (Latouche, 1998, pp.321, 326-27; Keating, 1997b, pp.81-82). Finally, nationalism may enhance a competitiveness policy to the extent that it promotes cross-class partnership in two ways. First, the national fact is likely to strengthen the organization of interests at the level of the minority nation (Latouche, p.324). Second, it encourages antagonistic social forces to look out for the 'broader good' of their shared nation.

The conjunction of minority nationalism and regional competitiveness strategies presents alluring prospects for labour movements and social democrats. Nationalism provides a series of additional public goods to help capitalists solve certain kinds of collective action and coordination problems standing in the way of high-wage, high-quality production paths. In a sense, it serves as a complement to the role of trade union power in terms of creating positive-sum agreements with capital, and may help push the capital-labour dynamic to what Wright calls 'social democratic utopia' (Wright, pp.976, 978). At the same time, nationalism generally seeks to represent the nation as a site of solidarity, which is likely to give labour movements and social democrats enhanced representation within the development coalition.

Competitiveness: Who Holds the Trumps?

Despite the rosy promise of competitive minority nationalism, it is less clear that regional competitiveness strategies fulfill their promise. There are a number of political and economic critiques of these strategies that suggest that the *promise* of creating a participatory and inclusive development model may serve to entangle the labour movement and social democrats in some very difficult and contradictory strategic positions.

The *political* arguments relate to the shift in the relative power of capital and labour. Given the structure of capitalist economies, particularly with respect to the institution of private property, business interests hold the power to make autonomous investment decisions (e.g. whether or not to invest, what to invest in, how much to invest). Progressive competitive strategies pre-suppose that business will be willing to share this decision-making power with other economic stakeholders on the grounds that they will reap benefits in the form of innovation and productivity gains. Yet, increased international capital mobility has created a situation where, to cite Coates' sporting analogy, 'national industrial bourgeoisies [across the advanced capitalist world] have taken their bat home. They will no longer play ball with local labour movements seeking to combine employment security with industrial and social rights'. Where corporatist institutions remain, they simply serve 'to ratchet down wages and labour rights in a slower and more negotiated way' than where they do not exist (Coates, pp.259-60). While this is a sweeping claim, it is supported by Bradford's assessment of attempts to create associative forms of governance in Ontario, Canada. His study underlined the difficulty of getting business to refrain from exercising its structural economic power – at least in the absence of significant political pressure (Bradford, p.564; Kuttner, 1994).

In a more strategic sense, competitiveness is a difficult project for the labour movement because it legitimizes a fundamental capitalist imperative. Competitiveness sets workers in different workplaces and societies (depending on the level at which it operates) against one another in what is likely a race to the bottom. Since firms in capitalist economies are in perpetual competition, progressive reforms can be continually delayed on the grounds of threatening the ability to compete (Gindin and Robertson, 1992, pp.32-33). Of course, the tensions involved in seeking to transform the system at the same time as making it work are inherent in the very roles that unions play in modern capitalist societies, and as such are not new. There are nonetheless two elements worth underlining here.

First, the prism of competitiveness redefines these tensions by moving the question of the survival and profitability of firms from being a *constraint* to being an *end* or a *goal* in itself. Second, the tension becomes even more complex in the case of minority nationalism. After all, the decline of the Keynesian (national) welfare state provides an opportunity for expanding regional economic strategies. Nevertheless, some things that the Keynesian state managed to partially remove from international competition and regulate domestically, such as wage rates, working conditions, and social provision, are no longer protected. The loss of these protections means that accepting competitiveness as an end in itself increases the risk of a race to the bottom. Regional strategies in regulated national economies may have produced gains for unions through productivity sharing; at present, they threaten to enhance the downward pressure on workers' living standards.

The combination of businesses' increased bargaining power and the adoption of capitalist norms leads to a new politics of regionalist development. Although there are a variety of responses, there is a general tendency to embrace the competitive ethos and market-reinforcing public policy, and to marginalize organized labour and questions of social inequality (Keating, 1998, p.157).

While the competitiveness agenda and capital mobility places business in a position of negotiating strength, it may paradoxically be businesses' *weakness* that pushes it to unilaterally exercise its power of economic decision-making. The 'structural competitiveness' of regional strategies is based on capturing niche rents from quality, custom or innovative products and then distributing these through high wages or corporate tax-financed social provision. However, with the acceleration of technological diffusion, the ability to outperform mass producers to the point of cancelling out the cost differential becomes more difficult. If mass producers can modestly increase their product customizability, they threaten to close this performance/cost gap, and to renew downward wage pressures even in economies on the purported high-wage/high-quality path (Coates, p.257; Knauss, 1998, pp.290-92). At the same time, as the number of economies adopting high-end strategies increases, competition for these niche rents is also bound to intensify. When the global macroeconomy shows a deflationary bias, the success of some regions' export-oriented strategies can only come at the expense of others. Attempts by 'losers' to adjust by ratcheting their cost structure downward are likely to further dampen demand, and to force even the 'winners' to eventually control their costs (Albo, 1997, pp.11, 22; Zuege, 1999, pp.97-100). The net result is to intensify cost competition, with its correlates of depressed incomes, work spreading, or reduced corporate tax income. 'Competitiveness' comes closer to the basic idea of ensuring the survival of firms than to the 'structural' definition of providing high and rising incomes in an open economy.

My analysis so far has shown a strong manufacturing bias, in large measure since progressive competitive economic and regional strategies have a manufacturing focus (Lovering, 2001, p.349).[1] It is not clear whether the adoption of a resource-based regional strategy would have greatly different effects, unless it was a resource from which significant rents could be captured and distributed, such as oil. In the Canadian potash and uranium mining sectors, for instance, the drive to compete through work reorganization has resulted in a similar dynamic of doing 'more with less', as employment levels and relative pay in the industry have taken a hit, while employment insecurity and job-related stress have increased. The *quid pro quo* of worker, household and community empowerment and participative, skilful jobs has emerged slowly, if at all (Russell, 1999, pp.161, 198-99).

The result is a rather bewildering situation for progressives. On the one hand, regional strategies promise to open decision-making power to a broader range of participants through more associative forms of governance. They promise to deliver the 'productive solidarities' that social democratic theorists argue are necessary to maintain high wage economies and advanced welfare states. Nationalism, in turn, promises a more inclusive community with less social inequality. Both partnership and nationalism are thus likely to represent important strands of social democratic strategy. Yet, as competitiveness comes to redefine these elements, their reflection of progressive goals may appear increasingly distorted as the gains of the competitive nation accrue to business, while labour is left to distribute the costs. According to Zuege, progressive competitive strategies may simply leave the union partner 'charged with controlling their most militant members and administering uneven development in an export-led growth model dependent on the intensification of labour' (Zuege, 1999, p.100). In the absence of an alternative strategy, competitive nationalism may involve gaining a seat at the table to sanction the repeal of past gains.

Competitive Nationalism in Quebec: A House of Mirrors

The interplay of nationalism, competitiveness strategy and labour responses in Quebec is of particular interest given that the national question has been *a* primary, if not *the* primary issue of Quebec politics and political debate since 1960. As a result, the representations of social relations and the integration of social forces within dominant representations of the minority nation have had significant effects on the actions and strategies of different actors. As we shall see, the labour movement was able to extract a number of gains by linking nationalism to a social democratic project. However, as the national project has turned to ensuring Quebec's survival in the international economy, the unions have borne the full brunt of competitive nationalism's contradictions.

The Labour Movement Comes to Competitive Nationalism

Labour's embrace of competitive nationalism is a relatively new phenomenon. The connection with competitiveness dates from the late 1980s, and the link to nationalism from the mid-1960s. The unions were initially wary of the nationalist surge in the early 1960s since many of the earlier nationalist politicians were of a reactionary character. Into the 1970s, they followed rather than led their membership in embracing nationalism, which meant they were unable to inject it with a strong working-class flavour. The political economy underlying the dominant strands of Quebec nationalism in the 1960s and 1970s varied from the mild welfare liberalism of the autonomist Quebec Liberal Party (QLP) to the social democratic platform of the sovereignist Parti Québécois (PQ). The PQ maintained hegemony over the 'left' of the political spectrum, and could thus rely on the active support of a majority of union members. Still, the closest formal links were the Fédération des travailleurs et travailleuses du Québec's (FTQ) – Quebec's largest labour federation, representing roughly 40 per cent of the unionized workforce) electoral endorsements in 1976 and 1981. While the FTQ supported the PQ's nationalism, with its social democratic vision of expanding the welfare state, creating tripartite consultative forums, and introducing worker-friendly legislation (e.g. health and safety, anti-scab laws, French-in-the-workplace provisions), the Confédération des syndicats nationaux (CSN) and the Centrale de l'enseignement du Québec (CEQ) (federations representing roughly 25 per cent and ten per cent of the unionized workforce) proposed an alternative nationalism based on an avowedly socialist political economy. In all cases, nationalism was valued for increasing social consensus behind a programme of social change. Increased sovereignty for Quebec within the Canadian federation was also felt to set the stage for a more substantive programme of reform (Guntzel, 2000, pp.370-79; Lipsig-Mummé, 1991, pp.85-93; Denis, 1998, pp.140-46).

These strategic choices paid dividends (at least for the FTQ) during the PQ's first term in power (1976-1980). The PQ delivered on many of its policy promises, since social democratic reforms were felt to strengthen the nationalist coalition behind the project of increasing Quebec's sovereignty. The government also launched a post-Keynesian, supply-side economic policy aimed at developing market niches through quality and innovation strategies. As part of this policy, it created peak-level tripartite and multipartite forums to help set the minority nation's strategic directions, although these never had much power or influence, particularly in the context of decentralized collective bargaining institutions. The recession of the early 1980s hung like an albatross over the PQ's second term (1981-85). Its response, consisting of welfare state retrenchment and unilateral public sector pay cuts, effectively ended the FTQ's dream of creating 'Sweden on the Saint Lawrence'. Both the PQ and the PLQ responded to the crisis of the post-war economic and social models by embracing a market-based political economy, and by redefining national affirmation around the success of a new class of Quebec-based entrepreneurs. This crisis also provoked strategic changes within the labour federations. The CEQ and the CSN's socialist alternative had never connected with the majority of their rank-and-file, and were beginning to undermine the leadership's credibility. The answer was to embrace FTQ-style social democratic strategies. The FTQ, in turn, embraced the idea of expanding sites of peak, sectoral and firm-level concentration between unions and business, and sought to use its newly-created labour sponsored investment fund as a lever to this end (Lipsig-Mummé, pp.94-101; Tanguay, 1995, pp.177-86).

By the late 1980s, this was coming together as a more coherent political economy. The class-conflict models of yesteryear were put aside in favour of new forms and institutions of dialogue whereby business and labour representatives could focus on achieving their common interests. The CSN, for instance, took up the question of new forms of work organization as a strategy for positive-sum labour-management relations. This referred to a grab bag of measures that were felt to break down Taylorist forms of work organization and the accompanying job-control form of unionism, such as teamwork, multi-skilling and multi-tasking, and participatory management in areas such as training and occupational health and safety. Given intense international competition, the CSN argued that labour-management cooperation in work reorganization was necessary in order to follow a high productivity/high wage/high employment trajectory that benefited all parties. Employers in highly competitive industries would be able to survive by increasing the flexibility of labour deployment and using a fuller complement of the workforce's skills. Meanwhile unions could maintain employment levels, improve training and workplace health and safety, and make strides in advancing workplace democracy. This was presented as a win-win proposition, since employers could only capitalize on the creativity, responsibility and commitment of their workers if they recognized workers' autonomy and power, and provided quality jobs and work environments (CSN, 1991). The FTQ was less confident in the potential of such positive-sum trade-off around the organization of work, stressing the decisive importance of power in making workplace gains. Nevertheless, the FTQ continued to push for labour-capital concentration to define the direction of Quebec's economy. This was echoed in the 1987 pronouncements by the CSN's president in favour of 'the negotiated society' (Denis, p.155). In both cases, the idea was that partnership could reap gains for workers without compromising the competitiveness of the nation's firms.

The shift to embracing competitiveness, reinforced by nationalism, appeared strategically promising, particularly as it coincided with the policies of the major political parties. The PQ was grasping towards a political economy that could provide a wide national consensus despite global competitive pressures. The result was to extol the nation [i.e. Quebec] as a prime site for *managing adjustment*. The proposed development strategy for a sovereign Quebec involved an emphasis on training, infrastructure provision, research and development, and cooperation between all social actors. In this view, social solidarity became a condition of success. The role of nationalism in this scheme was to foster the 'broad consensus' required to implement the strategy. The pay-off to the nation, as well as to labour, was the ability to compete while maintaining social cohesion through adjustment policies (Parti Québécois, 1994, pp.1-4, 11, 25).

The ruling PLQ, despite its ongoing flirtation with neoliberalism, also recognized the danger that market liberalism posed given the province's weak industrial and skilling structures. The government's industrial cluster-based development policy made a similar argument: 'all decision-makers and participants in the domain of economic development admit that solidarity and cohesion are essential for the development of a small economy in a changing world' (Gagné and Lefèvre, 1993, p.76).[2] Starting in about 1990, the government's initiatives in economic development and training policy consistently called on all social actors, and particularly business and labour, to cooperate towards the achievement of economic success (and the associated employment gains). These calls had extra weight because they were implicitly made in the name of the Quebec nation. This direction appealed to the labour movement because it involved a break from the ambient climate of neoliberalism, and the invocation of the nation opened spaces to bring collective projects to the fore (Gagnon and Lachapelle, 1996, p.181).

The imbrications of the labour movement, progressive competitive strategy and nationalism were cemented by exchanges between the labour leaders and leading business representatives during the highly publicized and closely followed Commission on Quebec's Political and Constitutional Future, held in 1991. This experience reinforced the feeling of the labour leadership that they could work together relatively harmoniously with business to lay out the broad lines of the nation's development. It seemed possible to strike agreements even while respecting the needs of the other party (Piotte, 1998, p.269).

The Promise Betrayed?

The union federations backed competitive nationalism for its promise of achieving progressive aims, but evidence is accumulating to suggest that it has provided few benefits. Business interests have managed to turn competitive nationalism to their own ends by stressing the narrower version of profitability over Coates' 'structural competitiveness' of high and rising living standards. The unions, on the other hand, have placed such a stress on partnership and on the need to compete, that they cannot credibly critique damaging initiatives cloaked in the 'necessity to compete'.

A striking example of the limits of competitive nationalism's progressive potential is the experience of the 1996 social and economic summits. The summits responded to the labour federations' demand that the state convoke the major social actors in order to agree to a collective response to the 1990s jobs crisis. Yet, at every step of the way, the labour movement found itself outmanoeuvred as the state lined up with business representatives. Indeed, to ensure the participation of business, the government tacitly promised that the Summits would not lead to increased taxes or regulation. This decision was justified on the grounds that the competitiveness of Quebec firms in fact required deregulation and reduced taxes (Chantier sur l'économie et l'emploi, 1996, p.10). As a result, when it came to the key topic of deficit reduction, the only debate left was the technical one about when to bring the deficit to zero. Given the tax promise, the only deficit-fighting approach on offer (barring miraculous rates of economic growth) was to make substantial cuts in the public sector, which was manifestly not what the unions had in mind. The *quid pro quo* for labour's assent to the deficit-fighting agenda was a second summit focussed on arriving at a jobs pact. While the unions claimed that the resulting 'Declaration for employment' was an important gain, it was in fact a non-binding document calling on all social partners to work towards surpassing Canada's job creation rate, so as to eliminate the Canada-Quebec unemployment rate differential. The Declaration was soon forgotten, but the deficit-reduction agreement was deemed binding enough for the state to reopen public sector contracts in order to extract money-saving concessions (Piotte, pp.257-69; CEQ, CSN, FTQ, 1996; Charest, 1999).

Events since the summit seem to confirm this tendency. On the one hand, the PQ continues to uphold competitive nationalism and sell its promise of inclusive development and national consensus. For example, an important restatement of Quebec's economic development policy in 1998 declared that the government pursued three goals: to create '*a competitive economy* capable of staying ahead of competitor economies and of meeting the challenge of becoming a knowledge-based economy'; to create '*a humane and solidaristic economy* which provides the largest possible number of Quebecers with the possibility to participate in the labour market and to maximize their benefits from this participation'; and to ensure sustainable development (Québec, Ministère des Finances, 1998, p.5).[3] On the other hand, despite the rhetoric of partnership and high quality inputs, the report also touted deregulation, cheap energy, low payroll taxes, and an inexpensive skilled labour as major competitive advantages. The promise of a humane economy solely reflects the commitment to active labour market policy and measures to make low-wage work more palatable (Ibid., pp.48-52, 151-6). The invocation of the shared challenge of remaining competitive shields the shift away from associative forms of economic organization and governance towards market-based ones.

This worldview is understandable since it comes from the Ministry of Finance, but it permeates actions elsewhere. For instance, Quebec's decree act, which allowed the Minister of Labour to extend a collective agreement to an entire sector of workers, was changed so that the Minister must now base decisions 'on consideration of criteria which focus on the need to take into account the context of increased international competition'. Considerations of competitiveness have led to the gutting of this system of bargaining coverage (Vallée and Charest, 2001, p.85). Similarly, despite twenty years of union demands for an overhaul to the labour code to protect union representation from subcontracting and to ease the organization of new workplaces (for instance, through multi-employer bargaining), successive governments have refused to act. The PQ finally decided to make modifications, but insisted it would only act where there was consensus. This event clearly illustrated where the power lay in the partnership, as the major business associations refused to make any concessions despite the importance of these changes for the health of their labour 'partner'. The need for a national consensus thus acted as a brake, particularly once the employer associations argued that the freedom to subcontract was necessary for their competitive success. The union federations were of divided opinion over whether or not to support the actual legislation, but in all cases, the result falls far short of initial demands (Conseil du Patronat du Québec, 2000, p.11; CEQ, CSD, CSN, FTQ, 1999; Ministère du Travail, 2000). Again, in these cases, competitiveness is invoked to support movement in a neoliberal direction, and the institutions for representing the social partners tie the labour leadership to this end. Lacking a guiding strategy, the labour leaders have difficulty in elaborating alternatives, particularly when proposed reforms come crowned with Quebec nationalism (Piotte, p.10).

An Alternative Approach?

The labour movement currently appears incapable of jettisoning its strategy of national consensus and social partnership, even as it turns to its disadvantage. Having adopted nationalism in the past as an element of social progress, there is a tendency to hold fast to competitive nationalism's promise of inclusive development, even as concrete gains grow ever thinner. The unions appear to lack an alternative political economy that could challenge the capitalist logic of competitiveness and give a new meaning to the nationalist project. This strategic paralysis has slightly reduced their hegemony over the broader left in Quebec. The women's movement and the community movement, by contrast, are increasingly setting the agenda for an alternative project. While this alternative still presumes that Quebec is the relevant community for building citizenship and solidarity, there is a clearer contestation of the dominant national project's political economy. The modern women's movement in Quebec is closely intertwined with modern Quebec nationalism since they both arose as emancipatory projects in the 1960s, and they both considered building the welfare state as a means towards this emancipation. Competitive nationalism presents particular dilemmas for this movement since it now involves attacks on the welfare state and the instrumentalization of women's groups providing autonomous social services. Yet, at the same time, it opens representation to women's organizations at peak-level summits and on regional development bodies on the grounds of expanding partnership and consultation (Lamoureux, 2001, pp.145-48, 157-59, 169-73).

Nevertheless, having not promoted and invested in the idea of the nation as the site for creating (a progressive) competitiveness, women's groups have found spaces for advancing elements of an alternative political economy. This alternative rose to prominence with the 1995 Bread and Roses March, with its poverty-fighting programme of investment in the social infrastructure (e.g. recognizing, consolidating, and regularizing women's paid and unpaid work in socially useful activities), higher minimum wages, pay equity, social housing, affordable higher education, and the application of minimum work standards to employability-cum-workfare programmes (David and Marcoux, 1995). The role of the women's movement and the community movement in providing an alternative was strengthened during the 1996 Summits. First, their representatives successfully lobbied for a working group on the social economy. They then raised fighting poverty as an essential agenda item. Finally, they walked out of the October Summit when this demand was largely ignored. As a result, the Women's movement inherited the mantle of legitimate leadership in the coalition opposed to the 1996-98 social assistance/workfare reforms (Fédération des femmes du Québec, 1998) and its actions suggest that challenging consensus politics on the basis of an autonomous agenda may open some interesting possibilities.

It is perhaps in engaging with these ideas of solidifying social infrastructure, fighting poverty, building community capacities to plan development and rethinking work-time and work-family responsibilities, that the labour movement will find an exit from the house of mirrors. These projects provide elements of an independent analysis, allowing for a critique of partnership for the simple sake of competitiveness. In the process, they would start to put the dominant nationalist project, of using the nation as a factor of production for high-end development, also into question. Rather than portraying the blossoming of the nation as resulting from the competitiveness of domestic capitalists, this alternative might suggest that increasing social rights and building citizens' democratic capacities contributes to the real strength of the nation.

Conclusion

For the time being, however, Quebec's labour movement remains trapped in competitive nationalism's house of mirrors. After all, the possibilities that the current context offers are quite entrancing. On the one hand, the weakening of the broader national state and the strengthening of regional scales of economic coordination conspire to provide an opening for minority nationalist projects, which often possess a lightly social democratic flavour. On the other hand, contemporary regionally-based development, with its emphasis on trust, association, and networks, holds out the promise of being inclusive, both in terms of stakeholder decision making and in terms of distributing benefits. Putting minority nationalism and regional competitiveness strategies together promises further synergies as the nation reproduces extra-economic elements facilitating high-end production, and regional economic success strengthens identification with the minority nation as the relevant economic unit.

Competitive nationalism becomes a house of mirrors when these optimistic claims distort the reality of shifting balances of power between labour and capital. As capital mobility strengthens the hand of business interests, and as ferocious international competition erodes the niche rents that regional competitiveness strategies seek to capture, the interest in the survival and success of firms will trump labour's demands for more inclusive forms of development. At the same time, the mainstream national project, once a vector for a more solidaristic social model, risks legitimizing a stagnation or roll-back of social development on the grounds of the need for the nation to remain competitive.

As our look at Quebec indicates, there are no easy ways of sorting out these tensions and contradictions. The old answer of a regionally-based progressive competitive strategy fortified by a social democratic nationalist project no longer delivers what it did twenty-years ago, while consensus-based policy-making has become a convenient cover for the PQ's lack of social democratic conviction, as seen in the 1996 Summits and the 2000-01 labour law reform. As competitiveness fails to deliver what it promised to progressives and the labour movement, and as it transforms the national project from being part of a broader social transformation to being a survival strategy in a turbulent global economy, the labour movement may do well to look to an alternative political economy. The efforts of the women's movement and the community movement, and their attempts at building the Quebec nation's political economy on a foundation other than that of competitiveness, would be a promising place to start.

Notes

1 This is indeed another limitation with much of the regional competitiveness literature, where the emphasis on manufacturing prevents the consideration of the regional economy as a territorially defined aggregate where high-end manufacturing play but a small part.

2 My translation.

3 My translation, emphasis in original.

References

Albo, G. (1994), '"Competitive Austerity" and the Impasse of Capitalist Employment Policy', in R. Miliband and L. Panitch, *The Socialist Register 1994*, Merlin, London.

Albo, G. (1997), 'A World Market of Opportunities? Capitalist Obstacles and Left Economic Policy', in L. Panitch, *The Socialist Register 1997*, Fernwood, Halifax.

Amin, A. (1999), 'An Institutionalist Perspective on Regional Economic Development', *International Journal of Urban and Regional Research*, Vol. 23.

Braczyk, H.J. and Heidenreich, M. (1998), 'Regional Governance Structures in a Globalized World', in H. J. Braczyk, P. Cooke and M. Heidenreich, *Regional Innovation Systems: The Role of Governances in a Globalized World*, UCL Press, London.

Bradford, N. (1998), 'Prospects for Associative Governance: Lessons from Ontario, Canada', *Politics and Society*, Vol. 26.

Brown, D. (1998), 'Why is the Nation-State so Vulnerable to Ethnic Nationalism', *Nations and Nationalism*, Vol. 4.

CEQ, CSN, FTQ (1996), *Sommet sur l'économie et l'emploi: Bilan intercentrales*, Montréal, Mimeo, 25 November.

CEQ, CSD, CSN, FTQ (1999), *Réforme du Code du Travail: Demandes de la partie syndicale*, Conseil Consultatif du travail et de la main-d'oeuvre, Québec.

CSN (1991), *Prendre les devants dans l'organisation du travail*, CSN, Montréal.

Chantier sur l'économie et l'emploi (1996), *La relance de l'emploi au Québec: Agir dans la compétivité et la solidarité*, Sommet sur l'économie et l'emploi, (n.p), 10 October.

Charest, J. (1999), 'Le mouvement syndical', in R. Boily, *L'année politique au Québec 1997-1998*, Presses de l'Université de Montréal, Montréal.

Coates, D. (2000), *Models of Capitalism: Growth and Stagnation in the Modern Era*, Polity Press, Cambridge.

Cooke, P. (1997), 'Regions in a Global Economy: The Experiences of Wales and Baden-Württemberg', *Review of International Political Economy*, Vol. 4, pp. 358-64.

David, F. and Marcoux, L. (1995), *Du pain et des roses: Cahier de revendications et guide d'animation*, Marche des femmes contre la pauvreté, Montréal.

Denis, S. (1998), '"De l'apolitisme à la souveraineté": l'action politique de la CSN, essai de synthèse', in Y. Bélanger and R. Comeau, *La CSN: 75 ans d'action syndicale et sociale*, Presses de l'Université du Québec, Sainte-Foy, pp. 140-46.

Gagné, P. and Lefèvre, M. (1993), *L'entreprise à valeur ajoutée: Le modèle québécois*, Publi-Relais, Montréal.

Gagnon, A.G. and Lachapelle, G. (1996), 'Quebec Confronts Canada: Two Competing Societal Projects Searching for Legitimacy', *Publius*, Vol. 26.

Gindin, S. and Robertson, D. (1992), 'Alternatives to Competitiveness', in D. Drache, *Getting on Track: Social Democratic Strategies for Ontario*, McGill-Queen's University Press, Montréal and Kingston.

Guntzel, R.P. (2000), '"Rapprocher les lieux du pouvoir": The Quebec Labour Movement and Quebec Sovereigntism, 1960-2000', *Labour/Le Travail*, Vol. 46.

Hollingsworth J.R. and Boyer, R. (1997), 'Coordination of Economic Actors and Social Systems of Production', in J.R. Hollingsworth and R. Boyer, *Contemporary Capitalism: The Embeddedness of Institutions*, Cambridge University Press, Cambridge.

Hueglin, T.O. (1989), 'Better Small and Beautiful than Big and Ugly? Regionalism, Capitalism and the Postindustrial State', *International Political Science Review*, Vol. 10, No. 3.

Jenson, J. (1995), 'Mapping, Naming and Remembering: Globalization at the End of the Twentieth Century', *Review of International Political Economy*, Vol. 2

Jessop, B. (2000), 'The Crisis of the National Spatio-Temporal Fix and the Tendential Ecological Dominance of Globalizing Capitalism', *International Journal of Urban and Regional Research*, Vol. 29.

Keating, M. (1997a), 'The Political Economy of Regionalism', in M. Keating and J. Laughlin, *The Political Economy of Regionalism*, Frank Cass, London.

Keating, M. (1997b), *Les défis du nationalisme moderne: Québec, Catalogne, Écosse*, Presses de l'Université de Montréal, Montréal.

Keating, M. (1998), *The New Regionalism in Western Europe: Territorial Restructuring and Political Change*, Edward Elgar, Cheltenham.

Knauss, J. (1998), 'Modular Mass Production: High Performance on the Low Road', *Politics & Society*, Vol. 26.

Kuttner, R. (1994), 'Don't Forget the Demand Side,' in D. Miliband, *Reinventing the Left*, Polity Press, Cambridge.

Lamoureux, D. (2001), *L'amère patrie: Féminisme et nationalisme dans le Québec contemporain*, Remue-ménage, Montréal, pp. 145-48, 157-59, 169-73.
Latouche D. (1993), '"Quebec, see under Canada", Quebec Nationalism in the New Global Age', in A. G. Gagnon, *Quebec: State and Society*, 2nd Ed, Nelson, Scarborough.
Latouche, D. (1998), 'Do Regions Make a Difference: The Case of Science and Technology Policies in Quebec', in H. J. Braczyk, P. Cooke and M. Heidenreich, *Regional Innovation Systems: The Role of Governances in a Globalized World*, UCL Press, London.
Lipsig-Mummé, C. (1991), 'Future Conditional: Wars of Position in the Quebec Labour Movement', *Studies in Political Economy*, Vol. 36.
Lovering, J. (1999), 'Theory Led by Policy: The Inadequacies of the "New Regionalism"', Illustrated from the Case of Wales, *International Journal of Urban and Regional Research*, Vol. 23.
Lovering, J. (2001), 'The Coming Regional Crisis (And How to Avoid It)', *Regional Studies*, Vol. 35.
Parti Québécois (1994), *Quebec in a New World: The PQ's Plan for Sovereignty,* Lorimer, Toronto.
Peck, J. and Tickell, A. (1994) 'Searching for a New Institutional Fix: The After-Fordist Crisis and the Global-Level Disorder', in A. Amin, *Post-Fordism: A Reader* Blackwell, Cambridge.
Phillimore, J. (2000), 'The Limits of Supply-Side Social Democracy: Australian Labor, 1983-96', *Politics & Society*, Vol. 28.
Piotte, J.M. (1998), *Du Combat au partenariat*, NotaBene, Montréal.
Québec, Conseil du Patronat du Québec (2000), *Avoir les moyens de ses ambitions pour mener la course: Programme d'action du Conseil du Patronat du Québec,* Conseil du Patronat du Québec, Montréal.
Québec, Fédération des femmes du Québec, (1998), 'La bataille de l'aide sociale: Un bilan provisoire,' Montréal, mimeo, 22 August.
Québec, Ministère des Finances (1998), *Québec objectif emploi: Une stratégie de développement économique créatrice d'emplois,* Finances, Québec.
Québec, Ministère du Travail (2000), *Pour une Code du travail renouvelé: Orientations ministérielles*, Ministère du Travail, Québec.
Rogers, J. and Streeck, W. (1994), 'Productive Solidarities: Economic Strategy and Left Politics', in D. Miliband, *Reinventing the Left*, Policy Press, Cambridge.
Russell, B. (1999), *More with Less: Work Reorganization in the Canadian Mining Industry*, University of Toronto Press, Toronto.
Storper, M. (1997), *The Regional World: Territorial Development in a Global Economy,* Guilford Press, New York.
Tanguay, A.B. (1995), 'Social Democracy on Trial: The Parti Québécois, the Ontario NDP, and the Search for a New Social Contract', in J-P. Beaud and J-G. Prévost, *Late Twentieth Century Social Democracy*, Presses de l'Université du Québec, Sainte-Foy, pp. 177-86.
Vallée, G. and Charest, J. (2001), 'Globalization and the Transformation of State Regulation of Labour: The Case of Recent Amendments to the Quebec Collective Agreement Decrees Act', *International Journal of Comparative Labour Law and Industrial Relations*, Vol. 17.
Vavakova, B. and Wolfe, D. (1999), 'Regional Innovation Policy: Rhône-Alpes and Ontario', *Regional and Federal Studies*, Vol. 9, No. 3.

Wolfe, D. (1992), 'Technology and Trade: Finding the Right Mix', in D. Drache, *Getting on Track: Social Democratic Strategies for Ontario*, McGill-Queen's University Press, Montréal and Kingston.

Wright, E.O. (2000), 'Working-Class Power, Capitalist-Class Interests and Class Compromise', *American Journal of Sociology*, Vol. 105.

Zuege, A. (1999), 'The Chimera of the Third Way', in L. Panitch and C. Leys, *The Socialist Register 2000*, Merlin, London.

Chapter 9

Emerging Transnational Coalitions Around Diamonds and Oil in Civil Conflicts in Africa

J. Andrew Grant, Sandra J. MacLean and Timothy M. Shaw

Introduction

At the beginning of the new century, civil war in the continent of Africa constitutes one of the most serious human security challenges, with global as well as national and international implications. In terms of numbers alone, the problem is extensive; indeed, about half of the wars currently being waged around the world are in Africa.[1] Moreover, the cost of these wars has been astronomical, in national military and financial terms certainly, but more importantly, in terms of lost human lives and livelihoods.

This chapter argues that traditional, state-centric approaches to analysis and practice fail to address adequately either the root causes of these contemporary African conflicts or the various venues though which remediation may occur (Wade, 2001, pp.72-74; *The Economist*, 13 January 2001, p.44). We opt instead for a broader analytical approach that situates the sources of African war within the nexus of deep-seated development difficulties and deficiencies (Duffield, 2001). Here, we draw on material from an emerging literature on the political economy of violence that recognises that conflict in the current context of Africa is not aberrant or irrational, but rather a functional response to the imperatives of underdevelopment, international norms and structures, and neoliberal forces of globalization. As suggested below, this approach needs to be situated in the context of changes within the broader fields of international political economy and development as well as security and peace-keeping studies (Reno, 1998; Reno, 2000, pp.433-459; Stein, 2001, pp.80-95).

The insights that emerge from these analyses present challenges for devising appropriate responses to the conflicts from both African and international agencies. In particular, we contend that states alone cannot sufficiently deal with the underlying causes of conflict, but that new 'mixed actor' coalitions of representatives from states, civil societies, and increasingly, corporations, offer a promising alternative to state-only solutions. Emerging partnerships among the three groups of actors that comprise the governance triad (Shaw and Nyang'oro, 2000, p.274) – states/inter-state organisations, civil societal organisations, and multinational corporations – at the global, regional, national, and local levels should be encouraged, as it is evident that many African states can no longer provide and ensure human security.

In an attempt to highlight the potential of such coalitions, the chapter explores, for reasons of both analysis and praxis, several initiatives that involve state and nonstate actors in a variety of peace-keeping, peace-building or peace-making responses. Specifically, we investigate the cooperative activities of state agencies and nonstate organisations that include domestic and international nongovernmental organisations (NGOs), think-tanks, and the corporate sector in the formation of epistemic communities (Haas, 1992, pp.1-35) and transnational advocacy networks around issue-areas central to African conflicts (Mbabazi, MacLean, and Shaw, 2002, pp.31-47), especially 'blood' diamonds and oil. Our theoretical framework departs from traditional conceptions of epistemic communities associated with work on international regimes by scholars such as Steven Krasner (1983, pp.1-21). Instead, we draw on a cognitivist theory of epistemic community to introduce a broader and more intersubjective concept of 'governance' that emphasises the importance of ideas and knowledge. As well, we rely on a constructivist approach to explore the importance of transnational coalition-building.

The Political Economy of Conflict: National, International, and Global Dimensions

Over the past few years, the body of literature on the political economy of violence has grown steadily (Carbonnier and Fleming, 2000; Keen, 1998). This development has coincided with increasingly sophisticated analyses of resource-fuelled civil conflicts in Africa, particularly in Sierra Leone, the Democratic Republic of the Congo (DRC), Angola, and Sudan. Various scholars, but also increasingly, several NGOs such as Global Witness, Human Rights Watch, Partnership Africa Canada and think-tanks such as the Institute for Security Studies (South Africa) and United Nations bodies have examined the underlying economic factors that contribute to the continuation of civil strife in war-torn regions of Africa (*Conflict Diamonds*, 2000; *A Crude Awakening*, 1999; *Angola Unravels*, 1999; *Rough Trade*, 1998; Cilliers and Dietrich, 2000; Smillie, Gberie and Hazleton, 2000; Field, 2000).

Most analyses from a political economy of violence perspective point to globalization forces as having either eroded or altered the policy-making capacity of states. Clearly, the nature and extent of globalization are debatable. But, for developing countries in particular, neoliberal policies associated with economic globalization challenge governments' ability to provide public goods, such as domestic security. Philip Cerny explains that:

Use quote

> Globalization is creating a growing range of complex challenges to the autonomous policy-making capacity, authority and legitimacy of nation-states, while a new security dilemma is challenging the ability of states and of the states system to provide both international and domestic security as a public good (Cerny, 1998, p.36).

Within this changed security environment, elites in weak states are able 'to pursue their economic agendas through trade, investment, and migration ties, both legal and illegal, to neighbouring states and more distant, industrialized economies' (Berdal and Malone, 2000a, p.3). Indeed, globalization has increased the 'greed factor' in intrastate conflict as organized crime networks and mafia-type guerrilla groups are increasingly able to establish global connections linking both formal and informal sectors. For example, extensive trade routes have been established over the past decade to smuggle diamonds from rebel groups, such as Sierra Leone's Revolutionary United Front (RUF) through Liberia, and *União Nacional para a Independência Total de Angola* (UNITA) through the DRC, the Republic of Congo (ROC), Togo, Burkina Faso, and other states and onto world markets. Now, in the civil wars of the post-Cold War era, rebel groups as well as governments fight for control of airports, sea ports, roads, rivers, telecommunication facilities, mines and agricultural areas as these transit points for goods provide both direct revenue to the groups that export various goods and indirect revenue through taxes, tolls, and other fees.[2]

Given the complicated state and nonstate relations as well as the inter-state dynamics, the application of the term 'civil war' to these situations may not be appropriate. Although the term continues to be used, it denotes a conflict within national boundaries, whereas most, if not all, of Africa's recent conflicts have important regional dimensions. Ian Smillie *et al* point out, for instance, that Liberia has been notorious in its support of the RUF rebels in the Sierra Leonean civil war (Smillie, Gberie, and Hazleton). And, in March 2000, a UN commission, chaired by then-Canadian ambassador Robert Fowler, published a report containing the names of individuals and states accused of disregarding UN sanctions levied against UNITA. The report identifies the presidents of Togo and Burkina Faso as major purchasers of UNITA's diamonds. The report also cites the governments of Rwanda, Zambia, Côte d'Ivoire, and Gabon as countries whose officials have various illicit ties to the UNITA rebels ('Shaming the Sanctions-Busters, 2000, p.46; United Nations, 2000, which was established pursuant to Security Council Resolution 864 (1993) and Resolution 1237 (1999)). Similarly, the April 2001 UN Security Council expert panel on the DRC (United Nations, 2001) established that the mineral and timber resources in the country have been exploited by the occupying forces of Burundi, Rwanda and Uganda, while 'allied' states – Zimbabwe, Angola, and Namibia – received a variety of mineral rights from the DRC government in return for their military support of the late Laurent Kabila's regime.

The regional links surrounding trade in minerals that fuel recent African wars are matched by broader inter- or trans-national connections. The diamond industry estimates that 'conflict diamonds' or 'blood diamonds' represent approximately four per cent of all diamonds on the global market. This contrasts with estimates by human rights NGOs that place the figure around 15 per cent. Regardless of the precise proportion of conflict diamonds that comprise the US$ 7 billion-per-year global diamond industry, the human cost of 'blood' diamonds is staggering. According to various estimates, the international trade in conflict diamonds has funded wars resulting in the death of approximately four million Africans and the displacement of six million more (Hall, 2001).

Taken together, these factors point to the need for a political economy of violence approach to understand the nature of, and rationale behind, the current civil wars in Africa. While recognising that greed certainly is manifested in the current crises, this analytical approach transcends a crude 'politics of greed' explanation that situates the source of these conflicts in venal leadership. Rather, it recognises that contemporary African conflict results from the complex mixture of international and global political economies with particularly African forms of statehood, political culture, and economy. The result is a political environment and structure that allows African government and military leaders to use the weakness of their states in conjunction with the international convention of sovereignty to extract resources for personalistic gain. In many African cases, conflict may actually enhance opportunities to profit from these circumstances.

This appears to be true of the four cases of Sierra Leone, the DRC, Angola, and Sudan. Similar regional and international dynamics characterize the 'civil' wars in each of these countries and the extraction of minerals has been at the heart of the political economies of violence that have emerged. However, there are interesting variations among these countries in terms of different interests, relations and modes of extraction.

Sierra Leone

Sierra Leone's civil war began in 1991 when rebel leader Foday Sankoh led his lightly-armed RUF forces into the country from neighbouring Liberia. Since then, Liberian President Charles Taylor has supported the RUF by training new conscripts, allowing the rebel group to maintain rear bases within its borders, and most importantly, by providing weapons and fuel in exchange for diamonds originating from RUF-controlled parts of Sierra Leone, such as Kono. A brief peace was achieved when the Lomé Agreement was signed between the government and the RUF on 7 July 1999, but despite the UN peacekeeping mission (UNAMSIL) that was installed as a condition of the accord, fighting resumed shortly thereafter. In several instances, peacekeepers were detained and even disarmed. In September 2000, the violence that broke out in the 'Parrot's Beak' region of southern Guinea between various armed factions supported by Liberia, Guinea and Sierra Leone lent a regional complexion to the conflict.

On 7 May 2001, the international community took a significant step to stem one of the major external causes of instability and warfare in Sierra Leone when the UN Security Council levied a variety of sanctions against Liberia.

President Taylor has denied that his government is involved either in supporting the RUF or in trading weapons for diamonds. However, during a two-month grace period, he was unable to demonstrate that he had complied with the Council's demands to stop supporting the RUF through arms-for-diamonds trading. Thus, under UN Security Council Resolution 1343, the importation of rough diamond from Liberia was prohibited. As well, a travel ban was imposed on senior government officials and their spouses and an arms embargo which had been imposed earlier on Liberia was extended. Currently, relative calm has returned to Sierra Leone, largely due to the presence of over 17,000 UNAMSIL military personnel. With the assistance of the UN and others, presidential and parliamentary elections will be held in Sierra Leone in May 2002.

The Democratic Republic of Congo (DRC)

A tentative peace currently exists in much of the DRC also, and the military forces of five countries have begun to withdraw from the civil war that has raged from the mid-1990s. The opposing sides consist of Angola, Namibia, and Zimbabwe that supported the late Laurent Kabila's governing regime, now headed by his son Joseph, while Rwanda and Uganda have supported separate sets of anti-Kabila rebel groups. The current attempts to end the conflict are through the reinvigorated Lusaka Agreement, signed originally in July 1999. Peace was never really established, even briefly, after the accord was signed and, as tensions remain high with the new round of negotiations, it remains to be seen whether sustainable peace can be achieved.

The costs in terms of people and resources from the relatively short war are astronomical as was pointed out by *The Report of the Panel of Experts on the Illegal Exploitation of Natural Resources and Other Forms of Wealth of the Democratic Republic of the Congo* (2001). This report was established to investigate charges of the illicit mining of precious minerals such as diamonds, gold, cobalt, and coltran, as well as other natural resources such as tropical timber and endangered animal species. It notes that the countries are involved in the DRC for a mix of reasons: mostly, ostensibly, and to some extent legitimately, to protect national interests, but in all cases, almost certainly for leaders' personalistic gain. Rwanda's officially-stated reason for being involved was to capture the perpetrators of the 1994 genocide; also, like Uganda, it has cited concerns about the security of its border with the DRC. Angola's participation in the DRC civil war has enabled the government to attack the rear bases of its long-time foe, UNITA. Zimbabwe's official reason for entering the war was to help protect the sovereignty of a neighbouring state. However, as the UN Report makes very clear, one of the main reasons why all of these countries are involved is to create opportunities for elite groups to plunder the DRC's rich resources. Indeed, prospects for economic gain appear to the only logical reason for involvement by countries such as Zimbabwe and Namibia ('Defence Defends Congo Kinshasa Mine', 2001).[3]

Angola

If the civil war in Sierra Leone demonstrates the brutality and the DRC the level of rapaciousness that may feature in Africa's political economies of violence, the war in Angola, on-going for over a quarter of a century, demonstrates how intractable these conflicts can be. As in the DRC, minerals have fuelled Angola's war. While the government has used oil revenues to support their military, alluvial diamond mining has provided the Angolan rebel faction, UNITA, with a lucrative source of income. The mode of extraction is distinctive to, and relevant for, the type of war being fought. Alluvial mining is especially suitable for a rebel movement because it does not require much in the way of skill, expensive tools, or machinery. Hence, in addition to civilian diggers (known as *garimpeiros*), rebels are also known to participate in alluvial diamond mining. While underground diamond deposits (known as kimberlite pipes) do exist in Angola, the extraction of these diamonds necessitates a great deal of investment in order to purchase specialized equipment and employ skilled technicians. UNITA's 'transient' civil war campaign has prevented the rebel group from engaging in kimberlite diamond mining.

The lucrative nature of UNITA's diamond mining is illustrated in figure 9.1, below, a composite of estimates by the UN and Global Witness. Aside from a sharp dip in 1995 when UNITA was expelled from some of the diamond-producing areas in north-eastern Angola, the rebel movement earned US$ 600 million to US$ 700 million per year from 1992 to 1997. This graph also shows that UNITA's diamond production has declined recently. The reduction coincides

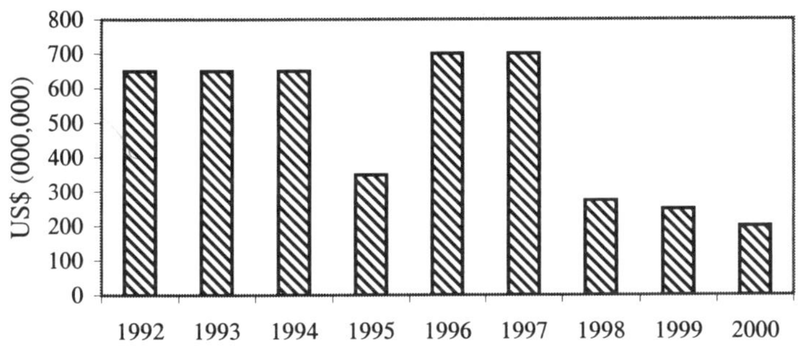

Figure 9.1: UNITA's Income from Diamond Sales, 1992-2000

Source: Estimates by the UN and Global Witness.

with the implementation on 29 October 1997 of UN sanctions on UNITA diamonds and condemnation of any party found purchasing diamonds from the rebel movement, an initiative that had been promoted by the transnational coalition of state and nonstate actors that had organized rapidly but efficiently around the 'blood/conflict diamond' issue.[4]

Sudan

The Sudanese government has been embroiled in a civil war against the Sudanese People's Liberation Army (SPLA) since 1983. The government has attempted to undermine the SPLA in its traditional stronghold in the southern part of the country by deliberately exacerbating ethnic cleavages in the region. Using a campaign of rhetoric, it has fostered a sense of marginalization among the Baggara in the northern and western parts of the country, while placing the blame on the Dinka and Nuer peoples in the south. To back up the rhetoric, the government supplied members of the Baggara with weapons and rudimentary military training, thereby transforming them into one of several ethnically-based militias aligned with the government ('Sudan – Global Trade, Local Impact', 1998).[5] When the newly-armed Baggara attacked the Dinka and Nuer, many members of these groups fled, leaving behind cattle as well as fertile farming and grazing land which their attackers confiscated. The government also benefited from the dislocation of the Dinka and Nuer by gaining control of the area after these groups were removed. Importantly, the land contains significant oil resources.

Since 1999, the relatively high price of oil (see figure 9.2) has enabled the Sudanese government to purchase armaments to further its war effort against rebel groups, as revenues from oil production are estimated at about US$ 500 million per year.[6] The inter-/trans-national connections of this war came to public attention when the Canadian oil company, Talisman Energy, came under criticism for its investments in Sudan, namely its 25 per cent stake in the Greater Nile oil project. Jim Buckee, Talisman's chief executive, has argued that his firm's presence in the country is a means to promote human rights protection; however, several reports, particularly the 'Harker Report', disputes this claim (Harker, 2000; Forcese, 2001, pp.37-56; Field). The Harker Report disclosed that the contract under which Talisman and other oil multinationals operate allows the Sudanese military to use roads and airstrips, such as the Heglig (Hajlij) airstrip, as it sees fit.

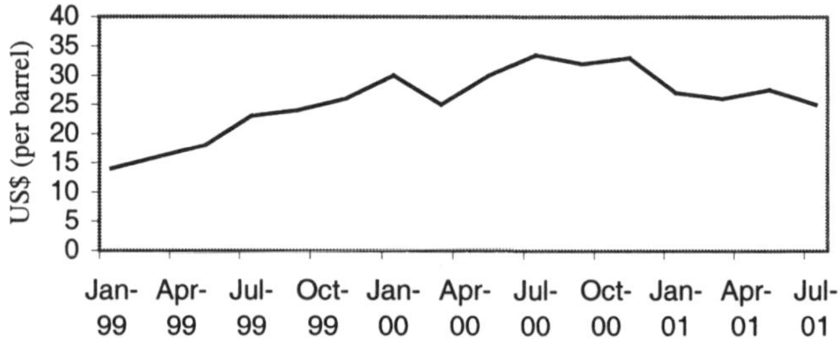

Figure 9.2: Recent Trends in World Oil Prices, 1999-2001

Source: The Economist; Crude Oil North Sea.

Moreover, it is quite clear, according to the Report, that these roads and airstrips had indeed been used by the Sudanese military to launch attacks on the SPLA and to forcibly displace local populations from the region (Harker, p.64).[7]

Human Security and the Political Economy of Violence

These and other civil wars in Africa justify the move toward a human security agenda that places the needs of humans above the interests of states. In the regional conflicts in Central Africa alone, more than a million people have died in the past decade and the recent wars in Western Africa and the Horn have taken the lives of equally large numbers of people. Even where lives are spared, war has been extremely destructive in terms of quality of life: economies have been devastated, governance institutions weakened and social structures strained beyond the ability to maintain the most basic societal requirements of dignity and respect. The debasement of humans that has occurred in all of these conflicts has serious implications for long-term rehabilitation of social fabric. Also, the damage to forests and ecosystems has been devastating, from the destruction that results from the exchange of mortars, rockets, and bullets, to the virtual strip-mining of areas surrounding alluvial diamond beds in Sierra Leone, Angola, and the DRC, and the indiscriminate cutting of rainforests in the DRC and Liberia.

These circumstances alone, however, as brutal as they are, provide insufficient reason to place human need rather than national interest as the basic security concern – they are, after all, conditions that have been common to some degree in all wars. What is different about most recent wars, including the majority of those in Africa, is that civilians have often been the *target* of aggression, and, in extreme cases, victimized by the very officials who had been sworn in as their protectors. The traditional view of security rests on the assumption that giving the state a monopoly on the use of violence protects people and that the measure of individual freedom which is lost is the necessary price to pay for the security of citizens that is guaranteed in exchange. Yet, the structures of governance that have evolved in post-colonial Africa have allowed leaders to use the notion of sovereignty – legitimized by being the most fundamental of international norms – as a vehicle for establishing lucrative rent-seeking arrangements (Clapham, 1996). The character of these arrangements has taken on a decidedly more sinister turn in recent years, in response to forces of globalization, which have contributed to both the downsizing of official economies in Africa and the emergence of informal, covert networks of extraction (MacGaffey and Bazenguissa-Ganga, 2000) that are fuelling most of Africa's current wars (Berdal and Malone, 2000b; Bayart, Ellis, and Hibou, 1999; Chabal and Daloz, 1999; Reno, 1995).

The complex, multidimensional nature of these conflicts that are fuelled, if not necessarily caused, by exploitation provides further justification for rethinking traditional state-centric approaches on security. The events and sequelae of the 11th September 2001 terrorist attacks on New York and

Washington, DC, have highlighted the saliency, not to mention urgency, of the human security approach, that was explicated nearly a decade ago in the United Nations Development Program (UNDP)'s 1994 Human Development Report. By the UNDP definition, a *human security* agenda takes human beings – not states – as the basic security referent, and is concerned with protecting people from unstructured, unanticipated, and unwelcome violence, which may accompany war, but also events such as mass migration or scarcity due to environmental catastrophes or degradation (Nef, 1995). In short, the concept of human security broadens the notion of security agenda beyond concerns for national interest to include issues of economy, food, health, environment, personal and community well-being.

In general, but especially given the conditions surrounding the political economy of violence in Africa, we argue that the notion of security at the beginning of the new century makes sense only if viewed from the lens of human security. And given the complexity and dimensions of human security, its protection requires policy development on several fronts and involving several types of actors. To move toward an agenda for the enhancement of human security in Africa, we stress the importance of considering nonstate players, both in terms of understanding the roles of guerrilla movements, private armies, and mercenaries in the fomentation of war, as well as the potentially positive roles of various NGOs, think-tanks, and some transnational corporations in developing effective global public policy to reduce the sources and fuelling agents of war (Grant, 2000; pp.1-131; Grant and Söderbaum, 2003, forthcoming).

Prospects for Transnational Coalitions around Conflict Diamonds and Oil

Already, NGOs have become recognised as partners to blue berets in myriad peace-support operations (Weiss, 1998). And, NGOs are increasingly engaged in 'peace-building governance', which brings together states and interstate agencies, private companies and civil societies (Mbabazi and Shaw, 2000, pp.187-197). Also, the growing set of think-tanks focusing on conflict, security and peace-keeping (Mekenkamp et al, 1999, pp.435-513) is beginning to address the emerging issue of policy responses to the political economy of violence. A recent proliferation in African think-tanks represents a second wave of such institutions, with a shift in emphasis from initial preoccupations with development, ecology, and gender to a concentration on current concerns like blood diamonds, the debt burden, landmines, small arms, HIV/AIDS, and so on. From the development of epistemic communities, formed around NGOs and think-tanks, both at a local level and with international partners, there are emerging novel forms of 'security communities' concerned about the causes and consequences of conflicts on the continent (Adler and Barnett, 1998).

These new security communities and the mixed-actor coalitions that comprise them have had some significant impacts on policy development. For example, in May 2000, 38 states, NGOs, and representatives from the diamond industry met in Kimberley, South Africa, to devise a system of regulations and safeguards that would prevent the trade of conflict diamonds. Now referred to as the 'Kimberley Process',[8] the movement has gained momentum, first from the optimism that followed from the inaugural gathering, and then as stakeholders ranging from diamond-producing countries to NGOs to industry heavyweights, such as De Beers and the World Diamond Council, came on-board during several subsequent meetings. The involvement of international NGOs such as Global Witness, Fatal Transactions, Human Rights Watch, Partnership Africa Canada, World Vision, and Amnesty International has led to greater public awareness concerning conflict diamonds and their linkage to various African conflicts (Smillie et al; Field). And, in December 2000, the African-led Kimberley Process was bolstered when the UN General Assembly voted unanimously in favour of the protocols to tighten certification standards on diamonds (Resolution 55/56) in order to trace their origins to official sources, rather than rebel groups or third-party states that produce little or no diamonds of their own. The latter group includes countries such as Liberia that are directly involved in conflicts financed by diamonds, but also countries such as Switzerland, which are removed from the conflicts, but benefit from the trade that fuels them. Indeed, reports abound that satchels of diamonds have made their way onto the world market through either the De Beers-controlled Central Selling Organisation (CSO) in London or the *Hoge Raad voor Diamant* (HRD) in Antwerp with customs documentation that indicate Switzerland as their origin – a country that produces no diamonds. These diamonds are imported into Switzerland through various channels, some of which originate in one of the many war-torn regions of the world, particularly in sub-Saharan Africa. After a year of negotiations during a total of thirteen meetings with each one being held in either a diamond-producing country or major trading market – including such major producers as South Africa and Russia – the Kimberley Process endorsed a 'final agreement' in Botswana in November 2001. The Kimberley document will be revised throughout most of 2002, with final meetings set for Canada and Switzerland in March and November 2002, respectively. Participants will focus on technical clarifications, national implementation schemes, and revisions to ensure that the document is compliant with World Trade Organisation regulations. Given the UN Security Council's efforts to impose sanctions on blood diamonds, a strong possibility exists that it will initiate the necessary procedures to transform the Kimberley Agreement into international law by 2003 (Partnership Africa Canada, 2002).

The aforementioned UN Security Council sanctions on Liberia recently received a boost as US President George W. Bush extended Executive Order 13194 (first established by then-President Bill Clinton in January 2001), which prohibits the importation of rough Liberian diamonds into the US. Having the Americans on side is doubly important as the US market represents about 65 per cent of the global demand for diamonds (Silverstein, 2001). Further support from the US comes in the form of the Durbin-DeWine-Feingold bill (Clean Diamonds Act, S2027). The objective of this bill echoes that of the Kimberley Process in that it aims to prohibit the import of diamonds from either illicit sources or states that do not abide by strict international control measures.[9] The Durbin-DeWine-Feingold bill is a companion bill to the Clean Diamonds Trade Act (HR2722), which has been promoted heavily in Congress by Representative Tony P. Hall. In November 2001, a compromise version of the Clean Diamonds Trade Act was passed by the House of Representatives by an overwhelming majority of 408-6. However, the Durbin-DeWine-Feingold companion bill has remained stalled in the Senate. The Bush administration has announced provisional support for domestic legislation on 'clean diamonds', which is contingent upon the establishment of an international agreement on conflict diamonds. Mirroring the Kimberley Process, both bills have benefited from the input of representatives of the diamond industry, such as the World Diamond Council, and NGOs such as the Council and Campaign to Eliminate Conflict Diamonds.

In addition to the findings of the aforementioned Harker Report, pressure on oil companies operating in Sudan has come from an unlikely source. In 2001, the US Congress passed a bill that, among other things, prohibits companies operating in Sudan (most notably petroleum firms) from participating in American capital markets. Upon Presidential approval, the bill – known as the Sudan Peace Act – would bar petroleum companies such as Talisman Energy from trading on the New York Stock Exchange under what is referred to as 'capital market sanctions'. The Sudan Peace Act has remained in limbo following the September 11th terrorist attacks, as the Bush administration has voiced a number of concerns ranging from the US' access to global oil reserves to the implications of what it perceives as political interference in capital markets.

Despite the foot-dragging by the Bush administration, on balance, the aforementioned initiatives are steps in the right direction. And it is largely efforts by mixed-actor coalitions of state and nonstate actors around issues of conflict diamonds and venal oil production, as well as the ongoing negotiations to ban the use of landmines and the recent progress on curbing the illicit trade of small arms that have created the impetus for new policies and new policy directions on security.[10] Indeed, the relatively successful mixed-actor Ottawa Process on landmines may be used as a template for the current efforts on conflict diamonds (with implications for future efforts on conflict oil). Moreover, while the small arms issue is not quite so amenable to the same process, certainly it has been the actions of various nonstate actors in cooperation with state actors that are responsible for much of the progress that has been made to date on this issue.[11] To be sure, state initiatives on issues of security have continuing relevance and certainly there is a case to be made for looking to 'African solutions for African problems' through both multilateral and bilateral initiatives. However, formal, state-formulated and state-administered solutions *alone* are inadequate, as was made evident, for example, by the initial failure of the Lusaka Accord in the DRC, the fragility of negotiations to forge a new agreement for that conflict, and the weak external support for peace initiatives in the region. Such efforts are heavily weighted toward failure as focus is on the cessation of hostilities among state actors, while the sources, fuelling agents and perpetrators of the conflict extend well beyond national and statist interests and boundaries and, in many cases, are the very agents that support the institutionalization of violence for profit.

Conclusion

This essay has argued that tracking the linkages of the multi-level/-sector/-actor nature of conflict in Africa is critical to understanding both the risks to humans and the dimensions of governance that feature in the region's current security dilemmas. The future of security in Africa is contingent upon containing the large and rapid increase in the regional arms market by official actors, such as Uganda and South Africa, but as well the arms trade involves an extensive informal trade in weapons for drugs and/or minerals along global supply chains. The costs to human security of both the formal and informal dimensions of the escalating arms trade are enormous, in terms of revenue diverted from social spending to weaponry, loss of business confidence and foreign investment, deepening rifts between citizens and governing elites, and increased destabilisation of the region. Moreover, the privatization of security in the region – which includes countries such as Zimbabwe 'selling' their troops to the Kabila regimes in the DRC as well as the proliferation in the use of private armies – is a growing phenomenon that undermines human security, especially because of the association with various gangs or mafias that trade illegally in drugs and minerals.

Throughout much of Africa, the structural impediments of outdated or lax legislation, government corruption, lack of resources and infrastructure, ongoing conflicts, and geographically large and porous borders all serve to constrain the ability of countries to effectively monitor and capture sanction-busters and arms traffickers. While the problem of capacity-building in Africa is daunting, the need to address it provides more impetus on like-minded actors to continue their efforts through multi-faceted coalitions and partnerships between states, international organisations, NGOs and think-tanks, and domestic and transnational firms. The dynamic and complex nature of African conflicts also provides the imperative to promulgate creative analyses and policies, which includes the promotion of epistemic communities. Traditional approaches to international political economy tend to overlook informal and illegal economies, which now account for approximately ten to twenty per cent of the world economy, and involve extensive trade in diamonds and small arms. Monographs by NGOs, think-tanks, as well as the Smillie *et al*, Fowler, and Harker reports which highlight the issues of political economy that contribute to the violence, reflect a positive redevelopment and redirection in approaches to security.

This essay represents a contribution to the growing collection of analyses on the 'new realism' of the changing and interrelated international and global political economies (Dunn and Shaw, 2001; Naylor, 1994; Klein, 2000; Cox, 1999, pp.3-28). We are optimistic about the possibilities for peace and stability in Africa, but cautiously so, as the various multi-faceted coalitions on issues such as conflict diamonds and oil must continue to develop and it is yet uncertain that they will. The Kimberly Process has lacked the leadership of an Axworthy, so it may not proceed like the Ottawa Process. Nor can embryonic efforts to highlight the role of oil in civil conflict count on a consumer boycott to spur action in the petroleum industry. While UN- and NGO-sponsored reports continue to cultivate an epistemic community with respect to conflict diamonds and oil, state-led action on this all-important commodity remains tenuous at best. The extreme value of both diamonds and oil also presents a significant challenge to efforts of transnational coalition-building. The physical properties of diamonds make them extremely easy to smuggle, and once cut and polished, it is very difficult to establish their point of origin. Despite the ostensibly altruistic legislation that is under consideration in Washington, it is important to recognise that the impetus for the US sanctions originates from the lobbying efforts of the evangelical right, which frames the civil war in Sudan as one in which the Islamic government in Khartoum is suppressing the Christians in the southern part of the country ('Doing the Right Thing for the Wrong Reasons', 2001). In addition to this rather alarming point, it should be stressed that no major American petroleum companies are currently operating in Sudan. Conversely, Angola provides approximately 10 per cent of US oil imports. Indeed, these uncertainties highlight our position that no single recommendation will solve the problems of human insecurity in Africa. If human security is of paramount concern, new forms of governance that include international organisations, states, civil societal organisations, private firms, and consumers are required to initiate positive change in Africa.

Notes

1 According to the statistics gathered by the Stockholm International Peace Research Institute (SIPRI), seven of 14 major conflicts worldwide took place in Africa in 1999: Algeria, Angola, the Democratic Republic of Congo (DRC), the Republic of Congo (ROC), Eritrea-Ethiopia, Sierra Leone, and Sudan, see: *SIPRI*, 2001.

2 Bribes are also paid which end up in the pockets of one or a small number of individuals in charge of these transit points. Though usually a governmental practice, rebel groups are known to impose and collect taxes on various products. During the Liberian civil war, Charles Taylor's rebels collected taxes on the flow of diamonds through the country.

3 For instance, the Namibian government received the rights to a diamond mine at Tshikapa, located in the southern part of the DRC near the Angolan border, in return for sending in troops to help sustain Laurent Kabila's regime in 1997. A Namibian parastatal company – August 26 Holding Namibia – was then given a contract to oversee the actual operations of the diamond mine from 1999 until 2004, although there are conflicting reports as to whether or not diamond mining has commenced in and around Tshikapa. In 2000, Namibian Minister for Mines and Energy Jesaya Nyamu was quoted as saying that the diamond mine had been in operation for some time, while the Ministry of Defence continues to deny that any mining has taken place, stating that only exploration projects have been carried out thus far.

4 It should be noted, however, that while the sanctions have contributed to the reduced outflow of diamonds from UNITA, political and business elites in Togo and Burkina Faso have continued to purchase UNITA-produced diamonds by way of illicit trade routes through the DRC and other neighbouring countries.

5 Despite the prominence of the main rebel group, the SPLA in the south, the Sudanese government was still able to support ethnically-based militias consisting of the Toposas and Mandaris peoples. Human Rights Watch estimates that over one million casualties have occurred in Sudan since its civil war began in 1983.

6 Amnesty International reports that the Sudanese government allocates most of its budget to military expenditures at approximately 84 billion dinars – an increase of 96 per cent since 1998.

7 Harker's findings have been confirmed by several NGOs operating in Sudan.

8 Another 'diamond summit' was held in London in October 2000, which was much more inter-state in terms of participants. Subsequently, the 'London Process' has not generated nearly the momentum as the 'Kimberley Process', owing to South Africa's boycott of the former (due to discussions of sanctions) and the apprehensive attitude of several nonstate actors, such as Global Witness and De Beers.

9 The full texts of Clean Diamonds Act Bills S2027 and HR2722 are accessible under 'Search, Bill Text 107th Congress', The Legislative Process, U.S. House of Representatives, web page.

10 See, for example, recent issues of *Africa Confidential*, and *Africa Research Bulletin*, available on-line, respectively.

11 A UN global conference on the illicit trade in small arms and light weapons was held in New York on 9-20 July 2001 to work on a 'Programme of Action' to guide efforts to halt the illicit trade in small arms and light weapons. The Protocol Against the Illicit Manufacturing of and Trafficking in Firearms, Their Parts and Components and Ammunition was established and will enter into force after 40 states have ratified the document. However, the US has opposed the Protocol based on the constitutional right of American citizens to bear arms (although US production of and lucrative trade in light weapons is undoubtedly another contributing factor). Various documents are available on the conference website: United Nations Conference on the Illicit Trade in Small Arms and Light Weapons in All Its Aspects, New York, 9-20 July 2001 (A/CONF.192/15).

References

A Crude Awakening: The Role of Oil and Banking Companies in Angola's Civil War and the Plunder of State Assets (1999), Global Witness, London, December.

Adler, E. and Barnett, M. (eds) (1998), *Security Communities*, Cambridge University Press, Cambridge.

Africa Confidential (n.d.), Patrick Smith (ed), London, UK.

Angola Unravels: The Rise and Fall of the Lusaka Peace Process (1999), Human Rights Watch, New York, September.

Bayart, J.F., Ellis, S. and Hibou, B. (1999), *The Criminalization of the State in Africa*, The International African Institute/James Currey & Indiana University Press, Oxford.

Berdal, M. and Malone, D.M. (eds) (2000b), *Greed and Grievance: Economic Agendas in Civil Wars*, Lynne Rienner, Boulder.

Carbonnier, G. and Fleming, S. (eds), (2000), *War, Money and Survival*, International Committee of the Red Cross, Geneva, February.

Cerny, P.G. (1998), 'Neomedievalism, Civil War and the New Security Dilemma: Globalization as a Durable Disorder', *Civil Wars,* Vol. 1, No. 1, Spring.

Chabal, P. and Daloz, J.P. (1999), *Africa Works: Disorder as a Political Instrument,* The International African Institute/James Currey & Indiana University Press, Oxford and Bloomington, Indiana.

Cilliers, J. and Dietrich, C. (eds), (2000), *Angola's War Economy: The Role of Oil and Diamonds*, Institute for Security Studies, Pretoria.

Clapham, C. (1996), *Africa and the International System: The Politics of State Survival*, Cambridge University Press, Cambridge.

Conflict Diamonds: Possibilities for the Identification, Certification and Control of Diamonds (2000), Global Witness, London, June.

Cox, R.W. (1999), 'Civil Society at the Turn of the Millennium: Prospects for an Alternative World Order', *Review of International Studies*, Vol. 25, January, pp. 3-28.

'Defence Defends Congo Kinshasa Mine' (2001), *The Namibian*, 28 February.

'Doing the Right Thing for the Wrong Reasons' (2001), *Globe and Mail,* 20 June.

Duffield, M.R. (2001), *Global Governance and the New World Wars: The Merging of Development and Security*, St. Martin's Press, London.

Dunn, K.C. and Shaw, T.M. (eds) (2001), *Africa's Challenge to International Relations Theory*, Palgrave, London.

Field, S. (2000), *Civil War in Sudan: The Role of the Oil Industry*, Occasional Paper 23, The Institute for Global Dialogue, Braamfontein, South Africa, February.

Forcese, C. (2001), '"Militarized Commerce" in Sudan's Oilfields: Lessons for Canadian Foreign Policy', *Canadian Foreign Policy*, Vol. 8, No. 3, Spring, pp.37-56.

Grant, J.A. (ed) (2000), 'Special Issue: Globalizations/New Regionalisms/Development', *International Insights*, Vol. 15, No. 3, Fall, pp. 1-131

Grant, J.A. and Söderbaum, F. (eds) (2003), *New Regionalisms in Africa*, Ashgate, Aldershot, forthcoming.

Haas, P.M. (1992), 'Introduction: Epistemic Communities and International Policy Coordination', *International Organization*, Vol. 46, Winter, pp. 1-35.

Hall, Tony P. (2001), 'Congressional Leaders Urge Action on Conflict Diamonds', Press Release, U.S. House of Representatives, 3 July.

Harker, J. (2000), *Human Security in Sudan: The Report of a Canadian Assessment Mission*, DFAIT, Ottawa, January.

Keen, D. (1998), *The Economic Functions of Violence in Civil Wars*, Adelphi Paper 320, Oxford University Press for the International Institute of Strategic Studies, Oxford.

Klein, N. (2000), *No Logo: Taking Aim at the Brand Bullies*, A. A. Knopf, Toronto.

Krasner, S.D. (1983), 'Structural Consequences and Regime Consequences: Regimes as Intervening Variables' in S.D. Krasner (ed), *International Regimes,* Cornell University Press, Ithaca, New York, pp. 1-21.

MacGaffey, J. and Bazenguissa-Ganga, R. (2000), *Congo-Paris: Transnational Traders on the Margins of the Law*, The International African Institute/James Currey & Indiana University Press, Oxford and Bloomington, Indiana.

Mbabazi, P. and Shaw, T.M. (2000), 'NGOs and Peace-building in the Great Lakes Region of Africa: States, Civil Societies and Companies in the New Millennium', in D.

Lewis and T. Wallace (eds), *New Roles and Relevance: Development NGOs and the Challenge of Change*, Kumarian, West Hartford, pp. 187-197.

Mbabazi, P., MacLean, S.J., and Shaw, T.M. (2002), 'Governance for Reconstruction in Africa: Challenges for Policy Communities and Coalitions', *Global Networks*, Vol. 2, No. 1, January, pp. 31-47.

Mekenkamp, M., et al, (eds) (1999), 'Directory', *Searching for Peace in Africa: An Overview of Conflict Prevention and Management Activities*, European Platform for Conflict Prevention and Transformation with ACCORD, Utrecht, pp. 435-513.

Naylor, R.T. (1994), *Hot Money and the Politics of Debt*, 2nd Ed, Black Rose, Montréal.

Nef, J. (1995), *Human Security and Mutual Vulnerability: An Exploration into Global Political Economy of Development and Underdevelopment*, IDRC, Ottawa.

'Oil, Diamonds and Danger in Africa' (2001), *The Economist*, Vol. 358, No. 8204, 13 January, p. 44.

Partnership Africa Canada (2002), 'Kimberley Process Working Document,' 20 March.

Reno, W. (1995), *Corruption and State Politics in Sierra Leone*, Cambridge University Press, New York.

Reno, W. (1998), *Warlord Politics and the African State,* Lynne Rienner, Boulder.

Reno, W. (2000), 'Clandestine Economies, Violence and States in Africa', *Journal of International Affairs*, Vol. 53, Spring, pp. 433-459.

Rough Trade: The Role of Companies and Governments in the Angolan Conflict (1998), Global Witness, London, December.

SIPRI (Stockholm International Peace Research Institute) (2001), *Yearbook 2001: Armaments, Disarmament and International Security*, Oxford University Press, Oxford.

'Shaming the Sanctions-Busters' (2000), *The Economist*, Vol. 354, No. 8162, 18 March, p. 46.

Shaw T.M. and Nyang'oro, J.E. (2000), 'African Renaissance in the New Millennium? From Anarchy to Emerging Markets?' in R. Stubbs and G. R. D. Underhill (eds), *Political Economy and the Changing Global Order*, 2nd Ed, Oxford University Press, Toronto.

Silverstein, K. (2001), 'Diamonds of Death', *Nation*, 23 April.

Smillie, I., Gberie, L. and Hazleton, R. (2000), *The Heart of the Matter: Sierra Leone, Diamonds and Human Security*, Partnership Africa Canada, Ottawa.

Stein, N. (2001), 'The De Beers Story: A New Cut on an Old Monopoly', *Fortune*, Vol. 143, March, pp. 80-95.

'Sudan – Global Trade, Local Impact: Arms Transfers to all Sides in the Civil War in Sudan' (1998), Report 10:4A, Human Rights Watch, New York, August.

United Nations Development Programme (1994), *Human Development Report 1994*, Oxford University Press, New York.

United Nations (2000), 'Report of the Panel of Experts on Violations of Security Council Sanctions Against UNITA', S/2000/203.

United Nations (2001), 'Report of the Panel of Experts on the Illegal Exploitation of Natural Resources and Other Forms of Wealth of the Democratic Republic of the Congo', S/2001/357, 12 April.

Wade, R. (2001), 'Winners and Losers', *The Economist*, Vol. 359, No. 8219, 28 April, pp.72-74.

Weiss, T.G. (ed) (1998), *Beyond UN Subcontracting: Task-sharing with Regional Security Arrangements and Service-providing NGOs*, Macmillan, London.

Chapter 10

Foreign Migrant Workers and Civil Society in South Korea: The Search for Power in an Era of Global Turbulence

Timothy C. Lim

Introduction

According to the International Organization of Migration (IOM), there are presently 150 million international migrants worldwide. Of these, about one-third cross national borders specifically to find work. These 50 to 60 million transborder migrant workers constitute only a small percentage of the global workforce of 2.6 billion people. Yet, while the number of transborder or foreign migrant workers is relatively small – even insignificant – from a global perspective, their impact often is not: in many countries, the presence of and need for foreign migrant workers can have far-reaching political, economic and social consequences. This is particularly the case in East Asia, where major 'host' societies, such as Japan, South Korea and Taiwan, have struggled to maintain a strong degree of ethnic homogeneity and cultural insulation in the face of large inflows by outsiders. 'Globalization' and rapid capitalist development, however, have helped to break down the social and political barriers that, for decades (if not centuries), have served to keep foreigners and foreign influence on the outside, or at least partly constrained. At the same time, the increasing porousness or instability of these traditional barriers has not gone unchallenged by national authorities. Indeed, in most East Asian countries, governments continue to impose – or attempt to impose – exclusionary immigration policies designed to keep foreign migrant workers isolated, marginalized, and disempowered. For this reason, foreign migrant workers continue to occupy vulnerable positions throughout the region.

The vulnerability of foreign migrant workers is neither new nor surprising. And there is good reason for this: the economic imperatives that drove, California farmers to exploit and marginalize Chinese and Japanese workers in the late 1800s (or Mexican workers in the 1920s), still drive Japanese, Korean, and Taiwanese capitalists (and their governments) to exploit and marginalize workers from the Philippines, China, Nepal, Bangladesh, Myanmar, Sri Lanka, Vietnam, Pakistan and other poor countries today. The reoccurrence of past patterns, however, does not mean that everything has remained or will remain the same. Quite the contrary. As I argue in this paper, ongoing changes in the global system have helped destabilize historically entrenched patterns of social relations through which certain groups, including foreign migrant workers, are marginalized and subordinated. Today, in other words, subordinate social groups have greater opportunities – or at least different potential – to exercise power in a concrete and meaningful manner. The purpose of this paper is to provide an understanding of the process by which seemingly powerless social groups can take advantage of changes in the global system to challenge and perhaps overturn historically reproduced practices of exploitation and subordination. This is not to say that changes in the global system only offer opportunities for oppressed groups. Of course this is not the case – increased global competition and capital mobility, for instance, has clearly had a profoundly negative impact on even the most powerful of labour organizations, much less largely unorganized and oftentimes ethnically divided groups of foreign workers. Rather, my intention is to discern and highlight the prospects for agency in the face of what has often been portrayed as, the overwhelming structural process of globalization.

To achieve the purposes of this paper, I will focus on the specific case of foreign migrant workers in South Korea. My choice of South Korea is driven by a number of factors, the most important of which is simply that, over the past decade, the position of foreign migrant workers in South Korea has improved substantially. While still relegated to 'difficult, dirty, and dangerous' work (the so-called 3-D jobs), foreign migrant workers have achieved meaningful gains in terms of wages, benefits, and coverage for industrial and job-related accidents, and protection from abusive and exploitative employers. Just as importantly, foreign migrant workers are on the path (albeit a rocky one) toward securing legal recognition from the South Korean government, which would not only guarantee protection of their basic 'human rights', but would also provide them the same rights and legal protections as domestic workers. My choice of South Korea is also driven by the manner in which these changes have come about. As I will discuss in the analysis that follows, the improvement in the position of migrant workers is the product of actions and strategies undertaken by a range of actors, including foreign migrant workers themselves, but also religious and civil organizations in South Korea. My major contention is that the critical element of change for foreign workers in South Korea derives from the linkage that has developed between the workers and a network of domestically based non-governmental organizations (NGOs) in Korea's civil society. It is through this linkage that foreign migrant workers have been able to use certain aspects of globalization to their advantage – such as the globalization of a common discourse on human rights and democracy – while minimizing, or at least moderating, the more negative aspects of global turbulence.

Migration to South Korea and East Asia: An Overview

Once a significant net exporter of labour, South Korea is now a significant destination for and net importer of foreign migrant labour. The reason for this is easy to discern: as with a number of other industrially developed economies in East Asia (e.g., Japan, Singapore, Hong Kong, and Taiwan), South Korea reached a turning point in migration due to changes in the structure of the national economy. Scholars refer to this phenomenon as the migration transition. For South Korea, the migration transition occurred in the late 1980s and is symbolized by the country's hosting of the 1988 Olympic Games. Before 1988, the only 'foreign workers' in Korea were a handful of white collar professionals, artists, and teachers. There were virtually no 'unskilled' or 'low-skilled' foreign workers in Korea's small factories, maritime sector, farms, or construction industries. By 1997, however, the number of unskilled or low-skilled foreign workers had shot up to more than 270,000, the largest percentage of which come from China (and are ethnic Koreans). From the beginning, however, Korea has also attracted workers from the Philippines, Nepal, Bangladesh, Myanmar, Pakistan, Indonesia, and Sri Lanka. More recently, migration to South Korea has become a truly global phenomenon, with workers coming from at least 54 countries, including Nigeria, Iran, India, Vietnam, Uzbekistan, Kazakhstan, Afghanistan, Ghana, Morocco, Egypt, Congo, Algeria, Hungary, Russia, Yugoslavia, Brazil, Peru, and Jamaica.

After reaching a peak in 1997, the number of foreign migrants – including both illegal workers and industrial 'trainees'[1] – declined by almost half, to less than 150,000, by the end of 1998. The main reason for this reversal is obvious: the Asian financial crisis. The Asian crisis, as one observer notes (Varona), forced migrant workers throughout Asia to confront the 'devil and deep blue sea'. In the major sending countries (e.g., the Philippines, Indonesia, Thailand, Sri Lanka, and Bangladesh), the 'devil' was record unemployment, hyperinflation, widespread bankruptcy among businesses, stagflation and so on. In the major receiving countries, on the other hand, migrant workers faced the 'deep blue sea' of forced deportation and 'voluntary repatriation', as the jobs that they typically filled either disappeared or were taken over by native workers. The Asian crisis, in short, created a 'double push', squeezing out and displacing workers in both the sending and receiving countries (Ibid.). In South Korea deportations and voluntary repatriation provide most of the explanation for the short-term reversal of worker migration. Yet, the reversal proved to be short-lived; by 2001, the number of foreign migrants in Korea had exceeded the peak in 1997, reaching roughly 300,000.[2]

The relatively quick recovery of worker migration to South Korea (and elsewhere) needs to be highlighted. For, despite the inevitable up-and-down movements in patterns of migration, the trend is fairly clear: East Asia will likely remain a significant destination for migrant workers for many decades. The reason, as I noted above, stems from the structural changes reflected in the migration transition. This does not mean, however, that foreign workers have become a dominant force in the East Asian economies. Rather, it means that foreign labour fills a void in the domestic industrial structure that could not otherwise be filled. Thus, while accounting for only one to two per cent of the economically active population in most of the East Asian economies (with the exception of Singapore), foreign labour serves a critical, even indispensable, role in key sectors. This is particularly true in South Korea, where among the country's small and medium-sized manufacturing enterprises (SMMEs), labour shortages were a severe and seemingly irresolvable problem before the arrival of foreign migrants.

A quick look at the relevant figures bears this out. Beginning in the mid-1980s, the labour shortage rate for small firms (10-29 employees) grew steadily from 1.50 in 1985 to 7.78 per cent by 1990. For 'unskilled' labour, the shortage rate was even more severe, growing from 4.90 to 20.13 per cent during the same period.[3] Moreover, in certain industrial sectors – such as plastics, electrical machinery, and commercial fishing – the vacancy rate was even higher, reaching upwards of 30 and even 40 per cent ('Influx of Foreign Labor Leads to Harsh Lessons for South Korea Bosses', 1996, p.A-27). Overall, by 1991, there were approximately 222,000 production jobs (of all skill levels) for which domestic workers could not be found (KLI, 1996). Shortly after South Korea opened its borders to foreign migrant workers, however, the vacancy rates in the SMME sector quickly declined. In the case of 'unskilled' labour, for instance, the rate fell by almost half in just one year, from 20.1 to 10.9 per cent. For 'low-skilled' positions, the change was almost as dramatic, going from 10.4 per cent to 6.6 per cent in the same period (Ibid.).

With the onset of the Asian crisis the severity of the labour shortage diminished even further. Yet, significantly, the labour 'shortage' did not completely disappear, even though the number of unemployed Korean workers jumped from 660,000 at the end of 1997 to an estimated 1.8 million by February 1999. Indeed, despite an initial 'crackdown' on foreign migrant workers, which was meant to force them out of South Korea during the early stages of the crisis, the Korean government quickly reversed course – largely at the behest of the Korean Federation of Small Businesses (KFSB) – and began to encourage more foreign workers to enter the country. This is evidenced, in part, by the re-expansion of the industrial trainee program, which is the only officially-sanctioned method of importing industrial workers from abroad to South Korea. Under this program, the number of 'trainees' peaked at 90,369 in 1997, but declined drastically to 48,355 in 1998. By the end of 1999, though, the number had rebounded to 79,000.[4] This reversal contradicted the predictions of Korean policy-makers and business representatives, many of whom believed that the crisis would help permanently 'correct' the country's increasing reliance on foreign workers. As a spokesperson for the KFSB put it during the early stages of the crisis, 'We expect a temporary vacuum in jobs occupied by foreign workers because Koreans are still reluctant to work in the sweatshop sector, known here as the three-D sector – dirty, dangerous and difficult. But after a time the three-D market will be swamped with South Korean applicants' ('South Korea expects mass exodus of foreign workers this year', 1998).

The Political Impact of the IMF Crisis on Foreign Workers

The financial crisis in South Korea had no significant consequences aside from the short-lived exodus of foreign workers. One of the most important political consequences of the crisis was a weakening of basic and hard-won labour benefits and rights for *all* Korean workers. On this point, the complete rewriting of Korea's labour laws regarding layoffs and the hiring of substitute workers was a particularly significant change. Prior to the crisis, layoffs were permitted only under conditions of 'corporate emergency' (i.e., imminent bankruptcy or failure). Moreover, companies were allowed to hire substitute workers, in case of labour disputes, only with other non-striking workers in the same company (Kim and Moon, 2000).[5] As a result of the crisis, however, the law governing layoffs was amended to include cases of merger and acquisition, handover, and restructuring, while the law governing substitute workers was amended to allow for unrestricted hiring for up to two years for professional positions and six months for manual positions. These two revisions not only constituted, as two Korean scholars argue, a fundamental restructuring of the internal dynamics of organized labour, but also created the basis for the massive and rapid increase in unemployment and the concomitant deterioration of the quality of life for most Korean workers during (and following) the crisis. The overall effect was to make the 'marginalization of workers … more pronounced than ever before' (Ibid., p.66).

For foreign migrant workers the Asian crisis helped to negate many of the gains made in the first part of the decade. Korean employers used the crisis as a pretext to return to many past practices of exploitation: non-payment of wages, excessive work hours, no overtime pay, no severance pay, and so on. Yet, the most damaging setback was the scrapping of an initiative for a 'Foreign Worker Employment and Human Rights Protection Law' (FWPL). The FWPL, which was first introduced by a coalition of civic and religious organizations in 1996 was designed to create a legal basis of equality for foreign migrant workers in Korea. While passage of the law was always in doubt, prior to the onset of the Asian crisis, the prospects were fairly good. Indeed, after collecting roughly one million signatures[6] through a nationwide signature campaign, support for the law seemed solid even within the government – both the ruling and opposition parties, as well as key ministries (including the Ministry of Labor), favoured passage of a new law along the lines proposed by Korean NGOs. The Asian crisis, however, effectively destroyed official and public support for the law. More than this, the KFSB used the crisis to argue that existing laws and institutions designed to control foreign migrants be adjusted to better meet the needs of the Korean economy. To make this point, the KFSB even conducted its own 'civil protests' in front of government offices.[7]

The political impact of Asian crisis helps to underscore the continuing vulnerability and weakness of foreign migrant workers in South Korea (and throughout Asia). In this regard, it is important to recognize that the crisis unleashed structural forces over which foreign workers and their social allies could exercise little or no direct control. At the same time, the structural effects of the crisis are not necessarily permanent; as the crisis has subsided, it is likely that new or reconfigured opportunities will emerge. On this point, Rex Varona (the Executive Director for the Asian Migrant Centre) provides a useful perspective. For all its damaging effects, Varona asserts, the Asian crisis provided opportunities for raising consciousness, for better organizing, and for more cohesive collective action. While 'consciousness raising' may not seem like an effective weapon against global processes, it would be wise not to dismiss Varona's assertions out of hand. For, as I discuss in the next section, the ability of foreign workers and Korean NGOs to appeal to an increasing 'global consciousness' regarding human rights and democracy likely played an important role in their early – and fairly successful – efforts to create a more just and equitable working environment in South Korea.

Working for Change and the Politics of Everyday Resistance

Foreign workers make up only a tiny proportion of South Korea's total workforce, yet they play a significant and structurally important role in the country's SMME sector. Occupying a 'structurally important' role in the Korean economy, however, does not mean that foreign migrant workers are in a position of strength; this is true in large part, because the potential supply of foreign workers is virtually unlimited. In other words, if foreign workers already in South Korea demand too much, it is theoretically possible for employers to simple fire them and bring in or hire additional workers from the vast 'global pool' of surplus labour. It is also true because foreign workers in South Korea are generally divided by language, ethnicity and nationality, – historically, the ability to play one group of migrant workers off against another has been a tried-and-true method of disempowerment. Lastly, the capacity of foreign workers to exercise power is limited because migrant work, by its nature, is transitory, thereby making it difficult to sustain a coherent strategy over time.

Despite the apparent weakness in the position of foreign migrants in Korea, a number of significant changes have occurred over the past decade (notwithstanding the backslide during the Asian crisis). One of the most mundane of these changes is also one of the most important to the majority of foreign workers, namely, an increase in price of their labour. This change is apparent both in the cases of legal workers, or technical trainees, and of illegal workers. Trainees, for example, saw their basic wage (or 'allowance') rise from roughly $200-260 a month in 1994 to $772 in 1997 (just before the onset of the Asian crisis), while, for illegal workers, their average monthly wage rose from 300,000 *won* in 1992, to 600,000 *won* in 1994, and to almost 800,000 *won* in 2000 (in some cases, illegal foreign workers are able to earn as much as 1.2 million *won* per month).[8] While one might argue that these wage increases merely reflect the forces of supply and demand, it is important to understand that both the Korean government and the KFSB had attempted to construct an employment system under which wages were to be intentionally depressed and tightly controlled. This effort failed, however, because foreign trainees were unwilling to abide by the conditions imposed upon them. They did this by exercising power through 'everyday acts of resistance', of which the primary one was simply to desert their positions: in 1993, almost 60 per cent of all industrial trainees left their positions without authorization. Significantly, this trend only began to diminish when the government and KFSB agreed to substantially increase the basic 'allowance'. (In October 1997, for example, after the trainee allowance had reached a comparable, although not equal, level to the average wage for 'illegal' workers, the desertion rate dropped to just 16 per cent ('One of Three Imported Foreign Trainees Working Here Illegally', 1997).

The ability to affect an increase in government-mandated wage levels, by itself, is a significant achievement. Still, it did little to address the underlying vulnerability of foreign migrants, much of which derives from the contrived and duplicitous distinction between 'trainees' and 'illegal workers'. For the industrial trainee system, the issue is clear: the system was never meant to provide technical training and instruction; it was, instead, designed to bring foreign workers into Korea in a regulated manner, and to institutionalize a substandard wage-level and substandard treatment. After all, by definition, 'trainees' are not workers and therefore are not entitled to the same wages, benefits, or protections as regular employees. For 'illegal workers', the issue is equally clear: from the very beginning, the majority of undocumented migrant workers in Korea – other than those who deserted their positions as trainees – were essentially given permission to work illegally in the country. One official from the Ministry of Justice so much as admitted this policy in stating, 'As far as we know, the United States also relaxes control on illegal Mexican workers during the orange harvesting season. Afterwards, it repatriates them on the reports of employers. *That could be cited as a model case for maximizing the nation's interest*' (my italics) ('Justice Ministry Postpones Plan to Expel Illegal Foreign Workers', 1998). The tacit permission for foreign migrants to work in South Korea is also reflected in the government's annual offer of 'amnesty' for migrant workers to leave the country without penalty. Amnesty offers have typically been offered twice a year, every year, since 1992.[9]

As with the distinction between trainees and workers, the contrived distinction between legal and illegal workers serves an obvious and useful purpose: 'illegal' workers ipso facto have little or no claim to protection under Korean labour laws, to compensation for industrial accidents and injuries, and to other basic rights. It is also easier for employers, the government, and society to justify their subordination and exploitation. For foreign workers, then, increasing the price of their labour was only a first, albeit very important, step. The key question was how more far-reaching changes could be achieved. The answer was found in adopting a more self-conscious, broad-based, and public strategy. The first element of this new strategy was manifested in a series of protests initiated by foreign workers themselves, but strongly aided by one of South Korea's most prominent civic organizations, the Citizens' Coalition for Economic Justice (CCEJ).[10]

Appealing for Change: Local Action in a Global Context

The first significant public protest by foreign workers occurred in 1994, when a group of 14 migrants from Bangladesh, Nepal, the Philippines, and Ethiopia staged a sit-in at the headquarters of the CCEJ. This demonstration lasted for 29 days and ended when the government (agreed to 'improve the human rights problem of foreign labourers' ('The Abuse of Foreign Laborer's Human Rights', 1994). The government's reference to 'human rights problems' was no accident: in organizing the sit-in, a clear decision was made by the workers and the CCEJ to appeal to the global discourse on human rights as the main basis for their claims. Members of the CCEJ knew that a *peaceful* appeal to 'human rights' would be, perhaps, the most effective strategy for the workers to use. It was not, however, a matter of simply putting words into the mouths of the 14 foreign migrants. It was the migrants themselves who first identified and approached the CCEJ – they were fully aware of the CCEJ's reputation as a progressive, democratic organization, and thus they sought to use the organization's reputation to achieve their own purposes.[11]

This first protest, however, had mixed results. While the government promised to protect *all* foreign workers 'who do not get paid for their work, who are injured at work or who are hit by employers...' ('S. Korea to Treat Foreign Workers Equally', 1995), only the 14 workers involved in the sit-in (as well as six others) received assistance. For the most part the general condition for foreign workers in Korea remained unchanged. Yet, the limited success of this first protest tended to encourage more activism. Thus, less than a year later, in January 1995, a second protest was staged, this time by a group of 13 Nepalese 'trainees' at the Myongdong Cathedral, a common site of non-violent protest. During this very quiet protest, in which the CCEJ also played an important role, the Nepalese workers made only a few public statements. In one joint statement, the workers stated: 'We may be from a poor country and that's why we are working here in Seoul like slaves. *But we have our basic human rights as well*' ('Cardinal Kim Apologizes to Foreign Workers in Seoul', 1995). For the most part, though, their point was made with a series of posters that contained statements (with pictures) such as: 'I lost three fingers on my right hand working in a factory. What will I do for the future?' Or, 'Please don't beat me'. 'We are not slaves'.[12] Despite the passive nature of this protest, it had an almost immediate impact. In fact, after only a few days – and following a public apology to the Nepalese workers by South Korea's Cardinal Stephen Kim – then Prime Minister Lee Hong-Koo ordered a 'thorough study' of the case and of the working conditions of foreign workers more generally ('Cardinal Kim Apologizes').

The sit-in ended when the government, along with the KFSB, agreed to implement measures to protect foreign trainees from beatings and to provide compensation for work-related injuries. The government also agreed to allow technical trainees to retain possession of their passports, to be paid directly, and to set up a special court to handle labour disputes. To be sure, none of these promises ended the exploitation and abuse of foreign workers, but they did mark the beginning of far more significant and long-term changes in the status of foreign workers in Korea. Before discussing what these changes were, however, it would be useful first to examine the primary reason that the government so readily agreed to meet the workers' demands for better treatment and more protection.

One of the most important reasons stems from the ability of the foreign migrants (and the CCEJ) to use the global discourse on human rights as a political resource and to use their marginalized status as a powerful ideological weapon. On this point, the ability of the workers to 'humanize' themselves was critical. For, prior to the two protests, foreign workers had been largely perceived as potential threats to the homogeneity and 'harmony' of South Korean society. This is the major reason for the relatively high proportion of ethnic Koreans from China who came to South Korea as migrant workers. This, too, was no accident, but instead was part of deliberate government strategy. The thinking was that as ethnic Koreans, these workers would pose less of a threat to South Korea's tight-knit, homogeneous society than workers from other, more 'alien' cultures. Interestingly, Chinese-Koreans were first portrayed as long lost brethren who should be magnanimously and warmly received into South Korean society. Despite 'blood ties' and an initial sense of cultural affinity, however, the relationship between South Koreans and their 'brothers' from China quickly deteriorated.[13]

It is not difficult to discern why the relationship deteriorated so quickly, namely, the harsh realities of migrant work and the ideals of 'brotherhood' simply did not mix. The contradictory nature of these two forces was well-illustrated by a series of violent and sometimes deadly incidents on Korean fishing vessels. In one notorious case, the captain of a South Korean tuna boat, the *Pescamar 15,* was murdered, along with ten other sailors (including seven Koreans and three Indonesians), after one of the Chinese-Korean crew members complained about harsh working conditions. Moreover, this was not an isolated incident: in 1995 alone, there were at least 125 violent incidents on Korean ships, resulting in the deaths of 12 Korean nationals ('Mutiny on High Seas', 1996). Most of these incidents involved clashes between South Koreans and Chinese-Koreans. The situation became so bad that the South Korean government was compelled to ban all crews in which foreign workers outnumbered native Koreans. The violence that occurred on fishing boats tended to confirm the worst fears Koreans harboured about foreign migrants. In this regard, then, the peaceful and decidedly non-violent nature of the sit-ins in 1994 and 1995 also served as an important symbol, demonstrating in unequivocal terms that foreign workers were victims, rather than threats to Korean society.

In staging peaceful, almost passive sit-ins, the protesters from Nepal and other countries were also purposely playing on the importance South Koreans attached to the country's international image and reputation. That this influenced government policy is fairly clear: time and time again, government officials and leading media and business figures have tied the rights of foreign workers to the requirements of living in an increasingly global civil society, where human and labour rights have begun to take centre stage. In 1994, for example, an editorial in the influential *Korea Economic Daily* stated, 'taking advantage of cheap foreign labour [would] hurt our international prestige in terms of human rights' ('Migrant Foreign Workers', 1994). The same sentiment was expressed in an editorial by the *Korea Herald*: 'Some disturbing reports regarding the unfair and inhumane treatment of foreign workers have attracted the concern of international labour organizations ....While this is clearly a moral issue, the unethical practices of some employers reflect poorly on Korea's international reputation' ('Remedy for Alien Workers', 1997).

By itself, relying on threats to tarnish Korea's 'international reputation' has only limited utility. After all, when the spotlight shifts, it is easy for the government and business to avoid actually implementing promised changes. This is what happened after both protests. More than failing to live up to its promises, however, the government actively sought to 'discourage' additional protests by rounding up and then deporting those who participated in the original sit-ins. This tactic certainly had the potential to undermine, if not completely defeat, the broader goals for better treatment and legal protection, but it failed because the workers were not alone in their struggle. From the very beginning, the workers had an important ally within Korean civil society: the CCEJ. Moreover, after the second sit-in (which received broad-based media coverage in South Korea and internationally),[14] a range of labour, religious, and civic organizations (NGOs) suddenly coalesced to actively and publicly support and promote the rights of foreign workers. The almost overnight emergence of this support not only marked the beginning of a strong and enduring linkage between foreign migrant workers and civil society in South Korea, but also offers the best (and, perhaps, only) prospect for achieving long-term and progressive change.

The effectiveness of NGOs in South Korea is tied to the broader process of democratization in Korean society, and especially to changes since 1987. Prior to 1987, civic organizations or NGOs like the CCEJ (which was founded in 1989), did not exist, much less exercise significant influence. By the year 2000, however, there were an estimated 70,000 civic groups in Korea (Narkarmi, 2000). The largest and most active of these organizations have proven to be quite effective in pushing for social, economic and political reforms. One reason for this, argues the Rev. Kyung-Suk Soh (1994), General Secretary of the CCEJ, stems from the ability of NGOs to transcend the class-based divisions that used to characterize South Korean society. Forging links between the middle and 'lower' classes, in other words, has enabled NGOs to develop broad consensus and legitimacy, which has translated into political power.

The link between foreign workers and Korean NGOs is a critical one. It has not only provided foreign migrants with resources they would otherwise not have access to, but it has also, almost automatically, imbued their 'struggle' with an important degree of legitimacy in the eyes of many South Korean citizens. Although this has not necessarily translated into widespread and active popular support, it has helped to limit strong public opposition to the legal gains made by foreign workers.

NGO's = give cause legit

Foreign Workers and Civil Society in South Korea

As I noted above, the CCEJ is not the only Korean NGO involved with foreign migrant workers. According to a survey by the Christian Institute for the Study of Justice and Development, at least 150 civil, religious, and labour organizations in South Korea are presently engaged in improving migrant workers' rights and supporting their interests. Virtually all of these organizations devote the bulk of their efforts to 'labour counselling' – e.g., helping foreign workers collect unpaid wages or severance pay, obtain medical assistance and financial compensation for work-related incidents, receive legal advice, etc. Labour counselling is a vital service that not only has helped thousands of individual workers receive compensation and benefits that would otherwise not have received, but also has slowly, led to broader legal-institutional changes within South Korea. This is no accident. In fact, for the Seoul Archdiocesan Labor Counselling Office, or LCO (the largest counselling centre for foreign workers in Korea), the effort to protect and expand worker rights through the use of existing legislation has long been an explicit strategy, one used effectively in the 1980s when the LCO dealt exclusively with Korean workers.

In the case of foreign migrant workers, the LCO, like the CCEJ, used a 'global' or international strategy.[15] In other words, the LCO appealed, not to domestic labour law, but to international labour standards, with which the Korean government had only recently agreed to comply as a member of the International Labour Organization (which the country joined in 1991). Specifically, the LCO argued that even if foreign workers were in Korea illegally, the fact that they were employed made their work contracts legally binding. In one particularly important case based on this principle, South Korea's supreme court upheld a lower court's decision that declared that all foreign workers, including those working illegally, are entitled to severance benefits, a basic right under Korea's labour law. Specifically, the court ruled that even though a Bangladeshi worker clearly violated immigration-control laws, his employment contract was valid and he was, therefore, entitled to 3.67 million *won* in severance pay ('Illegal Foreign Workers Awarded Severance Pay', 1997). A series of similar court cases, almost all of which were decided in favour of migrant workers, eventually compelled the government to adopt a more general policy position: on 14 October 1998, the Ministry of Labor announced that foreign migrants in Korea illegally would be protected under the Labor Standards Act. According to a ministry spokesperson, the act was amended because '[t]he relevant Supreme Court's judicial precedents regard illegal foreign workers as workers to whom the Labor Standards Act applies ....Accordingly, when employers ...violate the Labor Standards Act against illegal foreign workers, the employers are subject to the same level of punishment as that against domestic workers' ('Illegal Foreign Workers Protected by the Labor Standards Act from Now On', 1998).

The gradual extension of legal protections does not mean that the problems plaguing migrant workers have gone away. Employers continue to withhold payments, to deny responsibility for industrial accidents and injuries, to physically abuse their employees, and so on. Unlike the early 1990s, however, the legal and bureaucratic system is now generally (albeit not entirely) slanted in favour of the migrant workers. In addition, the network NGOs that assist foreign workers has become an indispensable tool for pressing claims against recalcitrant employers and the relevant government agencies. Prior to the development of this network the large majority of workers had little recourse when faced with job-related problems. With over 150 organizations providing free counselling and legal services (including the Lawyers for a Democratic Society, or *Minbyun*, and the Seoul Bar Association), however, migrant workers no longer just need to 'endure' unfair or discriminatory treatment, injury, or abuse.

The result, in practice, has been improvement in rights and protections for the majority of workers. Since the late 1990s, for example, migrant workers who bring claims against their employers for work-related injuries receive fair compensation in most cases – in fact, the LCO, which handles more cases than other any other counselling centre, claims a 100 per cent success rate on this particular issue.[16] Ten years earlier, by contrast, very few industrial accident claims were granted.[17] Just as important, illegal workers who bring claims are not reported to immigration authorities (as they were in the past), but are instead allowed to continue working.

Taken together, the increase in wages and extension of legal rights to foreign workers constitute a dramatic change – a change that clearly came about through the link between the workers and a burgeoning and proactive segment of Korea's civil society. The marginalized and vulnerable status of foreign migrants, however, has yet to be overcome. For, even though domestic labour laws have clearly been extended to cover foreign migrants, the Korean government and the KSFB continue to resist any formal effort to legalize the status of the workers or to do away with the fiction of the industrial 'trainee' system. Until this is done, the rights of workers will remain subject to abuse and arbitrary action by both employers and the government. This is the primary reason why a coalition of NGOs began the push for the Foreign Worker Employment and Human Rights Protection Law, which I briefly discussed above and which I examine in more depth in the remainder of this paper.

From Humanization to Legalization: The Next Challenge

The CCEJ was not the first Korean NGO to take up the cause of foreign worker rights. This honour belongs to the Labor Human Rights Center (LHRC), which was established in 1989 and which first began its work with foreign migrant workers in 1992. The LHRC was also the first organization to suggest the need for a new law.[18] According to the director of the LHRC, Seok-Won Park, the substance of a Foreign Worker Protection Law must include the following provisions: abolition of the trainee system, which unjustly and disingenuously classifies full-fledged workers as 'trainees'; implementation of a work permit system, which would also extend domestic labour rights to all foreign migrant workers; provision of social welfare benefits to foreign workers; and a grant of full amnesty to all foreign migrants currently in Korea 'illegally'.

The initiative of the LHRC was not done in isolation. Instead, the drive for the new law was taken up primarily by the Joint Committee for Migrant Workers in Korea (JCMK), which was established to coordinate the efforts of the various NGOs, including the LHRC, involved in promoting the rights of foreign migrant workers. As I noted above, the first attempt by the JCMK – which began with ten member organizations in 1995, but has since grown to 27 – failed to produce a new law. Despite this initial failure, the JCMK continued its efforts: in March 2000, the JCMK published a booklet entitled, *The Report on Oppressed Human Rights of the Migrant Trainee Workers*, which the JCMK sent directly to South Korea's current president and former human rights activist Kim Dae Jung.[19] Kim's initial response to the report was extremely positive; shortly after receiving the report, Kim ordered both his own party (the Millennium Democratic Party) and Ministry of Labor to study the issue and develop recommendations. Shortly thereafter, the head of the MDP and Ministry of Labor announced that the government would, in fact, enact a law to abolish the trainee system and legalize migrant work in Korea ('New Employment Scheme for Foreign Workers to be Introduced', 2000). The proposal was quite close to the proposal put forth by the JCMK. The new law was set to take effect in July 2001, but was later postponed until 2002.

The postponement proved prophetic, as the MDP announced in January 2001 that the new law would be shelved indefinitely ('MDP Shelves Introduction of Work Permit System', 2001). It is not clear why the MDP suddenly shifted its position, but constant pressure by the KFSB no doubt played a role. In addition, the timing of the MDP's announcement came almost immediately after Kim Dae Jung was awarded the Nobel Peace Prize. Sceptics of the president surmise that his support of the law promoting the 'human rights' of migrant workers was nothing more than a calculated effort to increase his chances to win the Nobel Prize. There may be some truth to this charge, since the shift was so abrupt, and since other progressive changes promoted by Kim were also abandoned around the same time. Whatever the case, the near-passage of a law abolishing the trainee system and establishing a 'guest worker' or work permit system was significant because it has established a much stronger foundation of legitimacy for the protection and promotion of foreign migrant worker rights in South Korea. It has established, moreover, the claim that the current system, by the government's own admission, violates the human rights of workers. Korean NGOs and foreign workers, therefore, are now better positioned to use the discourse on human rights as a political resource. They will need, however, to continue to look for the best opportunities under which to employ this resource. Fortunately, there are likely to be many, including South Korea's co-hosting of the 2002 World Cup.

Conclusion

The vulnerability and subordination of marginalized social groups is often taken for granted. In an era of neoliberal globalization there is a tendency to assume that the ability to exercise agency has become even weaker, if not entirely non-existent, for those groups at the bottom of the socio-economic ladder. Yet, this does not have to be the case: as the experience of foreign migrant workers in South Korea shows, a marginalized and seemingly powerless social group can, under certain conditions, effectively challenge historically entrenched practices of exploitation and subordination. Understanding how this has been accomplished is important, if only because transnational labour migration is an inexorable social process that is likely to grow more significant over time. It is also, as Stephen Castles puts it, likely to lead to 'some degree of permanent settlement in Asian recruiting nations ...' (Makabenta, 1994). In South Korea this is already beginning to happen. According to those who work closely with foreign migrant workers, not only are workers staying longer (in many cases, as long as eight or nine years), but also they are marrying South Koreans, having children, and beginning to raise their families in Korean society.

This is creating a whole set of new issues, which are already a focus of attention among the network of Korean NGOs involved in promoting the rights of migrant workers. Some of these issues are quite practical in nature – e.g., educational opportunities for the children of long-term but 'illegal' migrant workers – and some issues involve complex questions of national identity, citizenship, and culture. This paper is just one step toward building the foundation of knowledge necessary to adequately address these emerging issues.

Notes

1 In the first 'official' effort to deal with the need to import foreign workers, the South Korean government, together with the Korean Federation of Small Businesses, devised an Industrial Trainee system. This system, which was clearly patterned after a similar system established in Japan, was ostensibly meant to provide technical training to workers from developing countries. I discuss this in more detail elsewhere, see Lim (1999).

2 The figures in this paragraph are drawn from *Migration News* (various dates), available on-line.

3 Figures cited are from Korea Labor Institute (KLI), 1996.

4 The figures for 1997 and 1999 are from the Korea National Statistical Office (KNSO), 2000, p. 188; the figure for 1998 is from 'Justice Ministry Says Number of Illegal Aliens Rise', 1999.

5 These rules on layoffs and substitute hiring had only been passed shortly before the onset of the crisis, on 10 March 1997. Prior to this revision, layoffs were

generally handled on a case-by-case basis in the courts, while substitute hiring was prohibited.

6 Interview with Seong-Guen Ahn, Coordinator for the Joint Committee for Migrant Workers in Korea (JCMK), 26 June 2001. I was not able, however, to independently confirm the figure of one million signatures.

7 Interview with Seong-Guen Ahn.

8 The figure of 1.2 million *won* is based on interviews with anonymous foreign workers in South Korea during 14-26 June 2001.

9 Interview with Fr. Jack Trisolini, Director, Labor Pastoral Center Archdiocese of Seoul, 19 June 2001.

10 In an annual survey conducted by the *Sisa Journal*, a well-regarded weekly journal in Korea, the CCEJ was ranked as the most influential organization in South Korea. This put the CCEJ above the Federation of Korean Industries (FKI), which is comprised of the countries largest and most powerful business groups, *Sisa Journal*, 21 October 1993.

11 Interview with Jung-Hee We, Director of the Buddhist Coalition for Economic Justice, 21 June 2001.

12 Based on personal observation and translation by author.

13 I discuss this issue in more detail elsewhere, see Lim (1996).

14 The CCEJ played an instrumental role in making sure the protest received broad, and generally sympathetic, media coverage by calling press conferences and directly contacting reporters to make sure the protest was covered from the perspective of the workers (interview with Jung-Hee We).

15 Information about LCO activities is based on interview with Fr. Trisolini, Sr. Josephina Soon Ok Cheong, and Benedict Choe, all of the Labor Pastoral Center, on 19 June 2001.

16 Benedict Choe, General Secretary of the LCO, gave this figure to me. Among the other advocates for foreign workers whom I interviewed, however, none claimed a similar success rate, but all were unequivocal that the general conditions had improved significantly over the years.

17 The Korean government provided industrial accident compensation to foreign workers until mid-1990, before migrants began to arrive in significant numbers. In August 1990, however, the government revised its policy and denied coverage to all foreign workers. In 1994, foreign workers challenged the revised policy in court and won, although compensation was limited to companies with more than five employees. In July 2000, however, the law was amended again so that all companies, regardless of size, are required to provide industrial accident insurance (interview with Sr. Josephina Cheong and Benedict Choe).

18 Interview with Seok-Won Park, Director of the Labor Human Rights Center and the Association for Foreign Workers' Human Rights, June 22, 2001.

19 Interview with Seong-Geun Ahn.

References

Christian Institute for the Study of Justice and Development (CISJD) (n.d.), *Directory of NGOs for Migrant Workers in Korea*, CISJD, Seoul.

'Illegal Foreign Workers Awarded Severance Pay' (1997), *Korea Herald*, 8 August.

'Illegal Foreign Workers Protected by the Labor Standards Act from Now On' (1998), Ministry of Labor Press Release, 14 October.

'Influx of Foreign Labor Leads to Harsh Lessons for South Korea Bosses' (1996), *Los Angeles Times*, 10 November, p. A-27.

International Organization for Migration (IOM) (2000), *World Migration Report 2000*, IOM, Geneva.

'Justice Ministry Postpones Plan to Expel Illegal Foreign Workers' (1998), *Korea Herald*, 8 January.

'Justice Ministry Says Number of Illegal Aliens Rise' (1999), *The Korean Times*, 24 January.

Kim, Y.C. and Moon, C.I. (2000), 'Globalization and Workers in South Korea,' in S. S. Kim (ed), *Korea's Globalization*, Cambridge University Press, Cambridge, pp. 54-75.

Korea Labor Institute (KLI) (1996), *Labor Statistics*, KLI, Seoul.

Korea National Statistical Office (KNSO) (2000), *Social Indicators in Korea*, KNSO, Seoul.

Lee, C.W. (n.d.), 'Globalization and Labor Rights: The Case of Korea,' Korea Labor Institute Issue Paper.

Lim, T.C. (1999), 'The Fight For Equal Rights: The Power of Foreign Workers in South Korea,' *Alternatives*, Vol. 24, pp. 329-59.

Makabenta, Leah (1994), 'Asia Pacific Labor: In Denial Over Growing Migrant Labor', *Inter Press Service*, 8 December.

'Migrant Foreign Workers', Editorial, *Korea Economic Daily*, 3 May 1994.

'MDP Shelves Introduction of Work Permit System' (2001), *Korea Times*, 11 January.

'Mutiny on High Seas' (1996), *Korea Times*, 29 August.

Nakarmi, L. (2000), 'The Power of the NGOs: Civic Groups are the New Political Force', *AsiaWeek.Com Magazine*, Vol. 28, No. 5, 11 February.

'New Employment Scheme for Foreign Workers to be Introduced' (2000), *Korea Economic Daily*, 4 September.

'One of Three Imported Foreign Trainees Working Here Illegally' (1997), *Korean Herald*, 2 October.

Park, S.W., Lee, C.K. and Seol, D.H. (1995), 'A Survey of Foreign Workers in Korea 1995', in Korea Research Institute for Workers' Human Rights and Justice, *Policies and Protective Measures Concerning Foreign Migrant Workers*, Friedrich-Ebert-Stiftung.

'Remedy for Alien Workers', Editorial, *Korea Herald*, 3 March 1997.

Republic of Korea, Ministry of Labor (1997), *Employment Forecasting Survey*, Ministry of Labor, Seoul.

Republic of Korea, Ministry of Labor (1998), *Employment Forecasting Survey*, Ministry of Labor, Seoul.

Soh, K.S. (1994), 'The Meaning of "Civil Society" in the Korean Context', *Civil Society*, March-April, pp. 10-13.

'S. Korea to Treat Foreign Workers Equally' (1995), *Reuters World Service*, 7 February.

'South Korea expects mass exodus of foreign workers this year' (1998), *Agence France Presse*, 16 February.

'The Abuse of Foreign Labor's Human Rights' (1994), *Civil Society*, Vol. 1, No. 1, p. 3.

Varona, R. (n.d.), 'A Year After: Surveying the Impact of the Asian Crisis on Migrant Workers', n.p.

Chapter 11

Shaping 'Best Practice'? Union Responses to Lean Production in the North American Automotive Industry

Chris Roberts

Introduction

In the years following the December 1999 protests in Seattle, a worldwide movement has challenged the idea that anonymous forces of globalization are compelling governments everywhere to adopt neoliberal prescriptions. By targeting the corporate interests behind globalization, activists have contested the claim that privatization, deregulation, and economic liberalization are the necessary outcome of technological change or economic laws of nature. Yet the competitive pressure to outsource, downsize, and casualize employment seems a more ineluctable force marching economies towards a homogenous economic future. As market forces drive institutional adjustment everywhere, observers have asked whether intensified competition is leading firms, sectors, and entire economies to converge, willy-nilly, towards a single model of work and employment relations (Streeck, 1996).

The spread of production and employment systems has long been a source of fascination. Antonio Gramsci contemplated the political-economic, cultural, and physiological conditions and consequences of the diffusion of Fordism and 'Americanism' to Europe, while industrial relations specialist Clark Kerr and his colleagues posited a more conventional convergence thesis in the postwar era (Gramsci, 1971, pp.279-318; Rupert, 1995; Kerr, Dunlop, Harbison and Myers, 1960). Contemporary globalization renews this inquiry as downsizing, restructuring, and foreign direct investment reshape the Fordist landscape of employment patterns, labour markets and regional economies (Rubenstein, 1992; Holmes, 1993).

This paper examines the convergence debate through the lens of lean manufacturing in the North American automotive industry, widely considered the new 'one best way' to which all firms must adapt (Freyssenet, Mair, Shimzu, and Volpato, 1998). Just as Japanese competition destabilized North American mass production in the early 1980s, some have argued that the diffusion of lean production practices will lead to a world-wide convergence on 'global best practice', narrowing the competitive gap, restoring balanced trade, curbing the business cycle, and restabilizing the global auto industry (Womack, Jones, and Roos, 1990, pp.250, 253, 256). We argue that neither simple convergence nor stability is likely to result from the diffusion of lean techniques. On the one hand, lean production itself tends to diffuse not as a uniform package, but through incremental change, experimentation, continuous adjustment, and innovation in its social and organizational features, making continued divergence a by-product of the competitive process itself (Rubenstein, 2001). On the other, divergence in work organization and employment systems is reinforced by the resilience of institutions, diverse legislative and regulatory contexts, different firm strategies, and not least, the strength and orientation of trade unions (Elger and Smith, 1994a, p.35; Ruigrok and van Tulder, 1995). As a consequence labour can resist and shape lean production in ways that matter to workers, sustaining an independent role for strong trade unions.

The paper focuses on the experience of the Canadian Auto Workers to suggest that trade unions can continue to play a role in shaping 'best practice' in the industry. The first section describes the lean production process, and its consequences for workers and unions. The second section examines the competitive pressures for the adoption of lean production in the North American industry. The third section looks at the strategy of the Canadian Auto Workers in pursuing an independent union agenda towards lean production, and concluding remarks briefly draw lessons for thinking about convergence.

Lean Production and Its Emissaries

For three decades after World War II, the US automakers (especially the 'Big Three', General Motors, Ford, and Chrysler) pursued a relatively stable and highly profitable strategy of mass production, centring on increasing economies of scale, shop floor Taylorism, and relatively high levels of vertical integration. Sharpening competition from Japanese automakers coinciding with a deep recession in the late 1970s and early 1980s undermined this strategy, leading the auto majors to experiment with elements of the Toyota Production System, including quality circles, just-in-time programs, and statistical process control. However, it was only the experience with Japanese-US joint ventures (such as NUMMI, the GM-Toyota alliance in Fremont, California) and the arrival of Japanese transplants in North America that brought lean production as a system to the Big Three's North American plants in the 1990s. By the late 1980s, Japanese firms were building cars with American workers (some unionized, and sometimes in plants recently shuttered by US automakers) that were on a par in price and quality with those produced in Japan, suggesting the Toyota Production System could be transplanted to North American after all (Dassbach, 1996).

At the time, lean production was commonly believed to promise flexible and cooperative teams of multi-skilled workers, given expanded powers to problem-solve and identify efficiency gains within a less-hierarchical management structure. This understanding explained the more starry-eyed pronouncements of lean production as not merely 'a superior way for humans to make things', but one that 'provides more challenging and fulfilling work for employees at every level, from the factory to headquarters' (Womack et al., p.225). With rapid technological advance and shifting demand, mass production's 'job-control' focus was believed to stand in the way of flexible production and harnessing workers' knowledge and capacities to analyze, problem-solve, and actively participate in cost reduction (Adler, 1995).

A decade later, lean production emerges more clearly as a mass-production system retaining at its core the assembly line, time-and-motion study, and standardized job design. Lean production accomplishes high-volume output flexibly and with a high level of quality, not by entrusting workers with greater control so much as by means of standardizing jobs, and by recruiting workers themselves more systematically in continuously increasing production efficiency (Rinehart, Huxley and Robertson, 1997). The goal of the system is to reduce costs by minimizing resources, including labour-time, and especially, non value-added labour-time (or 'waste', defined as excess inventory, idle time, unnecessary movement, and indirect labour performed off-line). Production is reorganized on a 'pull' rather than 'push' basis, establishing a flow of production in which components are produced and delivered exactly when needed, in the exact quantity needed. Buffers and slack in the production process are eliminated (including inventories, stockpiles, and relief workers) as a means of eliminating 'waste' and revealing product defects immediately, with the goal of removing line imbalances and establishing a smooth, balanced and tightly-controlled production flow (Ibid., chapter 3; Moody, 1997, pp.87-8).

Jobs are redesigned to increase the portion of work-cycle time spent in value-adding effort. This is achieved through shorter work cycles, permitting more tightly-loaded jobs and more repetitive motions within the cycle (International Metalworkers Federation, 2001, pp.9-10). Through a process of continually 'stressing' the production process by reducing staffing levels, speeding-up production, and over-loading jobs, the line can continually be re-balanced and adjusted to a more intense pace of production (Moody, p.87; Parker and Slaughter, 1988).

The greater flexibility required to continuously cut costs is made possible by functional, numerical, and work-schedule flexibility, in the form of outsourcing, work teams, cross-training, and job rotation (Moody, p.95). Management substitutes the buffers of more flexible work schedules and overtime for hiring new staff to respond to market fluctuations; shift work, overtime, and even non-standard and temporary work schedules are needed for high utilization of plant and machinery.

Whereas traditional Taylorist management jealously guarded production information, workers in lean production are surrounded by cost-accounting data in an effort to shift 'from strictly top-down management driven processes aimed at lowering unit labour costs, to forms of work organization designed to get workers themselves to participate' in cost reduction (Blum, 1998, pp.54-5). Job definitions are more expansive, and include a variety of tasks complementing a flatter managerial hierarchy (IMF, 2001, pp.8-9). Cross-training is made possible by consolidated job classifications and the removal of job demarcations; widening the range of tasks skilled workers are trained for makes the skilled trades more interchangeable and flexible, even though many skilled tasks are likely to be specific to the firm and even the machine. Lower-skilled tasks performed by skilled workers (such as preventative maintenance) are in some cases shifted to the operators themselves, while higher-skilled work (e.g. troubleshooting machinery) is outsourced to outside vendors or shifted into management classifications (Parker, 1998, p.64). Incentives such as compensation, resting on levels of knowledge motivate workers to learn each job performed by their team, increasing flexibility and linking remuneration to individual and company performance.

At the level of the production process as a whole, lean management employs a system of activity-based cost accounting that analyzes and decomposes the production chain, allowing firms to divide up the production flow, reduce capital requirements, and increase profitability by deciding which business units to invest in, which operations to spin-off, and which work to outsource (Blum, pp.54-5). Accordingly, organizational restructuring has centred on identifying 'core competencies' comprised of the profitable and strategic functions of research and design, product development, final assembly, overall quality control, the manufacture of core components, and the overall organization of production, to be shared with first-tier suppliers (van Liemt, 1988, p.4). At the same time, the auto majors have spun off their captive parts manufacturers as independent suppliers (for instance, GM's Delphi and Ford's Visteon), and subassembly work, maintenance, and even management is outsourced or, when done inside the plant, 'insourced' to independent vendors. Increasingly, the vertically-integrated firm is being replaced by a network of firms and subcontractors as the paradigm of business organization (Flynn, Alkire, and Graham, 2001).

Not all ingredients of the lean production package are equally important, however. The primary efficiencies lie in production engineering and work reorganization, rather than its human resource management elements per se (such as teams, quality circles, suggestion programs, and labour-management committees) (Rinehart et al).[1] Moreover, in large part it is structural features like high capacity utilization and the large-scale outsourcing of parts production to low wage suppliers rather than management programs that explain the cost reductions of lean manufacturing (Moody, p.93; Babson, 1995a, p.18). This has important ramifications for the diffusion process, and the possibilities of an enduring, independent role for trade unions in the workplace.

Lean production's more enthusiastic advocates have argued that all firms will be forced to adopt it as 'global best practice' (Womack et al.). As firms have become internationally competitive, benchmarking firm performance against global best practice both within and across industries has become important to instilling continuous improvement towards the fastest, lowest-cost, most flexible, and highest quality production techniques and practices (Moody, p.91; Sklair, 2001, chapter 5).[2]

Globalization and the Diffusion of Lean Production

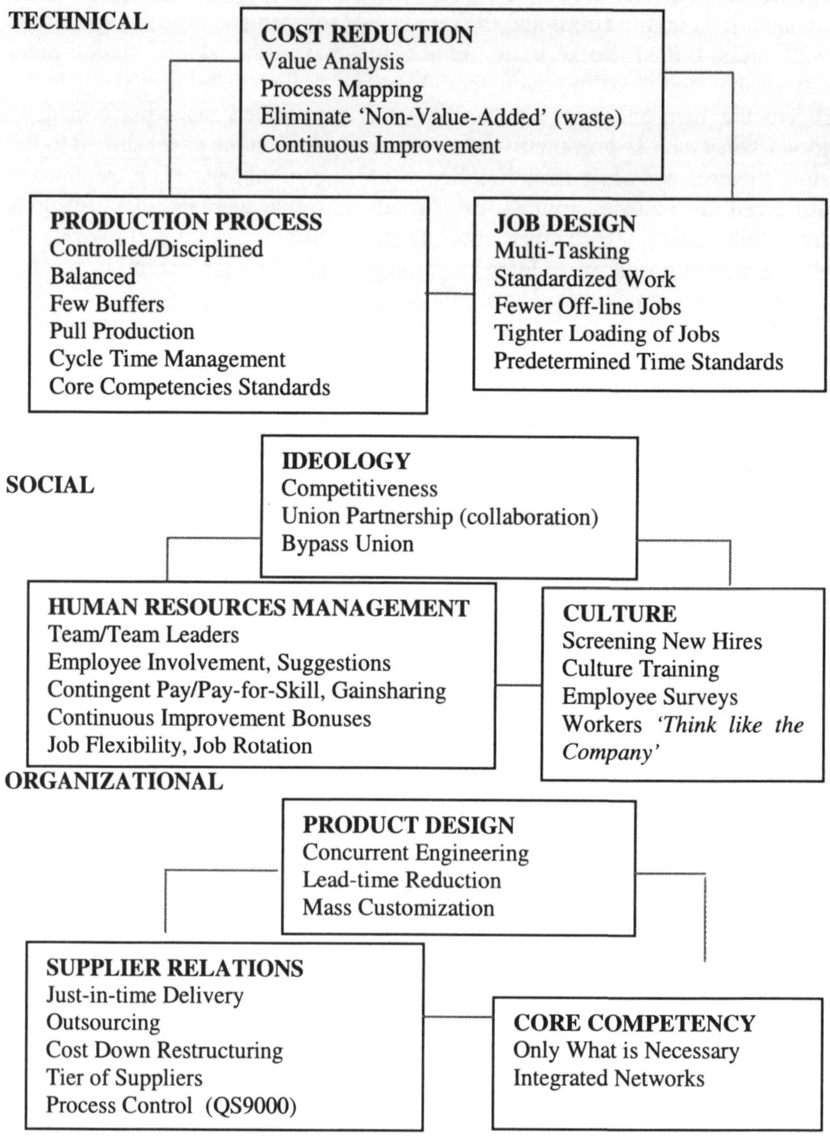

Figure 11.1: Technical, Social and Organizational Dimensions of Lean Production

Source: CAW, and IMF (2001), *Enterprise Restructuring and Work Organisation*, Research Paper, April.

Through the 1990s, more and more firms have adopted elements of lean production, and differences between national industries have become less sharp (Flynn, Alkire and Graham, 2001). Hopes for a progressive alternative to lean production building on craft traditions and genuine empowerment have been shaken, as lean organization has become the industry benchmark. However, no simple convergence on a single model is occurring. Rather, firms continue to develop differently based on their business models, trade union strategies, and the process of competitive adjustment itself.

Despite pressures to converge toward world-wide best practice, two consequences emerge from the primary significance of the manufacturing techniques of lean production. First, lean production's combination (or 'bundle') of elements will vary between firms and countries, as firms continuously seek improvements and innovations in work organization and management techniques in search of a competitive edge (Moody, 1998b, p.182). The varying pace of restructuring and the competitive pursuit of industry leaders is likely to lead not to convergence on a uniform model, but rather continuing divergence and uneven development (Botwinick, 1993). This is ensured by the piecemeal implementation of work intensification and cost minimization, in conjunction with retooling and new investment, and continuous changes resulting from market shifts, internal problems, worker resistance, and the practice of benchmarking.

Second, the lesser importance of the human resource management and ideological dimensions of lean production, compared to the core elements of lean production's organization of production, entails that trade unions can establish a basis from which to 'unbundle' and shape lean production, particularly with respect to work organization, in order to improve the quality of working life. Even as production is increasingly organized according to lean principles, the quality of working life will continue to differ between firms depending, among other things, on the strength and orientation of the union (Lewchuk, Stewart, and Yates , 2001, p.80; Babson, 1995a). Where unions can resist managerial programs integrating workers in the continuous improvement effort, for instance, they can stake out independent positions on work reorganization.

And indeed, greater divergence in auto industry employment relations is evident across countries as well as within them, as firms everywhere have been able to adopt the ingredients of lean production to varying degrees (Katz and Darbishire, 2000; Kochan, Lansbury, and MacDuffie, 1997). The initial thinking about lean production as a single 'package of organizational techniques which can be lifted from its original social and economic context and adopted and applied as a general recipe for enhanced productivity and competitiveness' has proven to be a poor predictor of the actual diffusion process (Elger and Smith, 1994b, p.2; Womack et al.).

Where existing institutions represent structural obstacles to diffusion, for instance in the form of training regimes that resist the confinement of skills to specific firms and workplaces, they are likely to form the basis for alternative visions of how lean production will be implemented (Boyer, Charron, Jurgens and Tolliday, 1998). In addition to 'each company's unique structural position in the automotive industry, together with the historical legacy of labour-management relations and systems of labour control,' trade union strategies matter to producing variation in the intensity, duration, and conditions of work (Lewchuk et al., p. 86).

Lean Production in the North American Auto Industry

Since the North American industry's crisis of 1979-82, intense competition in a slowly growing market has fuelled work reorganization and outsourcing to the southern US and Mexico. Nowhere have the pressures been more evident in the last decade than at General Motors, which has been losing market share steadily since the late 1970s. After pursuing a technology-based strategy of modernization and expansion in the 1980s, and experimenting with the wholesale introduction of labour-management partnerships at its Saturn plant in Springhill, Tennessee, GM has followed a piecemeal but more aggressive approach towards cost reduction in the 1990s (Adler et al., 1997, pp.62-6). GM experimented with lean production at Opel's Eisenach plant in the former East Germany in the early 1990s, circulating managers, engineers, and union leaders through the plant before importing lean techniques into its North American operations (Miller, 2000a). After closing a number of mostly US assembly plants in the early 1990s, GM has implemented its variant of lean production, Synchronous Manufacturing, and QS9000, GM's quality program at its remaining plants.

Historically more vertically integrated than its competitors, GM has followed its rivals in taking advantage of the de-unionization of parts manufacturing in the US (Dillon, 1998; Herzenberg, 1999). Since 1978, union density in the US parts sector has fallen 50 per cent to the point where one-fifth of US auto parts workers are unionized, while the purchasing power of hourly earnings in the sector has fallen 20 per cent (UAW, 2000). Remarkably, once the industry model for extensive union coverage and pattern bargaining, today fewer than half of US auto industry workers are unionized, down from 61 per cent of skilled and production parts and assembly workers at the beginning of the 1990s (UAW, 2001; Miller, 2001). Despite expansion outside of auto, the UAW's membership has fallen from 1,530,000 in 1979 to 702, 000 in 2001, even as employment in US auto has grown slightly since 1978 (Hudson, 2002). Outsourcing is consequently reinforcing a segmented industry structure in the US, generating a pattern of management-dominated employment relations in assembly plants and Tier 1 suppliers, and autocratic management and low-wage employment in Tier 2 and 3 suppliers (Herzenberg, 1996). As assemblers have rationalized their supplier base, the proportion of workers participating in high-productivity manufacturing diminishes.

Pressures for segmentation are likely to intensify with the spread within North America of modular production, which promises to raise outsourcing to new levels. GM first experimented with modular production at its Brazilian 'Blue Macaw' project and its Ramos Arizpe plant in Mexico before introducing it into the United States. Plans to introduce the modular production of small cars in the

US under the codename Project Yellowstone were initially resisted by the UAW, but an accommodation has been reached for a more low-key diffusion of modular production to the United States industry (Moody, 1999, pp.9-10; Miller 2000b ; Chappell, 2001). In place of a large number of suppliers delivering parts to the line where thousands of unionized assemblers assemble the vehicle, a modularized facility would see a smaller number of suppliers deliver 15-20 chunks of the vehicle (modules), each installed as a single unit in final assembly (Slaughter, 1999, pp.24-7; McAlinden, Smith and Swiecki, 1999).[3] Modular production therefore promises cost savings from simplified production and the transfer of highly-paid subassembly work (e.g. chassis and trim department work traditionally performed in-plant) to lower-paid, often non-union module suppliers or systems integrators, located in supplier parks or condominiums adjacent to the assembly plant (Ibid.; Abreu, Beynon and Ramalho, 2000). In the US, the gap between union assembler wages and non-union supplier wages has widened to approximately 95 per cent, and between union and non-union suppliers, 60 per cent (McAlinden et al).[4]

From the early 1980s, the UAW's strategy has been to accept the human resource aspects of the Toyota Production System, including labour-management 'jointness' at GM, lump-sum and profit-sharing payments, teams, consolidation of classifications, and job rotation. Signs of discontent have emerged in 1990s, however. Work intensification and insecurity over the ability to attract new investment sparked local strikes at GM in Flint, Michigan in 1994, a 17-day strike at two Dayton Ohio brake parts plants March 1996, and a two-month strike again at GM's Flint plants in summer of 1998. These skirmishes suggest accumulating grievances over local work conditions, and job insecurity associated with lean production and the movement to Mexico (Slaughter, 1998; Moody, 1998a; Babson, 1998). With the exhaustion of UAW hopes of removing labour costs from competition and stabilizing industry rivalry, competitive pressures on suppliers, not just in the maquiladoras of Northern Mexico or the industry of the American south, increasingly threaten to further undermine the high-wage regions of the Rustbelt themselves. As Kim Moody notes,

> The measure of this 'superior' production system cannot be calculated simply in the hours it takes to assemble a car in some high-tech assembly plant. Its real cost-cutting dynamics must include savings at its margins; for example, in the homes of the poor families in Cleveland, Ohio, who the United Auto Workers discovered twisting plastic nuts onto metal screws hour after hour (Moody, 1998b, pp.184-85).

The Canadian Industry and the CAW

The Canadian Auto Workers union split off from the UAW in the mid-1980s, after the International union embraced wage and work rule concessions, labour-management partnerships, and the principle of competitiveness (Gindin, 1989).

The Canadian union instead adhered to the postwar bargaining goals of an annual improvement factor, COLA, and a policy of wage solidarity, resisting contingent remuneration (profit-sharing, lump-sum payments), two-tier wages, and longer phase-ins for new hires.[5] Since the early 1980s, the union has viewed competitiveness as a constraint rather than a union objective, declining management's collaborative embrace and maintaining that competitiveness goals fuel competition among workers and weakens and dissuades the union from actions that jeopardize firm profitability (Ibid., p.14).

While the Canadian union emerged from an initial rejection of competitiveness and 'jointness' with management, the union has gone on to envisage a role for the union in engaging with and shaping the changing organization of work. In an effort to respond to new technology and forms of work organization in the 1980s, and strengthen the union's role on the shop floor, the CAW formed a work organization department and developed an independent position on work restructuring comparatively early on, rejecting team concept, and urging ergonomic job improvement and worker-centred training instead of job rotation and multi-tasking (CAW, 1990, 1993). The union has combined an emphasis on ideological opposition to competitiveness and alliances with management, with a determination to shape work reorganization in the interests of workers. Nevertheless, it is also pragmatic about local, informal change.

An investment boom, rapid productivity growth, and a two-to-one production to sales ratio have made the Canadian automotive industry a 'success story' over the past decade, although a wave of plant closures and layoffs has recently dampened enthusiasm (Stanford, 2000). Against this backdrop, employers have increasingly introduced lean practices. General Motors of Canada in particular has deepened its outsourcing, with the total GM workforce in Canada falling from 43,000 in 1990 to 29,000 in 1996 (Kumar, 1999, p.158).[6] Hourly-paid unionized employment has fallen from 35,000 to 22,000, mostly through attrition and early retirement. Union resistance to teams and 'jointness' generally has prevented the company from introducing as many elements of lean production's HRM programs as it would like to. Where changes require alterations to the collective agreement, progress has been slow, but where changes occur informally on the shop floor or as a result of new technology, engineering, and work reorganization accompanying lean manufacturing, pursuing a union agenda to improve the quality of working life has been more difficult.

In an attempt to respond to lean production, the union has pursued a strategy of 'engage and change' combining principled resistance to the system's HRM components with a union agenda on work organization. On this basis, the union has tempered a commitment to separate interests with a pragmatic openness to negotiating incremental change where workers can benefit (Holmes and Kumar, 1998). While bargaining work-time reductions and employment security measures in a bid to shield workers from the effects of outsourcing and productivity growth, the union has agreed to other elements that preserve the flexibility of management.

The union views outsourcing as a major challenge, eroding workers' skills reserve, threatening existing apprenticeship structures, increasing the proportion of workers on limited-term contracts, and expanding the range of tasks remaining workers are expected to perform (IMF, p.6). In 1996, the union struck GM for 26 days over the company's attempt to sell its Windsor trim and Oshawa fabrication operations; after briefly occupying the Oshawa plant, the union won 'work ownership' language permitting assemblers to outsource work to independent suppliers so long as the same terms and conditions of work apply to the employees performing the new work. The change to outsourcing language forced companies to defend changes as bringing demonstrable gains in operational or technological efficiencies, as opposed to attempts purely to avoid the collective agreement.

1) A Moratorium on Plant Closings:
'The company will not close or sell any plant, in whole or in part'. This language was bargained in 1996, and lasted for the life of the agreement before being renewed in 1999.
2) No Outsourcing of Major Operations:
'The company will not outsource any major operations'. This includes production as well as subassembly and support activities such as doors, instrument panels, material handling and repair.
3) Protecting Community Employment Levels against Outsourcing:
'There will be no reductions in community employment levels as a result of outsourcing'. The purpose of this language was to protect the employment level in a plant and community against incremental outsourcing of minor operations. The company's right to outsource under specific conditions is recognized, but with a protection for employment levels.
4) Protecting Skilled Trades Work:
This language limits the employer's ability to 'contract out' or to 'contract in' work customarily performed by skilled trades members of the union (tool and die makers, electricians, machinists, etc.).

Figure 11.2: Work Ownership Provisions

Source: CAW and IMF (2001), *Enterprise Restructuring and Work Organisation*, Research Paper, April.

In the 1999 round, the language was improved and updated to include modular production under the work ownership language, as well as changes in company structure and not just plant production. Umbrella language permits companies to introduce modularization, provided the union contract is extended to cover employment in the adjoining firms supplying modules for final assembly. The language in the 1996 agreement was also strengthened by specifying operations identified as 'major outsourcing' and establishing a process to notify the union of decisions to outsource minor tasks and how the company intended to maintain 'community employment levels' (Ibid., p.16.)

As modular production is introduced, the union's strategy is to extend work ownership to independent suppliers, incorporating them into existing bargaining units as the equivalent of 'satellite plants' of the original equipment manufacturers. At the same time, the union has stepped up efforts to organize non-union Tier I suppliers like Magna, a firm with 50 plants and 15,000 employees in Canada (Ibid.). The union bargained a letter from Daimler Chrysler in the 1999 bargaining round requesting Magna to refrain from interfering in the organizing effort underway at its Integram seat-manufacturing plant in Windsor, a move that was important to the successful outcome of the vote.

Counteracting some of the insecurity traditionally associated with downturns, but increasingly extending over the cycle with restructuring and outsourcing, the union has added early retirement incentives and other re-employment and income maintenance programs to its negotiated income security benefits (Ibid., p.22). With productivity growing faster than vehicle sales, the union has also emphasized maintaining overall employment numbers by reducing average hours of work, through arrangements that increase plant utilization rates. (Stanford, p.10). Workers with ten years' seniority currently are eligible for the equivalent of nine weeks annual leave, comprised of three or four long weekends a year (linked to holidays), 52 hours for personal days off, scheduled paid absences from work (two weeks a year), as well as 100 hours of vacation time and 56 hours of Christmas holidays. Thirty-and-out retirement packages for workers with 30 years service reduce hours over an employee's working life as a whole (IMF, p.3).

In addition to more time away from work, assembly plant operators on an eight hour shift can get rest periods at day work of seven minutes per hour, or in plants with three shifts, eight hours pay for seven and one half hours work. However, overtime remains crucial to lean production and highly valued by many workers; the CAW has accordingly had less success in reducing regularly scheduled overtime.

The union has long resisted the HRM aspects of the new employment relations, and has more recently negotiated a union awareness course that challenges the ideological offensive of lean production. While studies confirm that Canadian assembly plants have a lower incidence of the HRM aspects of lean production, the union maintains a commitment to high-quality, productive work. Holmes and Kumar report that compared with plants in the United States, Canadian plants have more job classifications and greater job-control focus, less teamwork, different training arrangements, and no contingent compensation, job rotation, or any form of jointness or partnership with management. However, the incidence of information sharing, consultation, and informal employee involvement in product quality and technology use remains high (Kumar and Holmes, 1998, p.164).

The CAW has been particularly active in pursuing an independent agenda on work reorganization. In bargaining, the union has sought better contract language on job design concerning ergonomics and production standards. In the assembly plants, the union bargained from the company full-time ergonomic and production standards reps, coordinated by full-time, trained union ergonomic reps paid for by the employer. In disputes centring on ergonomics and production standards, the union has sought better language and a faster resolution process for grievances (IMF, p.20). In addition to collective bargaining strategy, the union emphasizes education, including courses on ergonomics and production standards, and has negotiated a four-hour course for every Big Three union member delivered by the union, on company time.

The work organization department has also embarked on the study of stress-related health risks such as hypertension. This complements an earlier study which utilized benchmarking to measure the quality of working life in lean production Ontario assembly plants, developing a union 'best practice' and the potential for international comparisons to combat awkward, badly-designed and over-loaded jobs (CAW, 1996). In the lead-up to the 1999 bargaining round, the union developed a plan for responding to both the firms' lean operating systems and production standards, although differences between plants and chains make this a challenge (CAW, 1999ab). The union's plan is to develop a national strategy establishing safeguards and guidelines for local participation in company operating systems.

Management at GM's Canadian plants has emphasized greater flexibility, improved productivity, and high quality, and work reorganization has involved both formal and informal changes directed at greater flexibility and cost reduction (Kumar, 1999). The union has combined ideological resistance to HRM aspects of lean with a commitment to improving work conditions, but a pragmatic willingness to make changes where they bring improvements (such as three shifts) or do not fundamentally weaken the union. Contrary to the initial expectations around the diffusion of lean production, the CAW experience suggests that participation in lean's HRM aspects is unnecessary to the competitiveness and high-quality performance of lean production that the Canadian industry demonstrates (Rinehart et al). Consequently, Big Three workplace change has been piecemeal, and pragmatically and often informally negotiated.

Tensions are evident in the strategy. Even as the national union has continued to outline a workers' agenda in the workplace, changes continue to be negotiated informally in the plant and at the local level. The union's work on production standards has not eliminated shop floor discontent over the declining quality of working life, as evinced by wildcats at GM Oshawa in October 1999, and in August the following year. Competitive pressures continue to mount, as imports expand their share of the Canadian market and competition with Mexican plants for the US market promises to increase. The liberalization of trade and investment as NAFTA is phased in will further increase competitive pressures across North America. Despite the performance of the Canadian industry in the 1990s and the success of the CAW in maintaining union density in the independent parts sector, the pressures from the low-wage segment of the continental industry pose an ongoing challenge. Nevertheless, the union's strategy for responding to these pressures continues to distinguish the Canadian industry from workplaces organized by the UAW and other unions in the world auto industry.

Conclusion: Competitive Instability, and the Global Convergence of Production Systems

Two decades ago, international competitive pressures played a pivotal role in destabilizing North American mass production and the postwar pattern of union-management relations, ushering in an extended period of dislocation and adjustment. Now perceived as the competitive benchmark of 'best practice' in a growing number of firms and countries, lean production has diffused around the world, the phases of greatest restructuring often coinciding with crises induced by recession.

Despite the hopes of its leading advocates, the diffusion of lean production alone is unlikely to re-establish stability or competitive equilibrium in the industry. The long-term business horizons and more stable patterns of accumulation accompanying the rapid growth after World War II have long been superseded by sharp competition, enterprise restructuring, work intensification, outsourcing, and continued downsizing. The gaping US auto trade deficit, and the recent job cuts in the North American industry and abroad, arise from uneven growth rates, exchange-rate imbalances, and a host of factors intractable to the nostrums of 'best practice' and firm-level flexibility.

The experience of the auto industry suggests that even as 'best practice' diffuses across borders, intense competition and the search for advantage reproduce instability, unevenness, and divergence. Hopes for progressive yet competitive craft-based alternatives to traditional Fordism inspiring earlier criticisms of convergence have since been chastened, as firms everywhere seek cost reductions in shrunken workforces and greater effort from remaining workers. Yet although elements of 'best practice' are spreading everywhere, no homogeneity needs result. Far from the image of firms converging on a single, static 'best practice' through a process of perfect competition, and impeded by 'imperfections' of history, institutions and power, competition between firms itself reproduces disparities and differences in the manner in which work and production is organized.

In the absence of counteracting forces, however, this may simply result in the competitive ratcheting-down of the quality of working life. Until mechanisms emerge to contain competition in the North American auto industry, conceivably in the form of coordinated national bargaining and continental labour standards, greater inequality and instability are likely to accompany the deepening of lean production and the search for spatial advantage in low-wage zones.[7] Yet, even this process in the medium-term tends to spark the re-emergence of worker militancy in new locations, and with it the basis for containing competition on a new scale (Silver, 1997; Cowie, 1999).

The case of the CAW suggests that strong unions can continue to pursue an independent and creative agenda within lean production, even in the absence of industry-wide rules and restrictions on competition. This includes the 'unbundling' and contestation of features of lean management such as team-leader selection, as the CAW demonstrated in a five-week strike against the GM-Suzuki venture

CAMI automotive in late 1992. As the struggle to shift the frontier of control becomes a battle over the seconds contained in each work cycle, an independent position on work reorganization remains centrally important not least to the union's presence in the workplace and its ties to the membership. Nonetheless, the wider social and economic context for the diffusion of lean production do ultimately place limits on the pursuit of a workers' agenda solely at the level of informal negotiations and collective bargaining. Lean production diffuses in no small part through insecurity, and the labour shedding that is the hallmark of lean production continually poses the risk of isolation for remaining employees and their organizations . However, the instabilities accompanying the spread of lean production are likely to continue to provide openings to unions determined to play a role in shaping work and employment systems in the auto industry.

Notes

---

1 Accordingly, the belief that lean production entails job satisfaction and worker empowerment has given way to the argument that it simply demands 'high-involvement' from workers, see Rinehart, 2001.

2 These benchmarks rarely if ever contain worker-centred standards such as safe jobs, meaningful autonomy, and empowerment, and consequently remain 'partial, incomplete and ultimately ideological in nature', see Bowden and Russell, 2000, p. 109.

3 Examples of modules are the rolling chassis (comprising the frame, suspension, brakes and brake lines, tires, fuel system, and steering mechanism) or vehicle cockpit module (instrument cluster and panel, air bags, console, and pedals), see McAlinden et al.

4 The pay gap between all US parts supplier workers and all Big Three employees widened dramatically over the past two decades, from 50 cents an hour in 1978, to $7.20 by 1997, see Slaughter, 1999. Ironically, however, the union wage premium in the US auto sector fell in the 1990s, as non-union firms entered high-paying sectors such as assembly and engine production, and the boom brought up wages in non-unionized auto, see UAW, 2001. In Canada, the gap between assembly and parts sector real hourly wages also doubled in the decade after 1985, see Kumar and Holmes, p.134.

5 This section draws on IMF, 2001.

6 The union agreed to more large-scale changes at its Ste. Therese, Quebec assembly plant in the 1980s in an effort to keep the plant open.

7 For some proposals for continental rules, see Herzenberg, 1996.

References

Abreu, A. Beynon H. and Ramalho, J. (2000), '"The Dream Factory": VW's Modular Production System in Resende, Brazil', *Work, Employment & Society*, Vol. 14, No. 2, pp. 265-82.

Adler, P. (1995), '"Democratic Taylorism": The Toyota Production System at NUMMI,' in S. Babson (ed), *Lean Work: Empowerment and Exploitation in the Global Auto Industry*, Wayne State University Press, Detroit, pp. 207-19.

Adler, P., Kochan, T., MacDuffie, J.P., Pil, F., and Rubenstein, S. (1997), 'United States: Variations on a Theme', in T. Kochan, R. Lansbury, and J. MacDuffie (eds), *After Lean Production: Evolving Employment Practices in the World Auto Industry*, ILR Press, Ithaca, New York, pp. 62-6.

Babson, S. (1995a), 'Lean Production and Labor: Empowerment and Exploitation', in S. Babson (ed), *Lean Work: Empowerment and Exploitation in the Global Auto Industry*, Wayne State University Press, Detroit, pp. 1-37.

Babson, S. (ed) (1995b), *Lean Work: Empowerment and Exploitation in the Global Auto Industry*, Wayne State University Press, Detroit.

Babson, S. (1998), 'The 1998 Flint Strikes', mimeograph.

Blum, R. (1998), 'Investment Strategies and "Leaner" Production in the North American Auto Industry', in H. Juarez Nunez and S. Babson (eds), *Confronting Change: Auto Labor and Lean Production in North America*, Wayne State University, Detroit, Michigan. pp. 51-69.

Botwinick, H. (1993), *Persistent Inequalities*, Princeton University Press, Princeton, New Jersey.

Bowden, B. and Russell, B. (2000), 'Benchmarking, Global Best Practice and Production Norming in the Australian Coal Industry: The Impact of Globalization', in S. McBride and J. Wiseman (eds), *Globalization and Its Discontents*, St. Martin's, New York, pp. 97-110.

Boyer, R., Charron, E., Jurgens U. and Tolliday, S. (eds) (1998), *Between Imitation and Innovation: the Transfer and Hybridization of Productive Models in the International Automobile Industry*, Oxford University Press, London.

CAW (Canadian Auto Workers) (1990), *CAW Statement on the Reorganization of Work*, CAW, North York.

CAW (Canadian Auto Workers) (1993), *Work Reorganization: Responding to Lean Production*, CAW, North York.

CAW (Canadian Auto Workers) (1996), *Working Conditions Study: Benchmarking Auto Assembly Plants*, CAW, North York, May.

CAW (Canadian Auto Workers) (1999a), *Report to Auto Council from the Operating Systems Taskforce*, CAW, North York.

CAW (Canadian Auto Workers) (1999b), *Report to Auto Council from the Production Standards Taskforce*, CAW, North York.

Chappell, L. (2001), 'Nissan's Solution: Modules', *Automotive News,* 5 March, p. 1.

Cowie, J. (1999), *Capital Moves: RCA's Seventy-Year Quest for Cheap Labor*, Cornell University Press, Ithaca, New York.

Dassbach, C. (1996), 'Lean Production, Labor Control, and Post-Fordism in the Japanese Automobile Industry', in W. Green and E. Yanarella (eds), *North American Auto*

Unions in Crisis: Lean Production as Contested Terrain, State University of New York University Press, Albany, pp. 19-40.

Dillon, S. (1998), 'A 20-Year G.M Parts Migration to Mexico', *New York Times*, 24 June, p. D1.

Elger, T. and Smith, C. (1994a), 'Global Japanization? Convergence and Competition in the Organization of the Labour Process', in T. Elger and C. Smith (eds), *Global Japanization? The Transnational Transformation of the Labour Process*, Routledge, London, pp. 31-59.

Elger, T. and Smith, C. (1994b), 'Introduction', in Elger T. and Smith, C. (eds), *Global Japanization? The Transnational Transformation of the Labour Process*, Routledge, London, pp. 1-24.

Flynn, M., Alkire, K. and Graham, D. (2001), *OEM Parts Purchasing: Shifting Strategies*, The Office for the Study of Automotive Transportation, Transportation Research Institute, University of Michigan, January.

Freyssenet, M., Mair, A. Shimzu, K. and Volpato, G. (eds), (1998), *One Best Way? Trajectories and Industrial Models of the World's Automobile Producers*, Oxford University Press, London.

Gindin, S. (1989), 'Breaking Away: The Formation of the Canadian Auto Workers', *Studies in Political Economy*, Vol. 29, pp. 63-89.

Gramsci, A. (1971), *Selections from the Prison Notebooks*, Q. Hoare and G. Nowell Smith (eds), (trans), Lawrence and Wishart, London.

Herzenberg, S. (1996), 'Regulatory Frameworks and Development in the North American Auto Industry', in F. Deyo (ed), *Social Reconstructions of the World Automobile Industry*, St. Martin's, New York, pp. 261-94.

Herzenberg, S. (1999), *Constructive vs. Destructive Competition*, statement before Public Hearing of the U.S. Trade Deficit Review Commission: Trade in Manufacturing, Trade and Environment Issues, Pittsburgh, Pennsylvania, 29 October.

Holmes, J. (1993), 'From Three Industries to One: Towards an Integrated North American Automobile Industry', in M. Appel Molot (ed), *Driving Continentally: National Policies and the North American Auto Industry*, Carleton University Press, Ottawa, pp. 23-61.

Holmes, J. and Kumar, P. (1998), 'Chrysler Canada's Windsor Assembly Plant: Lean Production Through Bargained Incremental Change,' in H. Juarez Nunez and S. Babson (eds), *Confronting Change: Auto Labor and Lean Production in North America*, Wayne State University, Detroit, Michigan, pp. 257-78.

Hudson, M. (2002), 'UAW Gains as Auto Jobs Drop', *Detroit News*, 3 April, p. A1.

IMF (International Metalworkers Federation) (2001), *Enterprise Restructuring and Work Organisation,* Research Paper, April.

Katz, H. and Darbishire, O. (2000), *Converging Divergences: Worldwide Changes in Employment Systems*, Cornell University Press, Ithaca, New York.

Kerr, C., Dunlop, J., Harbison, F. and Myers, C. (1960), *Industrialism and Industrial Man*, Harvard University Press, Cambridge, Massachusetts.

Kochan, T., Lansbury, R. and MacDuffie, J. (eds) (1997), *After Lean Production: Evolving Employment Practices in the World Auto Industry*, ILR Press, Ithaca, New York.

Kumar, P. (1999), 'In Search of Competitive Efficiency: The General Motors of Canada Experience with Restructuring', in A. Verma and R. Chaykowski (eds), *Contract and Commitment*, Industrial Relations Centre, Queen's University Kingston, pp. 37-81.

Kumar, P. and Holmes, J. (1998), 'The Impact of NAFTA on the Auto Industry in Canada', in S. Weintraub and C. Sands (eds), *The North American Auto Industry Under NAFTA*, Centre for Strategic and International Studies, Washington, DC, pp. 92-183.

Lewchuk, W., Stewart, P. and Yates C. (2001), 'Quality of Working Life in the Automobile Industry: A Canada-UK Comparative Study', *New Technology, Work, and Employment*, Vol. 16, No. 2, pp. 72-87.

McAlinden, S., Smith, B. and Swiecki, B. (1999), *The Future of Modular Automotive Systems: Where are the Economic Efficiencies in the Modular Assembly Concept?*, Michigan Automotive Partnership Research Memorandum No. 1, Office for the Study of Automotive Transportation, University of Michigan Transportation Research Institute, November.

Miller, J. (2000a), 'Lessons for the General: GM Borrows From its New American Competitors to Create a New Cadillac Plant in Michigan,' *Automotive News*, 15 May, pp. 8n-d.

Miller, J. (2000b), 'Mexican Modules', *Automotive News*, 5 June, pp. 1.

Miller, J. (2001), 'UAW's Ranks Fall As Economy Sinks', *Detroit News*, 25 April.

Moody, K. (1997), *Workers in a Lean World: Unions in the International Economy*, Verso, London.

Moody, K. (1998a), 'On the Line in Flint', *The Nation*, 13 July, p. 6.

Moody, K. (1998b), review of 'Social Reconstructions of the World Automobile Industry,' *International Labor and Working-Class History*, Vol. 54, Fall, pp. 181-5.

Moody, K. (1999), 'Big Three Win a Modular Future: Contract Hype and Reality', *Against the Current*, November/December, pp. 9-10.

Parker, M. (1998), 'Skilled Work in an Era of Management-By-Stress', *Working USA*, September/October, pp. 56-72.

Parker, M. and Slaughter, J. (1988), 'Management by Stress', *Technology Review*, Vol. 91, No. 7, pp. 36-44.

Rinehart, J. (2001), 'Transcending Taylorism and Fordism? Three Decades of Work Restructuring', in R. Baldoz, C. Koeber and P. Kraft (eds), *The Critical Study of Work: Labor, Technology, and Global Production*, Temple University Press, Philadelphia, PA, pp. 179-85.

Rinehart, J., Huxley, C. and Robertson, D. (1997), *Just Another Car Factory*? *Lean Production and Its Discontents*, ILR Press, Ithaca, New York.

Rubenstein, J. (1992), *The Changing US Auto Industry: A Geographical Analysis*, Routledge, New York.

Rubenstein, J. (2001), *Making and Selling Cars: Innovation and Change in the U.S. Automotive Industry*, Johns Hopkins University Press, Baltimore.

Ruigrok, W. and van Tulder, R. (1995), *The Logic of International Restructuring*, Routledge, London.

Rupert, M. (1995), *Producing Hegemony: The Politics of Mass Production and American Global Power,* Cambridge University Press, Cambridge.

Sklair, L. (2001), *The Transnational Capitalist Class*, Blackwell, Oxford, chapter 5.

Silver, B. (1997), 'Turning Points of Workers' Militancy in the World Automobile Industry, 1930s-1990s', *Research in the Sociology of Work*, Vol. 6, pp. 43-71.

Slaughter, J. (1998), 'Too Little, Too Late for the UAW', *The Progressive*, August, pp. 20-1.

Slaughter, J. (1999), 'Modular Rage', *Multinational Monitor*, April, pp. 24-7.

Stanford, J. (2000), 'A Success Story: Canadian Productivity Performance in Auto Assembly', paper presented to the CSLS Conference on the Canada-U.S. Manufacturing Productivity Gap, Ottawa, January.

Streeck, W. (1996), 'Lean Production in the German Automobile Industry: A Test Case for Convergence Theory', in S. Berger and R. Dore (eds), *National Diversity and Global Capitalism,* Cornell University Press, Ithaca, New York. pp. 138-170.

UAW (United Auto Workers) (2000), 'Auto Parts Industry', *Jobs, Pay, and the Economy,* March/April.

UAW (United Auto Workers) (2001), 'Union Representation and Earnings in the Auto Industry', *Jobs, Pay, and the Economy,* January/February.

van Liemt, G. (1998), 'Applying Global Best Practice: Workers and the "New" Methods of Production Organization,' Employment and Training Paper No. 15, Employment and Training Department, International Labour Office, Geneva.

Womack, J., Jones, D. and Roos, D. (1990), *The Machine That Changed the World,* MacMillan, New York.

Chapter 12

'Decent Work': The Shifting Role of the ILO and the Struggle for Global Social Justice[1]

Leah F. Vosko

With the proliferation of supranational trade agreements and the concomitant deregulation of national labour markets many groups are calling for transparent, representative and democratically-accountable international organizations to improve workers' lives. Although the nature of struggles for global social justice differ, as do the ultimate goals of the actors moving them forward, collectively they raise the profile of deteriorating labour rights and standards worldwide. One outcome of this development is that international organizations, like the International Labour Organization (ILO), are rethinking their roles in globalization. Indeed, the ILO is an important case to examine since the organization has been criticized widely for perpetuating the hegemony of American capitalism, especially during the Cold War, and for neglecting the situation of marginalized workers in the global economy (Cox, 1977; Prugl, 1999, pp.199-97; Vosko, 2000; Whitworth, 1994).

This chapter examines the ILO's new platform of action known as *Decent Work* (1999) and explores whether recent changes inside the ILO, represent a genuine challenge to the hegemonic order in the organization. It asks, does *Decent Work* create space for alternative politics within the ILO and if so, could trade unions and labour-oriented NGOs use this transnational space to pry open the organization and challenge its historic 'hegemony-reinforcing' practices? The argument advanced in this chapter is that *Decent Work* reflects the evolving hegemonic order in the ILO under globalization, which continues to be influenced by the corporate/state-centric version of corporatism characterizing it for decades. Still, various facets of this platform, and struggles flowing from it, reveal a growing counter-hegemonic presence inside the ILO and especially at its margins, where transnational coalitions between organized labour, emerging labour organizations in the informal sector and NGOs are growing.

Decent Work represents a skillful effort at mediating escalating tensions inside the ILO between global capital, backed by a majority of industrialized states, and an increasingly vocal group of member states, trade unions, women's organizations and other NGOs concerned with improving the lives of marginalized workers. Two sets of initiatives underpinning the platform highlight Decent Work's mediating role and give definition to the struggles underway inside the ILO and at its margins. The first is the ILO *Declaration on Fundamental Principles and Rights at Work* and its Follow-Up (1998a) otherwise known as the Social Declaration – the ILO's recent and widely criticized attempt to compel member states to abide by core labour standards. The second is the commitment by the ILO to craft standard-setting instruments and use its extensive technical resources to contribute to improving working conditions and labour rights among marginalized groups of workers. The *Convention Concerning Home Work* (1996a) and the emerging standard on 'Workers in Situations Needing Protection' are among the first concrete measures flowing from this commitment.

A central pillar of the *Decent Work* platform, the ILO's new Social Declaration responds largely to the demands of the U.S. and various segments of the international trade union movement while avoiding several of the pitfalls of social clauses identified by women's groups, trade unions and other NGOs. Still, the danger that the Social Declaration could reinforce conventional corporate/state power relationships within the ILO remains acute since it neglects to provide member states with the tools necessary to target global capital and, consequently, fails to prevent downward harmonization in labour standards. Conversely, the platform's second pillar, reflecting its broad emphasis on 'decent work' for all, including 'people on the periphery of formal systems of employment', responds more directly to the concerns of a number of national trade unions, including unions of informal workers, and the new priorities of International Confederation of Free Trade Unions (ICFTU) as well as women's organizations, emerging labour organizations in the informal sector and other NGOs working on behalf of the unorganized (ILO, 1999, p.39). However, while new initiatives directed at marginalized workers represent a victory for those struggling to extend rights and protections to workers historically ignored by the ILO, they lack force. As a result, trade unions, emerging labour organizations in the informal sector, women's organizations and other NGOs confront considerable, although not necessarily insurmountable, challenges in their struggle to use *Decent Work* to move beyond 'labour and hegemony' (Cox).

In advancing this argument, the ensuing discussion unfolds in three parts. part one sets the backdrop for the inquiry by revisiting how Robert Cox used the notion of 'labour and hegemony' in depicting the ILO's role after World War II and by probing the salience of Cox's conception in the present era of global capitalism, drawing on recent feminist scholarship in international political economy. It also describes the growing counter-hegemonic presence inside the ILO and at its margins to frame the analysis of *Decent Work*. Moving to the case study, part two examines the contradictory tenor of *Decent Work* and two central initiatives of the platform. Finally, part three considers whether trade unions, emerging labour organizations in the informal sector, women's groups and other NGOs could use Decent Work to move beyond 'labour and hegemony' as Cox conceived of it, or if power relationships in the ILO, in which corporate/state objectives dominate, will continue to interfere with the creation of a meaningful structure for advancing the interests of marginalized workers. The chapter concludes by examining how the potentially negative effects of the Social Declaration could be minimized – through the construction of parallel instruments – and how strong standard-setting instruments directed at marginalized workers could be used to advance global social justice.

The purpose of this chapter is not to review debates over social clauses. Instead, it aims to critically evaluate events taking place inside the ILO parallel to developments in other international organizations, including the impasse in discussions at the WTO that fuelled the adoption of the ILO's Social Declaration, whose form resembles a social clause yet it is not attached to trade. Still, to be clear, I concur with analysts rejecting social clauses as a route to achieving global social justice. The problems flowing from tying labour rights and labour standards to market-generating agreements are far-reaching.[2]

'Labour and Hegemony' Revisited

In Robert Cox's 1977 essay, 'Labor and Hegemony', he used the case of the ILO to probe the hegemony of U.S. capitalism on an international scale, on the one hand, and the larger bureaucratic problems plaguing international organizations, on the other. His main contention was that despite the ILO's initial reformist spirit, the organization maintained hegemonic power relations after World War II and was poised to continue along this path even without the participation of the U.S. because of the institutionalization of a particular version of corporatism in the organization. This took expression in the ILO's tripartite structure – and, by extension, its support for the corporative state, Cox understood corporatism to be 'a form of productive relations, one based on an ideology of non-antagonistic relations and on bureaucratized structures of representation and control,' (Ibid., p.389) suggesting that it could exist at the state or the enterprise level. Yet, at the state level, he referred to the general category of the corporative state, which he argued took 'two forms… societal and state corporatism', and he linked tripartism to 'the societal form, emerging in countries of advanced capitalism'. Cox also viewed the AFL-CIO's contribution to the construction of the corporative state in the U.S. as crucial to 'labour and hegemony' and illustrated how its tacit support for corporativism translated at the international level inside both the International Confederation of Trade Unions (ICFTU) and the ILO.

Cox argued further that the hegemonic power relations operating in the organization 'prevented the ILO from confronting effectively the real social issues of employment creation, land reform, marginality and poverty in general' (Ibid., p.385). They inhibited the emergence of a strong counter-hegemonic force in the post-war era and led organized labour to neglect the interests of marginalized workers in the formal and informal economies in the North and the South. For Cox, 'labour and hegemony' inside the ILO reflected hegemony in international productive relations characterized by organized labour's participation in limited social reform rather than transformation and industrial relations under capitalism (Ibid., p.387). One major consequence of the acceptance of the corporative state in the ILO was the international trade union movement's abandonment of peripheral workers, echoing domestic tendencies in the U.S. (Ibid., pp.390-391).

Since Cox's incisive analysis of the ILO, dramatic changes have taken place in industrialized and industrializing countries propelled, in part, by the globalization of production, the feminization of the labour force and, most recently, the end of the Cold War. In turn, scholarship – especially feminist work on the ILO and scholarship probing the reconfiguration of the international trade union movement – now take Cox's work as a point of departure (O'Brien, 2000; Prugl; Whitworth, 1994).

The changing shape of productive relations is, at a minimum, altering the form of 'labour and hegemony' inside the ILO. While the connection that Cox made between U.S. capitalism in the ILO was certainly apt until the end of the Cold War, the current expression of both hegemony and counter-hegemony in global relations of production is in flux. Although U.S. capitalism remains dominant, nation-states are increasingly relinquishing their control over domestic capital. Correspondingly, in response to globalization, counter-hegemonic activity is becoming more visible inside international organizations. In the ILO, some member states belonging to the G-77 and key Northern states are coordinating their efforts to stem informalization in the South and casualization in the North and the South. The ICFTU is also expressing a growing commitment to addressing the needs of marginalized workers and a willingness to work cooperatively with trade unions of informal workers (David, 1996; ICFTU, 1999). Outside the ILO and at its margins, challenges are also increasing from trade unions representing informal workers and emerging labour organizations of formal and informal workers, especially trade unions like India's Self-Employed Women's Association (SEWA) and the UK-based organization HomeNet that made their common agenda known in discussions on the Home Work Convention (1996).

Consequently, there is growing space for resistance inside the ILO and especially at its margins, a space that Cox found largely absent in the post-WWII era. Still, while it may be true that a 'tentative transformation' is taking place in the international labour movement (O'Brien), an analysis of *Decent Work* suggests restrained optimism with regard to the ILO. What is new inside the ILO is the emergence of a vigorous struggle at the edges of its sphere of influence. National unions, women's groups and a variety of NGOs are receiving a genuine hearing, particularly on issues related to marginalized workers, in the corridors of the International Labour Office and in the ILO's official platform, albeit alongside the still louder voices of dominant actors.

In his recent work on the crisis in world order, Cox suggests that international organizations have the capacity to be effective 'interlocutors' in the struggle for re-regulation and re-politicization on the global scale. Correspondingly, feminist scholars argue that they represent important 'transnational spaces' for struggles for gender equality in the face of passive or active de-regulation. For example, a growing number of feminist works demonstrate how NGOs can agitate in multilateral forums to create appropriate norms on violence against women and women's health (Meyer, 1999; Meyer and Prugl, 1999). Scholars writing about gender politics in the labour field also reveal how interventions by the global women's movement can impact the standard-setting of organizations like the ILO which, in turn, influences labour policy and practice at the national level (Lotherington and Flemmen, 1991; Cohen, Ritchie, Swenarchuk and Vosko, 1999; Whitworth, 1994).

In 'Labor and Hegemony', Cox's point was not that the ILO was inescapably bound by the hegemony of American capitalism, although his analysis implied that corporatism can operate as a highly effective political shell for capitalist relations of production (Jessop, 1979, p.203), nor was it that international organizations were inappropriate sites of struggle for so-called traditional segments of organized labour or women's organizations. Instead, as Cox has indicated more recently, the point is 'that institutional change is more likely to follow than precede a new direction' (Cox, p.112). The pressing question is thus how can progressive segments of the international labour movement use the ILO to advance the cause of global social justice? Specifically, to what extent does *Decent Work*, and various initiatives underpinning the platform, offer potential to move this struggle forward given both the nature and operation of ILO structures and external factors?

The ILO's New Platform of Action: *Decent Work*

Decent Work is the product of a major organizational review; whereby the ILO examined its role and determined how it would best respond to member states and its constituents from labour and business given the challenges posed by globalization. This platform is not simply a new strategic plan, however. Rather, it reflects the ILO's attempt to gain some measure of institutional autonomy; it symbolizes a broader effort on the part of the ILO to remake itself given the end of the Cold War, the unraveling social pact around which its activities were organized in the post-World War II period and accelerating globalization.

'Decent Work'

The concept 'decent work' sets a paradoxical tone for the ILO's new platform. It is used by the organization as a metaphor to identify the need to improve the conditions of all working people, through efforts at re-regulation and the expansion of social and labour protections. As the official platform notes, the Decent Work agenda is shifting the ILO's attention beyond a narrow group of workers:

> Because of its origins, the ILO has paid most attention to the needs of waged workers – the majority of them men – in formal enterprises. But this is only part of its mandate, and only part of the world of work. Almost everyone works, but not everyone is employed.... The ILO must be concerned with workers beyond

> the formal labour market – with unregulated wage workers, the self-employed, and homeworkers (ILO, 1999, pp.3-4).

Yet, the concept 'decent work' is not intended to be synonymous with what has come to be known as 'standard work' and the labour and social protections and benefits flowing from it. Nor are the central features of 'decent work' equated with a standard employment relationship, which not only served as an emblem of the post-war period in industrialized countries but as a normative model of employment for the ILO in its standard-setting and technical cooperation activities supported by the international trade union movement. Rather, the central dimensions of 'decent work' laid out in the platform are left vague; they are said to be culturally- and regionally-specific and based on people's experiences in their daily lives. However, the protections surrounding 'decent work' are significantly inferior to those typically associated with a standard employment relationship.

For ILO Director-General Somavia, the goal of securing 'decent work' for all people arose partly out of the conviction that it was inappropriate to interpret the social challenges of the global economy only through the 'prism of the market'. This perspective, according to Somavia (1999, p.2), 'only provide[s] half the answer'.... 'the invisible hand of the market needs to be guided by a caring eye'. At the same time, Somavia (1999, pp.2-3) notes that:

> Decent work is not defined in terms of any fixed standard or monetary level. It varies from country to country. But everybody, everywhere, has a sense of what decent work means in terms of their own lives, in relation to their own society.... The immediate objective is to put in place a social floor for the global economy.

The relativist tone of Somavia's remarks reflect the ILO's effort to mediate the struggle between global capital and a vocal group of member states largely from the G-77, unions (especially unions of informal workers), emerging organizations of labour in the informal sector and NGOs concerned with improving the living and working conditions of marginalized workers.

As important as Somavia's own stance, is the play of the struggle between the forces of global capital and actors concerned with marginalized workers in initiatives associated with the platform. Under *Decent Work*, the International Labour Office is now organized on the basis of four strategic areas: the promotion of fundamental principles and rights at work; employment, enterprise creation and human resource development; social protection; and social dialogue. The struggle underway inside the ILO is especially clear in two initiatives underpinning the platform that reflect these strategic areas – the Social Declaration and measures to improve conditions for 'people on the periphery of formal systems of employment' (ILO, 1999, p.39).

The Social Declaration

The ILO crafted a new Social Declaration that was designed to set a floor of international labour rights and adopted it on 18 June 1998. This declaration was a response to the impasse in the debate over the appropriate relationship between international trade and labour standards, and particularly to the lack of consensus inside the WTO over whether it should address labour issues. Since the adoption of the Social Declaration, there have been several attempts to reintroduce discussion of a social clause-type mechanism inside the WTO, most notably the Green Room discussions in Seattle in 2000, but these attempts have resulted in entrenching divisions. Thus, with the exception of social clause type mechanisms in various regional trade agreements the Social Declaration is the closest that states have come to setting a floor of fundamental international labour rights with a formal monitoring mechanism attached.

However, the declaration advances no new obligations to member states, nor does it give the ILO or individual member states the power to introduce trade sanctions, even where a country has failed to ratify a core convention (ILO, 1998a: 8, S. 5).[3] Instead, the Social Declaration uses moral suasion to encourage member states to fulfill their constitutional obligation to advance fundamental principles and rights at work. The explicit objective of the Social Declaration is to promote adherence to conventions in the following areas (ILO, 1998a):

i) freedom of association and the effective recognition of the right to collective bargaining;
ii) the elimination of all forms of forced or compulsory labour;
iii) the effective abolition of child labour;
iv) the elimination of discrimination in respect of employment and occupation.

While the ILO's existing supervisory machinery already provides the means for ensuring that member states fulfill their constitutional obligations, the Social Declaration offers the ILO a new tool for promoting the ratification and enforcement of core conventions. By targeting nations that have not ratified core conventions, it establishes that they still have an obligation to respect the fundamental rights that are the subject of these conventions. Thus, the Social Declaration applies to all member states, all countries that have formally accepted the ILO Constitution.

To monitor progress towards the respect of fundamental rights and to promote ratification, the Social Declaration introduces a 'follow-up' mechanism. Through this follow-up, the ILO uses its constitutional procedure (Article 12) to require states that have not ratified core conventions to submit reports to allow the ILO to monitor progress made towards implementing the principles enshrined in these conventions (ILO, 1998b). The declaration also requires that the ILO publish annually a major report providing 'a dynamic global picture' on one category of fundamental principles and rights (ILO, 1998a), a report that also includes official observations of organized labour and business. The first Global Report on the subject of freedom of association and the effective recognition of the right to bargain collectively was released in June 2000.

Given the scope of the Social Declaration and its targets for action, the constraints on global capital are limited. Indeed, two dimensions of the declaration, in particular, indicate that it is unlikely to alter fundamentally the corporate/state-centric power relations characterizing the ILO historically. First, the Social Declaration's scope is limited. Despite the existence of nearly two hundred International Labour Conventions, the declaration targets the ratification of core labour standards in only four limited areas. It is clearly important that countries promote fundamental labour rights and while the ILO made an innovative move by using its Constitution to compel member states to abide by these rights, the Social Declaration sets aside the many important international labour standards adopted since World War II. Ironically, especially given *Decent Work's* renewed commitment to address the needs of marginalized workers, the core conventions largely leave this important area of standard setting untouched.

Second, the Social Declaration targets nation-states for adherence to core labour standards yet fails to enable states to challenge global capital collectively. In this way, it does not address the issue at the heart of the labour standards international trade debate – the erosion of basic labour rights and the weak enforcement of labour standards. Instead, it reflects an attempt by the ILO to balance the demands of global capital with a set of its vocal opponents. There is no question that states remain powerful actors in the international system but, to be effective and endow states with more control, any supranational measure designed to improve labour standards and labour rights must initiate market-controlling measures targeting global capital.

The profound tensions surrounding the Social Declaration are predictable given ongoing debates about the central purpose of the instrument. Paradoxically, however, the debate over the declaration generated a situation in which actors with divergent (even opposing) views and objectives often landed on the same side. Supporters of the Social Declaration take three distinct positions. First, the strongest supporters of its scope view it as, at best, a third-rate alternative to a social clause targeting states failing to comply with labour standards but are hopeful that it could ultimately lead to this type of mechanism. Member states like the U.S., some Western NGOs and the still Western-dominated ICFTU are on record as preferring an instrument that is more binding on governments yet they support a number of procedural and substantive dimensions of the Social Declaration (ICFTU, 1999; Grace, 2000). Their posture is based partly on the view that the Social Declaration's use of the ILO's Constitution does not rule out sanctions and partly on their support for moral suasion as a tool (Weisband, 2000).

A second group of more conditional supporters of the Social Declaration holds dramatically different views. Many countries tepidly accept this instrument for the very reasons that the U.S., the ICFTU and other groups are displeased with it. The majority of countries belonging to the G-77, for example, applaud the Social Declaration's clear rejection of protectionism and its promotional focus. These countries left their mark on the final text of the Social Declaration – and in other international forums like the WTO Singapore Ministerial Meeting and Copenhagen +5 – by opposing a more binding mechanism and the use of this instrument for protectionist purposes. For them, the Social Declaration is a trade-off, characteristic of the uneasy mediation achieved under *Decent Work*. The G-77's lukewarm support for the Social Declaration reflects an oppositional stance that aims to protect developing countries from Western domination.

A third group of supporters, especially many women's groups and development NGOs, take a more critical stance. They argue that the type of position offered by the G-77 should be rejected because a weak endorsement of the Social Declaration is not the same as support for international measures directed at controlling capital. They thus call for reforming this and other instruments, in tandem with struggling for labour rights and enforceable standards at the national level, with the aim of creating market-controlling mechanisms.

Similar divisions exist between those groups opposing the Social Declaration. There are ILO member states and NGOs who consider it insufficient because it is not a social clause and thus non-binding. Adherents to this view are most closely allied to the position adopted by the U.S. prior to the Singapore WTO Ministerial Meeting but altered thereafter, which named the ILO as the competent body for dealing with international labour standards. Conversely, there are trade union organizations and NGOs and women's organizations that reject social clauses, arguing that they will not extend sufficient protection to workers and, therefore, reject the Social Declaration because it is offered as a resolution to the trade and labour standards debate and deteriorating international labour standards more broadly. The activism of both groups of opponents takes different forms than those working for change through the declaration. Those advocating a social clause continue to focus almost exclusively on lobbying inside the WTO, and those seeking to challenge globalization outside existing international institutions – and, hence, vehemently rejecting a social clause – tend to use meetings of world leaders as sites of protest.

The positions of various actors on the Social Declaration, particularly the bifurcated views of *both* its supporters and its opponents, highlight the tensions that underpin it. They demonstrate that the interpretation and implementation of the declaration is itself subject to a complex struggle. In the context of the shifting role of the ILO, however, by targeting states yet failing to enable them to contribute to increased controls over global capital, and constructing an instrument of limited scope, the organization's use of the Social Declaration reflects an artful attempt at mediation. If groups manage to link it to extending social and labour rights and protections to marginalized workers and to increasing states' collective power over global capital the Social Declaration might become effective. However, without this type of intervention, the Social Declaration may be poised to reinforce conventional corporate/state power relationships in the ILO.

Extending Protection to Marginalized Workers

The identification of another priority group of workers in *Decent Work* – i.e., people on the periphery of formal systems of employment – also reflects prevailing tensions in the ILO. In aiming for 'decent work' for all, the platform makes it clear that the ILO is not attempting to encourage countries to extend the same level of benefits accorded to standard workers to all workers in need of protection. While this is a position that does not threaten global capital's demand for a 'flexible' workforce, it does extend some protections to marginalized workers by calling on governments to craft national legislation to prevent the use of contingent workers primarily as a means of escaping regulation. This approach is the product of longstanding efforts of officials in the International Labour Office aiming to 'mainstream gender', take seriously the conditions of workers in the informal economy and address the proliferation of non-standard employment. It also addresses some of the concerns of those determined to stem informalization in the South and casualization in both the North and the South. *Decent Work's* focus on marginalized workers is thus a display of the ILO's new commitment to bring workers once deemed to be outside of its constituency into its standard- and norm-setting activities. More than the preceding pillar of the platform, therefore, the substantive initiatives behind this pillar signal the growing presence of groups struggling on behalf of marginalized workers.

The new ILO *Convention Concerning Home Work*, No. 177 (1996) and current discussions on creating an instrument on Workers in Situations Needing Protection (2000) are cases in point. While the Home Work Convention has limitations and discussions on extending protections to marginalized workers are proceeding tediously slowly, these developments suggest that the ILO potentially offers a transnational space for greater coordination between women's groups, other NGOs, emerging labour organizations in the informal sector and the international trade union movement.

The ILO Convention Concerning Home Work

The *Convention Concerning Home Work* (1996), which arose before the ILO introduced *Decent Work* but whose promotion is central to it, is an important new international instrument. It is the product of collective efforts to address the conditions of workers in the informal economy and the gendered character of precarious employment worldwide. Since its adoption, this convention has been taken as a model by trade unions of informal workers like SEWA and groups like UK-based HomeNet for improving the conditions of marginalized workers in the global economy.

Given the ILO's longstanding neglect of workers falling outside standard employment relationships, the terms of the Home Work Convention are also relatively positive, although 'detailed guidelines as to how the situation of homeworkers should be improved' are relegated to the non-binding recommendation (ILO, 1996b). The preamble of the Convention is especially monumental as it recalls that 'many international labour Conventions and Recommendations laying down standards of general application are applicable to homeworkers' (ILO, 1996a: Preamble). Beyond this gesture, which makes it clear that the International Labour Code now applies to homeworkers, three other dimensions of the convention are worthy of emphasis. Article One defines an employer as a person who either parcels out homework directly or through an intermediary, making it difficult for employers in ratifying countries to escape regulation by defining homeworkers as independent contractors. Article Three, however, is the strongest dimension of the instrument as it requires ratifying countries to adopt, implement and periodically review a national policy on homework aimed at improving the situation of homeworkers. This provision also requires governments to work in consultation with the 'most representative' organizations of workers and employers and, where they exist, those organizations (not necessarily trade unions) concerned with homeworkers specifically, a pivotal opening for groups moving towards trade union status like SEWA. Building on Article Three, Article Four also requires national governments to promote equal treatment between homeworkers and other wage earners, taking into account the special characteristics of homework.

Owing to the Employers' Group rejection of any binding instrument on homework and to standard-setting more broadly, the Recommendation Concerning Home Work, No. 184 (1996) lays out much more comprehensive provisions. This instrument is a strong template for countries committed to introducing legislation and regulations. It proposes the introduction of a registry of employers using homeworkers and a parallel registry of workers, designed to enable association building or trade union formation and eventually collective bargaining. The recommendation also addresses questions of minimum age, collective representation, minimum wages, comparable treatment in remuneration, benefits and statutory entitlements and protections for homeworkers and regular waged workers as well as compensation for equipment and time for maintaining machinery. In a very significant move, the final recommendation proposes that nations establish joint and several liabilities between intermediaries and employers for the payment of remuneration to homeworkers. The recommendation also contains detailed provisions on social security, hours or work, weekly rest and sick leave and maternity protection as well as calling on governments to create special programs to facilitate freedom of association and collective bargaining. In combination with the Convention, therefore, the Recommendation Concerning Home Work is a powerful tool to extend protections to marginalized workers.

The unique dimensions of the new Convention on Home Work were the product of an unprecedented coalition between progressive unions of formal workers, unions of informal workers, emerging labour organizations in the informal sector, women's groups and other NGOs, an alliance absent in the creation and promotion of the Social Declaration. Homework was first discussed formally at the International Labour Conference in 1995 and, in response to this discussion, the ILO drafted an instrument that was modified and adopted on the floor of the ILO in 1996. Elizabeth Prugl (1997) argues that the Convention on Home Work represents a pivotal victory for both the global feminist movement and progressive segments of the international labour movement and signals a transformation away from 'fordist gender rules' inside the ILO. Various records suggest that the convention survived in spite of the negotiating tactics of the Employers' Group because of the nature of the coalition backing it – between HomeNet, trade unions of informal workers, emerging labour organizations in the informal sector, women's organizations and the ICFTU – and its effective lobbying efforts directed at governments. Notably, in their internal debates over both the convention and recommendation, mainstream unions took the stand that homeworkers need protection and SEWA and HomeNet and feminist NGOs, focused on the agency of women homeworkers. In contrast to the case of the Social Declaration, however, a coalition came together effectively here even though trade unions and feminist NGOs had different perceptions of homework and homeworkers. It was this opposition, combined with the support of many EU governments, as well as governments like South Africa, that contributed to the successful adoption of the convention. The emergence of the Home Work Convention is thus cause for moderate optimism and underscores the growing significance of emerging labour organizations in the informal sector as potential allies of the traditional trade union movement.

'Workers in Situations Needing Protection'

The evolving instrument on 'Workers in Situations Needing Protection' also reflects prevailing struggles inside the ILO. Discussions on the instrument concretize a central sentiment in the *Decent Work* platform, but they are proceeding slowly due partly to the contentious outcome of discussions on homework. In the early 1990s, there was a call for a new instrument on private employment agencies from employers to respond to the growth of the temporary help industry and, at the same time, an instrument designed to encourage states to regulate contract labour, principally supported by organized labour. Since both issues reflected priority areas of standard-setting identified by the ILO, the Workers' Group and the Employers' Group made a backroom deal: the Workers' Group agreed to submit to a revision of the Convention on Private Employment Agencies, 1949 (No. 97) in exchange for the Employers' Group agreement to discuss a convention on Contract Labour.

The re-opening of the Convention on Private Employment Agencies was a defeat for workers since it led to the adoption of a new Convention on Private Employment Agencies (No. 181) that legitimizes triangular employment relationships – involving an agency, a worker and an employer – connected to the rise of precarious employment (Vosko, 1997, 2000). Groups opposing the terms of this instrument, mainly trade unions, were unable to convince governments of the importance of retaining restrictions on the activities of private employment agencies. They were also ineffective in convincing the other social partners of the growing need to regulate employment relationships where responsibility does not rest squarely with one entity. As a result, the ILO adopted a convention focused on private employment agencies that undermines the aim of achieving parity between workers in standard and non-standard employment relationships overlooked in *Decent Work*.

The other side of the deal is still a matter under contestation. In 1997, the International Labour Conference held a preliminary discussion on Contract Labour, where the Workers' Group lobbied for a strong instrument. However, in the aftermath of the passage of the Home Work Convention, tensions were high between workers and employers and conceptual and political problems impeded progress. Since there were few observer organizations present at the discussion, virtually no attention was paid to the concerns of unions and other organizations representing workers engaged in contract labour. The result was a decision to abandon the term 'contract labour' but to solicit twenty-nine country studies on workers needing protection and initiate six regional meetings of experts (ILO, 2000d). The overarching goal of these studies was to identify workers in situations needing protection. In particular, they were asked to explore the gray area between formal and informal sectors and to highlight the situation of women workers.

The result was a technical report entitled 'Meeting of Experts on Workers in Situations Needing Protections' that was released in May 2000. The most significant feature of the report is its finding that:

> There is a category of workers who appear to be excluded from the protection provided by the employment relationship, but who in fact carry out their work within the framework of concealed or disguised employment relationships. At the same time, there are objectively ambiguous situations, which are on the increase, which merit protection, since the workers involved are placed in situations of dependency, but in respect of which the scope of legislation may be too narrow, in that it does not allow an identification of the employer of the persons who should assume responsibility vis-à-vis the worker.

This report was filed and discussed at the ILO's Governing Body in November 2000 and discussed again in March 2001 but is only set to reach the floor of the International Labour Conference in June 2003. The lack of agreement on a common definition of contract labour and the elusive character of the phenomena under consideration, present profound obstacles to the adoption of a convention on 'unprotected workers'. In the case of homework, delegates had a clear idea of whom the convention was designed to serve and a coalition of supporters evolved on this basis. In the shift away from 'contract labour' towards 'unprotected workers', the focus is less clear and this inhibits lobbying efforts. Little is likely to happen here without a clearer focus that then will enable a renewed alliance between labour supporters.

Beyond 'Labour and Hegemony'?: 'Decent Work' and the Struggle for Global Social Justice

The two central pillars underpinning *Decent Work* reflect the prevailing struggle inside the ILO. The shape of the Social Declaration and particularly the platform's new emphasis on extending protections to workers on the periphery of formal systems of employment indicate that trade unions of informal workers, emerging labour organizations in the informal sector, women's groups and other NGOs are receiving a greater hearing inside the ILO – than they have in the past. They are thus better positioned to resist hegemonic forces in the ILO than during the Cold War. Still, it would be an exaggeration to suggest that either pillar of *Decent Work* amounts to a significant challenge to the longstanding power relationships within the ILO. The Social Declaration is a relatively blunt instrument and although the groups pushing for the extension of international labour standards to the unorganized and to workers in the informal sector, emerging instruments are weak, especially in their capacity to generate lasting improvements for workers at the national level. *Decent Work*, therefore, represents an effort at mediating the demands of global capital with those of a vocal group of actors struggling to transform the ILO's agenda.

Recent developments in the ILO create an opportunity to advance the cause of global social justice at a number of levels. At a macro-level, taking advantage of this opportunity involves a two-fold strategy. As Greenfield (1998) argues, it involves first challenging the lack of democracy and transparency in international organizations – in the ILO's case, this also involves highlighting problems flowing from its tripartite structure and the corporate/state power relationships historically characterizing the organization – and seeking strategic exclusions from specific standards that threaten to lower the bottom of the labour market. A second strategy involves lobbying for stronger and more meaningful international labour standards as well as international and supranational instruments effective in monitoring and regulating the activities of global capital. If applied to the Social Declaration, this secondary strategy could assist ILO member states in enforcing improved labour standards in ways that enable workers to exercise their labour rights individually and collectively through their representative organizations.

A meso-level strengthening alliance is crucial to moving marginalized workers' issues to the centre of the ILO's agenda. This also involves increasing pressure on member states and reshaping the international trade union movement so that the debate over global social movement unionism goes beyond 'how unions should adapt to include unprotected workers'. Thus far, coalition-based strategies have been effective in making challenges at the margins of the ILO's traditional area of standard-setting activity. The debate over the hard-won Home Work Convention is a case in point. Given that the Social Declaration is already in force, coalitions inside the ILO could press to give this instrument a more meaningful role and, in so doing, pry open corporatist structures in the ILO and challenge its state-centric hegemony-reinforcing practices. To complement activities inside the

ILO, women's organizations, emerging labour organizations in the informal sector, trade unions of informal and formal workers and other NGOs and the ICFTU could also work collectively to develop a parallel report to the ILO's Global Report to assess the official observations of nation-states and business, and supplement the official observations of national labour organizations. This shadow report could then be submitted formally to the ILO but also circulated widely at the international, national and local levels to fuel activities aimed at improving the conditions of marginalized workers. A report of this sort could address both progress and setbacks in areas of common concern and follow models developed by progressive trade unions, emerging labour organizations in the informal sector, women's organizations, other NGOs and the ICFTU. UNIFEM's Biennial Report and alternative budget exercises offer a potential template.

Engagement with workers at the micro-level – through public forums as well as through detailed field observations – in devising this type of report is essential to developing finely-grained assessments of the situation in a given country or region and to improving ties between trade unions of informal and formal workers, emerging labour organizations in the informal sector, women's groups and other NGOs. It is also crucial for building momentum for the struggle underway inside the ILO.

Notes

1 This is a revised and summarized version of a chapter that first appeared in *Global Social Policy* (2002), Vol. 2, No. 1, April. Field research for this chapter was undertaken at the ILO in June 1997, and June and July 2000. This research was made possible by the Social Sciences and Humanities Research Council of Canada. Thanks also to Martha Chen, Judy Fudge, Gerald Kernerman, and Robert O'Brien for their comments on earlier versions of this chapter and to Arlene Dosen and Paula Trachy for their research assistance.

2 Embedding social clauses in trade agreements means that violation of labour and social standards will *only* be assessed on the basis of whether they constitute unfair trade practices. Other problems include the absence of democracy and transparency in the agencies responsible for crafting and monitoring social clauses and their use for protectionist purposes. The fact that social clauses target nation-states, which increasingly act as 'transmission belts' (Cox, 1992, p.31) for global capital rather than enabling governments to target capital, also represents a fundamental limitation.

3 However, while it has not been tested, the follow-up to the Social Declaration could result in such measures in the long term (i.e., after many rounds of a country's failure to abide by core labour standards).

References

Cohen, Marjorie Griffin, Ritchie, Laurell, Swenarchuk, Michelle and Vosko, Leah (1999), *Globalization: Some Implications and Strategies for Women*, National Action Committee on the Status of Women, Toronto.

Cox, Robert (1977), 'Labor and Hegemony', *International Organization*, Vol. 31, No. 1, pp. 385-424.

Cox, Robert (1994), 'The Crisis in World Order and the Challenge of International Organization', *Cooperation and Conflict*, Vol. 29, No. 2, pp. 99-113.

David, Natacha (1996), *Worlds Apart: Women and the Global Economy*, ICFTU, Geneva.

Grace, Brewster (2000), 'Briefing Paper on U.S. Initiatives in the WTO on Trade and Labor Standards', in *Focus: WTO and Labour Standards*.

Greenfield, Gerard (1998), 'The ICFTU and the Politics of Compromise', in Ellen Meinksins Wood, Peter Meinksins and Michael Yeats (eds), *Rising From the Ashes? Labour in the Age of 'Global' Capitalism*, Monthly Review Press, New York, pp. 180-189.

ICFTU (1999), *Building Workers' Human Rights into the Global Trading System*, ICFTU, Geneva.

ILO (International Labour Organization) (1994), *Record of Proceedings: Working Party on the Social Dimensions of the Liberalization of International Trade*, International Labour Office, Geneva, November.

ILO (International Labour Organization) (1996a), *Convention Concerning Home Work*, No. 177, International Labour Office, Geneva.

ILO (International Labour Organization) (1996b), *Recommendation Concerning Home Work*, No. 184, International Labour Office, Geneva.

ILO (International Labour Organization) (1996c), *Report of the Subcommittee on Home Work: Submission and Discussion*, ILO, Geneva.

ILO (International Labour Organization) (1998a), *ILO Declaration on Fundamental Principles and Rights at Work and Its Follow-Up*, International Labour Office, Geneva.

ILO (International Labour Organization) (1998b), *Constitution of the International Labour Organizations and Standing Orders of the International Labour Conference*, International Labour Office, Geneva, February.

ILO (International Labour Organization) (1999), *Decent Work: Report of the Director General*, International Labour Conference, 87th Session, International Labour Office, Geneva.

ILO (International Labour Organization) (2000a), *Your Voice at Work: Global Report Under the Follow-up to the ILO Declaration on Fundamental Principles and Rights at Work*, International Labour Office, Geneva.

ILO (International Labour Organization) (2000b), *Review of Annual Reports Under the Follow-Up to the ILO Declaration on Fundamental Principles and Rights at Work*, International Labour Office, Geneva.

ILO (International Labour Organization) (2000c), 'Measures Recommended by Governing Body under Article 33 of the Constitution – Implementation of Recommendations Contained in the Report of the Commission of Inquiry entitled Forced Labour in Myanmar (BURMA)', International Labour Conference, Provisional Record, International Labour Office, Geneva.

ILO (International Labour Organization) (2000d), *Meeting of Experts on Workers in Situations Needing Protection: The Employment Relationship; Scope*, Basic Technical Document, International Labour Office, Geneva.

Jessop, Bob (1979), 'Corporatism, Parliamentarism and Social Democracy', in Philippe Schmitter and Gerhard Lehmbruch (eds), *Trends Towards Corporatist Intermediation*, Sage, California, pp. 186-211.

Lotherington, Ann Therese and Flemmen, Anne Britt (1991), 'Negotiating Gender: The Case of the ILO', in Kristi Anne Stolen and Mariken Vaa, *Gender and Change in Developing Countries*, Norwegian University Press, Norway, pp. 273-308.

Meyer, Mary K. (1999), 'Negotiating International Norms: The Inter-American Commission of Women and the Convention on Violence against Women', in Mary K. Meyer and Elisabeth Prugl (eds), *Gender Politics in Global Governance*, Rowman and Littlefield, Oxford, pp. 58-71.

Meyer, Mary K. and Prugl, Elisabeth (eds) (1999), *Gender Politics in Global Governance*, Rowman and Littlefield, Oxford.

O'Brien, Robert (2000), 'Workers and World Order: The Tentative Transformation of the International Union Movement', *Review of International Studies*, Vol. 26, pp. 533-555.

Prugl, Elisabeth (1999), *The Global Construction of Gender: Home-Based Work in the Political Economy of the 20th Century*, Columbia University Press, New York.

Somavia, Juan Schmitter (2000), 'Decent Work in the Global Economy', speech delivered in Vigyan Bhavan, New Delhi, 18 February.

Vosko, Leah F. (1997), 'Legitimizing the Triangular Employment Relationship: Emerging International Labour Standards from a Comparative Perspective,' *Comparative Labor Law and Policy Journal*, Fall, pp. 43-77.

Weiss, Edward (2000), 'Discursive Multilateralism: Global Benchmarks, Shame, and Learning in the ILO Labor Standards Monitoring Regime', *International Studies Quarterly*, Vol. 44, No. 4, December, pp. 643-666.

Whitworth, Sandra (1994), *Feminism and International Relations*, St. Martin's Press, New York.

Index

Afghanistan, 16
Africa, 8, 17, 55, 124-127, 129, 131-136
    South Africa, 125, 133, 135
Alternatives for the Americas, 95, 98
Angola, 125, 126, 127, 128, 129, 131, 136
Argentina, 22, 46, 48, 54, 55
Asia, 16, 20, 42, 43, 47, 51, 54, 55, 142
    financial crisis, 19, 43, 92, 140, 142-145
Asia-Pacific Economic Cooperation (APEC), 42, 97, 99, 102
Australia, 59

banks, 18, 19, 21, 42, 50
barriers, 13, 21, 35, 48, 49, 50, 51, 52, 68, 91, 140
    informal, 51
Blair, Tony, 5, 73, 75, 79, 80, 82, 83
    administration, 72, 73-74, 80-82
Bolivia, 48
Brazil, 44, 46, 49, 50, 55
    financial crisis (1999), 43
Bread and Roses March (1995), 118
Bretton Woods, 18, 42
Britain, *also* United Kingdom, 28, 75-76, 79, 82,
Bush, George W., 133
    administration, 134

Canada, 7, 35, 36, 42, 49, 50, 51, 52, 59-71, 94, 95, 96, 106, 111, 117, 133, 164, 166
Canada-U.S. Free Trade Agreement (CUSFTA) 91, 93, 94, 95
capital, 6, 7, 8, 14, 15, 17, 18, 19, 20, 28, 30, 31, 32, 42-43, 49, 51, 60, 67, 72, 89, 90, 91, 92, 93, 94, 98, 100, 105, 106, 107, 108, 109, 111, 112, 115, 118, 119, 134, 140, 141, 159, 174, 175, 179, 181, 182, 187
    accumulation, 14, 15
    controls, 18, 22
    flows, 2, 3, 16, 18, 20, 43
    flight, 43
    social, 27, 64, 108, 109
capitalism, 2, 14, 16, 17, 18, 22, 24, 26, 27, 32, 69, 73, 90, 105, 174, 175, 176, 177, 178
Charter of Economic Rights and Duties of States, 18
Chile, 50, 95
China, 14, 16, 46, 52, 140
civil society, 20, 90, 96-98, 141, 148, 149, 151
civil war, 8, 99, 124, 126-131, 136
class, 4, 7, 14, 16, 22, 24, 27, 30, 32, 48, 66, 90, 92, 105, 106, 108, 110, 114, 115, 149
    capitalist class, 14, 15, 22, 27
Clean Diamonds Trade Act, 133-134
Clinton, William (Bill), 24, 80, 133
    administration, 23, 79, 81, 83
coalition(s), 31, 32, 44, 72, 73, 74, 75, 78, 79, 82, 83, 93-94, 108, 110, 111, 114, 119, 124, 125, 129, 132, 134, 135, 187
    transnational coalitions, 8, 94, 129, 136, 174
coalition strategies, 97, 191
communism, 14
comparative advantage, 47
competition, 4, 7, 18, 19, 21, 33, 45, 47, 48, 49, 50, 52-56, 74, 93, 105, 106, 107, 109, 110, 111, 112, 113, 115, 117, 119, 156-157, 162, 163, 164, 167-168
    competitiveness, 13, 14, 20, 22, 42, 48, 53, 54, 72, 73, 74, 91, 107, 108, 109, 110, 111, 112, 115, 116, 117, 118, 119, 120, 141, 161, 163-164, 167
    structural competitiveness, 107, 112, 116
conditioning, 4, 35, 93
Council and Campaign to Eliminate

Conflict Diamonds, 134
crisis, 18, 19, 20, 22, 45, 72, 73, 77, 100, 114, 116, 143-144, 162, 177
economic, 16
financial, 19, 43

debt, 15, 17, 43, 53, 61, 132
deficit, 15, 20, 61, 116-117, 168
democracy, 3, 4, 17, 26-27, 32, 60, 79, 80, 109, 115, 141, 145, 187
democratic governance, 4
democratizing, 18, 22
demonstrators, 93, 99
Democratic Party, 18, 80, 152
Democratic Republic of the Congo (DRC), 125, 126, 128
developing countries, 17, 21, 91, 125, 182
dollar, 42, 60
US, 15, 18, 19, 127, 129, 130
Durbin-DeWine-Feingold bill, 133-134

Egypt, 46
environment, 29, 37, 90-91, 97, 109, 115, 132, 145
environmental groups, 82, 92, 93, 94
policies, 91-94, 97
rights, 22
standards, 23, 94-95
equality, 80, 141
gender, 177
inequality, 30, 66, 92, 112, 113, 168
Europe, 33, 42, 43, 50, 51, 60, 74, 99, 156
Eastern Europe, 14, 91
European imperialism, 14
European Union (EU), 28, 42
Western Europe, 20, 49, 99

finance, 14, 18, 54, 60, 133
fiscal policy, 43, 55
financial instability, 19, 22
Fordism, 64, 107, 156, 168, 170
Fordist welfare state, 68, 69, 188
France, 16, 59
free trade, 14, 28, 29, 37, 52-53
Friedman, Milton, 18

G8 Summit, 99
General Agreement on Tariffs and Trade (GATT), 91
General Agreement on Trade in Services (GATS), 29, 42, 44, 90
General Motors (GM), 157, 159, 162-168
Germany, 16, 162
global discourse, 147, 148
global turbulence, 1, 72, 141
globalism, 5, 59
globalization, 1-9, 13, 14, 16, 17, 19-23, 30, 31, 32, 41, 43, 47, 51, 72, 73, 80, 89, 99, 100, 124, 125, 126, 131, 141, 153, 156, 174, 177, 178, 182
cultural, 2, 14
production, 2, 180
Gramsci, Antonio, 156
Gramscian, 32
Greenspan, Alan, 23-24

human rights, 94, 97, 127, 130, 141, 145-149, 152

India, 46, 177
indigenous peoples, 94
Indonesia, 49
inflation, 18, 23, 43, 81, 142
information technology, 49, 53
interest groups, 44, 48, 52, 75
international, 1, 2, 3, 4, 6-9, 15, 17, 26, 27, 36-37, 41-56, 60, 64, 72, 73, 74, 80, 90, 91, 94, 98, 99, 106, 107, 111, 112, 113, 115, 117, 119, 124, 127, 131, 132, 133, 134, 135, 148-150, 167, 168, 175, 176, 181-183, 187, 188
internationalism, 13
internationalization, 15, 18, 20
International Confederation of Free Trade Unions (ICFTU), 94, 175-177, 178, 181, 185, 188
international finance, 18
international institutions and organizations, 8, 21, 28, 29, 34, 89, 94, 97, 125, 135, 136, 174, 176, 177, 178, 182
international investors, 42, 43
International Labour Organization (ILO), 8, 175-188, *see also*
Convention Concerning Home Work, 175, 183

Decent Work, 174-175, 177-179, 181-183, 185-187
International Labour Conference, 184, 186
Social Declaration, 8, 175-176, 180-182, 185, 187
Social Union Framework Agreement, 68
International Monetary Fund (IMF), 20, 45, 91, 92, 93, 96, 97, 99, 144
international treaties, 18, 20, 21, 22, 34
internet, 41, 56
investment, 13, 15, 16, 19, 20, 21, 29, 30, 36, 41, 44, 45, 46, 54, 55, 59, 63, 64, 67, 81, 91, 92, 94, 96, 97, 98, 100, 111, 115, 118, 126, 129, 130, 161, 163, 164, 167
direct investment, 42, 54, 109
foreign investment, 15, 16, 17, 18, 36, 43, 54, 55, 92, 109, 135, 156,
investment law, 9,
portfolio investment, 42
Iraq, 46

Japan, 15, 16, 33, 46, 49, 50, 51, 52, 54, 140, 156, 157

Kimberley Process, 133-134
Korea, 19, 48, 50, 140
South Korea, 46, 54, 140-153
Foreign Worker Employment and Human Rights Protection Law (FWPL), 144, 151

labour, *also* work, 6, 8, 28, 32, 37, 43, 48, 49, 55, 61, 63, 65, 67, 72, 74, 81, 89, 90, 91, 92, 93, 94, 97, 110-120, 145, 146, 147, 149, 153, 157, 158, 159, 160, 162, 163, 169, 174-179
contract labour, 189, 190
feminization of labour force, 177, 180
labour market, 8, 33, 48, 117, 156, 174, 179
labour market policy, 22, 33, 34, 72-76, 80, 82-83, 117, 178
labour movement, 105, 106, 110-120
international labour movement, 94, 95, 149, 177-178, 185
labour organizations, 49, 55, 90, 141, 142, 143, 149-150, 174, 175, 177, 187, *see also*
Canadian Auto Workers (CAW), 157, 163-168
Centrale de l'enseignement du Québec (CEQ), 114
Confédération des syndicats nationaux (CSN), 114
Dana Worker's Alliance, 95
Fédération des travailleurs et travailleuses du Québec's (FTQ), 114
Frente Auténtico del Trabajo (FAT), 95
India's Self-Employed Women's Association (SEWA), 180
United Auto Workers (UAW), 162, 163, 167
United Electrical Workers (UE), 95
labour rights, 22, 97, 111, 144, 148, 151-152, 174, 175, 176, 180
labour standards, 8, 37, 94, 168, 174, 175, 176, 183
core labour standards, 8, 175, 184
international labour standards, 41, 150, 180-182, 184, 187
laissez-faire, 28, 77, 83
Latin America, 16, 20, 47, 55
legitimacy, 61, 107, 115, 126, 149, 152
liberal democracy, 2, 26-27
liberal democratic policies, 29
liberalism, 4, 27, 29, 32, 114
economic, 26, 29, 32
liberalization, 21, 43, 51, 52, 167
Liberia, 127-128

Maastrict Treaty, 92, 93
Macpherson C. B., 26-27
manufacturing, 15, 21, 49, 109, 112, 137, 143, 156, 159, 161, 162, 164, 166
lean manufacturing, 7, 156
Maquiladora, 94, 95, 163
marketization, 3, 9, 73
Marx, Karl, 14
Mercado del Sur (MERCOSUR), 42
Mexico, 13, 16, 41, 42, 43, 44, 50, 94, 95, 162, 163

financial crisis, 43
migration, 41, 126, 132, 140, 142, 153
Multilateral Agreement on Investment (MAI), 96
multinational corporations, 16, 17, 18, 30, 91, 93, 95

Namibia, 126, 128
national, 3, 5, 7, 8, 16, 30, 32, 35, 36, 37, 43-44, 45, 51, 52, 54, 55, 56, 65, 67, 68, 72, 74, 76, 90, 91, 92, 93, 94, 95, 97, 98, 100, 105-120, 124, 125, 126, 128, 131, 132, 133, 135, 140, 142, 153, 161, 167, 168, 174, 175, 178, 182-184, 187, 188
national monopoly, 51
nationalism, 13, 106, 110, 111, 113-115, 118
competitive nationalism, 7, 105, 106, 113, 116-119
minority nationalism, 105, 106, 107, 110, 111, 112, 119
neoliberal, 3, 5-6, 8-9, 20, 28, 32, 33, 34, 37, 59, 61, 62, 67, 69, 72, 73, 74, 76, 79, 80, 83, 97, 98, 99, 101, 109, 118, 124, 153, 156
neoliberal policies, 5, 6, 8, 72, 74, 79, 83, 90, 100, 125
neoliberalism, 5, 17, 19-20, 27, 72-73, 74, 83, 89, 90, 91, 92, 95, 97, 98, 100, 115, 116
Nixon, Richard, 18
nongovernmental organizations (NGOs), 7, 125, 127, 132-136, 137, 141, 144, 145, 149-150, 153, 174-175, 177-179, 181-185, 187-188, *see also*
Amnesty International, 133, 137
Citizens' Coalition for Economic Justice (CCEJ), 146-150, 154
Coalition for Justice in the Maquiladoras (CJM), 94
Global Witness, 125, 129, 133
Human Rights Watch, 125, 133, 137
Institute for Security Studies (South Africa), 125
International Organization of Migration (IOM), 140
National Anti-Poverty Organization (NAPO), 64
Partnership Africa Canada, 125, 133
World Vision, 133
North America, 30, 51, 92, 93, 94, 95, 99, 156, 157, 162, 167, 168, 171
North American Free Trade Agreement (NAFTA), 18, 28, 29, 42, 90, 91, 167
Chapter 11 (NAFTA), 30, 36

Organization for Economic Cooperation and Development (OECD), 32-34, 95
Jobs Strategy, 33-34

Paraguay, 46, 54
Parti Québécois (PQ), 114, 115
People's Summits, 95, 96, 97, 98
political, 2, 7, 16, 18, 19, 26-27, 29, 31, 32, 34, 41, 44-45, 47, 48, 51, 53, 61, 64, 65, 68, 74-77, 80, 89, 90, 97, 98, 100, 101, 106, 108, 109, 111, 113, 114, 115, 118, 120, 124, 125, 127, 129, 132, 134, 135, 140, 144, 148, 149, 152, 156, 175, 178, 186
choices, 4
decisions, 4, 5, 7
geo-political, 14, 15
popular sector groups, 89-94, 99
privatize, 21, 54-55, 81, 91, 92, 135, 156
production, 2, 13, 14, 15, 19, 22, 23, 41, 42, 47-48, 50, 51, 53, 93, 107, 108, 109, 110, 119, 129, 130, 134, 137, 143, 156-159, 161-168, 177-178
lean production, 7, 156-159, 161-164, 166-169
mass production, 156-158, 168
modular production, 162-163, 165-166
productivity, 15, 43, 48, 55, 109, 111, 112, 115, 161, 162, 164, 166, 167
property rights, 20, 29, 30, 35, 36
protectionism, 28, 181
protest, 6, 7-8, 53, 89, 90, 93, 95, 96, 97, 99, 100, 147-149, 156, 182
protestors, 97, 99, 148
protest strategies, 8, 89, 90, 93, 96, 98
civil protest, 144, 146
public protest, 93, 147
public sector, 21, 92, 93, 101, 114, 117

Québec, 114, 117, 118, 119
Québec Liberal Party (QLP), 114

reforms, 20, 21, 22, 23, 34, 35, 77, 78, 95, 111, 114, 118, 119, 149
regulation, 4, 21, 54, 55, 56, 90, 93, 94, 100, 105, 109, 116, 133, 177-178, 183-184
    deregulation, 2, 8, 18, 33-36, 52, 91, 116, 117, 156, 174, 178
regulatory policy, 5, 7, 41, 44, 157

Saudi Arabia, 46
Seattle, 89, 96, 97, 99, 100, 156, 180
sectoral policies, 47-50, 52, 53, 56, 115
September 11th, 1, 7, 13, 98, 100, 131, 134
Sierra Leone, 46, 126
social cohesion, 73, 109, 115
social justice, 22, 174, 176, 178, 187
social policies, 5, 32, 33, 59, 60, 61, 63, 66, 67, 68, 69, 79, 80, 107
social programs, 5, 21, 59, 64, 65, 67, 68, 69, 90, 92
sovereignty, 28, 31-32, 60, 106, 114, 127, 128, 131
Soviet Union (USSR), 2, 14, 91
state, 2-9, 11, 13, 15, 17-22, 26, 28-37, 49, 50-52, 54-56, 59, 60, 61, 62, 64, 65, 66, 67, 69, 72, 73, 81, 83, 89, 90, 92, 95, 96, 97, 98, 99, 100, 106, 107, 108, 109, 110, 116, 117, 119, 129, 131-136, 174-182, 185, 187, 188
    minimalist state, 20
    nation-state, 6, 7, 15, 16, 17, 21, 22, 37, 72, 74, 79-80, 89, 105, 106, 107, 109, 126, 177, 181, 188
state autonomy, 44, 46-50, 56
state intervention, 48, 51, 54, 72
stock market, 19, 91
students, 94, 100, 101
subsidy, direct, 51
subsidization, indirect, 51
Sudan, 125, 127, 130-136
sustainable development, 97
sweatshop, 97, 143
Sweden, 49
Switzerland, 49, 134

Taylorism, 157
Taylorist, 115, 158
tax, 5, 35, 42, 48, 51, 59, 60, 64, 65, 66, 68, 69, 79, 90, 92, 112, 116, 117, 126
    expenditures, 59-69
    indirect transfers, 51, 59
taxation, 20, 51, 55, 59, 60, 62, 66, 68, 69, 81, 106
Thatcher, Margaret, 5, 77, 78
    adminstration, 72-83
third world, 16, 18
trade, 2, 7-9, 13, 15, 16, 17, 20, 23, 29, 30, 34, 35, 37, 43, 44, 45, 61, 91, 94, 96, 97, 100, 126, 127, 130, 133, 134, 135, 157, 167, 168, 176, 180, 182
    international trade, 11, 16, 30, 42, 44, 181
trade agreements, 10, 30, 36, 42, 44, 46, 52, 54, 93, 94, 174, *see also*
    Asia-Pacific Economic Cooperation (APEC)
    Canada-U.S. Free Trade Agreement (CUSFTA)
    Clean Diamonds Trade Act
    G8 Summit
    General Agreement on Trade in Services (GATS)
    General Agreement on Tariffs and Trade (GATT)
    Mercado del Sur (MERCOSUR)
    Multilateral Agreement on Investment (MAI)
    North American Free Trade Agrcemcnt (NAFTA)
    Uruguay Round
    World Trade Organization (WTO)
trade protection measures, 51
    Trade Policy Review Mechanism (TPRM), 34, 35
trade union, 9, 94, 105-118, 157, 159, 161-162, 174-175, 182-185, 187, 188
trade union movement, 105
    international trade union movement, 175, 177, 179, 183, 185, 187
    transnational unionism, 95
    see also International Confederation of Free Trade Unions (ICFTU)

transnational corporations, 2, 32, 132
Trilateral Commission, 18, 19

Uganda, 126, 128, 135
unemployment, 22, 23, 33, 73-77, 81, 117, 142, 144
 non-accelerating inflation rate of unemployment (NAIRU), 33
 structural unemployment, 33-34, 82
United Kingdom (UK), *also* Britain, 16, 59, 109
 HomeNet, 177, 183, 185
United Nations (UN), 18, 125, 126
 United Nations Development Program, 132
 UNIFEM, 188
 United Nations Security Council, 129
United States of America (USA), 15, 16, 19, 20, 22, 31, 33, 42, 43, 44, 46, 49, 50, 51, 59, 74, 79, 80, 82, 91, 94, 95, 96, 98, 127, 129, 130, 133, 134, 136, 146, 162, 163, 166
American imperialism, 14, 18, 31
 US Treasury, 20, 81
Uruguay Round, 29, 37, 91
Uruguay, 54

wages, 21, 23, 43, 47, 62, 65, 92, 101, 109, 111, 112, 118, 119, 141, 144, 145, 146, 150-151, 163, 164, 184
Wall Street, 18, 23
Washington, 16, 97, 99, 132, 136
 Washington Consensus, 20, 22
welfare, 43, 61, 63, 68, 73, 79, 80-81, 114
 social welfare, 61, 90, 152
welfare programs, 43, 63, 76
welfare reform, 81-82
welfare state, 3, 18, 20, 59, 91, 107, 112, 113, 114, 118
 Keynesian (national) welfare state, 18, 112
 post-Keynesian, 114
women, 6, 8, 66, 67, 90, 93, 94, 118, 120, 175, 177-178, 184-188
women's movement, 90, 118, 119, 120, 181
work, 23, 63, 81, 83, 111, 113, 115, 117, 118, 119, 140, 152, 164-169, 178
 non-standard employment, 183, 186
 standard work, 179, 183
workers, 18, 21, 32, 33, 47, 49, 63-66, 92, 93, 94, 95, 111, 112, 113, 114, 115, 117, 165-168, 172, 174-188
foreign migrant workers, 7, 140-154
homeworkers, 179, 183-186
illegal workers, 142, 145-146, 151
marginalized workers, 7, 8, 177, 178
 racial minorities, 6
 women workers, 185, 186
 see also labour, women, trade union
workfare, *also* work-welfare, 72, 74, 80, 81, 82, 83, 118, 119
World Bank, 16, 18, 19, 21, 22, 96, 97, 99
World Economic Forum, 97
World Trade Organization (WTO), 28, 29, 30, 34-37, 42, 89, 91, 92, 93, 96, 97, 99, 100, 133, 176, 180, 182
 WTO Secretariat, 29
 see also GATS and GATTS

youth, 18, 73, 74, 78, 82
 youth labour market policies, 5, 73
 youth training, 72, 78, 81
 youth unemployment, 73, 74, 77, 81
Yugoslavia, 16

Zapatistas, 95
Zimbabwe, 126, 128,